T0305151

Central Banks and Monetary Regimes in Emerging Countries

THE ELGAR SERIES ON CENTRAL BANKING AND MONETARY POLICY

Series Editors: Louis-Philippe Rochon, *Full Professor, Laurentian University, Canada, Editor-in-Chief of* Review of Political Economy *and Founding Editor Emeritus,* Review of Keynesian Economics, Sylvio Kappes, *Assistant Professor, Federal University of Ceará, Brazil and Coordinator, Keynesian Economics Working Group, Young Scholars Initiative* and Guillaume Vallet, *Associate Professor, Université Grenoble Alpes and Centre de Recherche en Economie de Grenoble (CREG), France*

This series explores the various topics important to the study of central banking and monetary theory and policy and the challenges surrounding them. The books in the series analyze specific aspects such as income distribution, gender and ecology and will, as a body of work, help better explain the nature and the future of central banks and their role in society and the economy.
Titles in the series include:

The Future of Central Banking
Edited by Sylvio Kappes, Louis-Philippe Rochon and Guillaume Vallet

Central Banking, Monetary Policy and the Environment
Edited by Louis-Philippe Rochon, Sylvio Kappes and Guillaume Vallet

Central Banking, Monetary Policy and Social Responsibility
Edited by Guillaume Vallet, Sylvio Kappes and Louis-Philippe Rochon

Central Banking, Monetary Policy and the Future of Money
Edited by Guillaume Vallet, Sylvio Kappes and Louis-Philippe Rochon

Central Banks and Monetary Regimes in Emerging Countries
Theoretical and Empirical Analysis of Latin America
Edited by Fernando Ferrari-Filho and Luiz Fernando de Paula

Future volumes will include:

Central Banking, Monetary Policy and Income Distribution
Edited by Louis-Philippe Rochon, Sylvio Kappes and Guillaume Vallet

Covid 19 and the Response of Central Banks
Coping with Challenges in Sub-Saharan Africa
Salewa Olawoye-Mann

Central Banking, Monetary Policy and the Political Economy of Dollarization
Edited by Sylvio Kappes and Andrés Arauz

Central Banking, Monetary Policy and Gender
Edited by Louis-Philippe Rochon, Sylvio Kappes and Guillaume Vallet

Central Banking, Monetary Policy and Financial In/Stability
Edited by Louis-Philippe Rochon, Sylvio Kappes and Guillaume Vallet

Central Banks and Monetary Regimes in Emerging Countries

Theoretical and Empirical Analysis of Latin America

Edited by

Fernando Ferrari-Filho

Full Professor of Economics, Department of Economics and International Relations, Federal University of Rio Grande do Sul, Porto Alegre, and Researcher, National Council for Technological and Scientific Development (CNPq), Brasília, Brazil

Luiz Fernando de Paula

Professor of Economics, Federal University of Rio de Janeiro, Rio de Janeiro, and Researcher, CNPq, Brasília, and Rio de Janeiro Research Foundation (FAPERJ), Rio de Janeiro, Brazil

THE ELGAR SERIES ON CENTRAL BANKING AND MONETARY POLICY

 Edward Elgar
PUBLISHING

Cheltenham, UK • Northampton, MA, USA

Published by
Edward Elgar Publishing Limited
The Lypiatts
15 Lansdown Road
Cheltenham
Glos GL50 2JA
UK

Edward Elgar Publishing, Inc.
William Pratt House
9 Dewey Court
Northampton
Massachusetts 01060
USA

A catalogue record for this book
is available from the British Library

Library of Congress Control Number: 2022948500

This book is available electronically in the **Elgar**online
Economics subject collection
http://dx.doi.org/10.4337/9781802203981

ISBN 978 1 80220 397 4 (cased)
ISBN 978 1 80220 398 1 (eBook)
Printed and bound by CPI Group (UK) Ltd, Croydon, CR0 4YY

Contents

Contributors

André de Melo Modenesi is an Associate Professor at the Federal University of Rio de Janeiro (Rio de Janeiro, Brazil) and a researcher at the National Council for Technological and Scientific Development (CNPq) and at the Rio de Janeiro Research Foundation in Brazil.

André Moreira Cunha is a Full Professor in the Department of Economics and International Relations at the Federal University of Rio Grande do Sul (Porto Alegre, Brazil) and a researcher at the National Council for Technological and Scientific Development (CNPq) in Brazil.

Andrés Ferrari Haines is an Adjunct Professor in the Department of Economics and International Relations at the Federal University of Rio Grande do Sul (Porto Alegre, Brazil).

Antonio José Alves Junior is a Full Professor of Economics in the Economics Department at the Federal Rural University of Rio de Janeiro (Rio de Janeiro, Brazil).

Assilio Araujo is a PhD in Economics at the Federal University of Rio Grande do Sul (Porto Alegre, Brazil).

Bianca Orsi is a Teaching Fellow in the Economics Department/Leeds University Business School at the University of Leeds (Leeds, UK).

Eliane Araujo is an Adjunct Professor in the Department of Economics at the State University of Maringá (Maringá, Brazil) and a Visiting Professor in the Graduate Program of Economics at the Federal University of Rio Grande do Sul (Porto Alegre, Brazil) and a researcher at the National Council for Technological and Scientific Development (CNPq) in Brazil.

Elisangela Araujo is an Adjunct Professor in the Department of Economics at the State University of Maringá (Maringá, Brazil).

Ernani Teixeira Torres Filho is a Professor of Economics in the Institute of Economics at the Federal University of Rio de Janeiro (Rio de Janeiro, Brazil).

Fábio Henrique Bittes Terra is an Associate Professor at the Federal University of ABC (São Bernardo do Campo, Brazil) and an Associate

Professor in the Graduate Program in Economics at the Federal University of Uberlândia (Uberlândia, Brazil) and a researcher at the National Council for Technological and Scientific Development (CNPq) in Brazil.

Fernando Ferrari-Filho is a Full Professor of Economics in the Department of Economics and International Relations at the Federal University of Rio Grande do Sul (Porto Alegre, Brazil), a Visiting Professor at the Washington and Lee University (Lexington, USA) and at the Meiji University (Tokyo, Japan), and a researcher at the National Council for Technological and Scientific Development (CNPq) in Brazil.

Hernán Eduardo Neyra is an Adjunct Professor at the National University of Moreno (Buenos Aires, Argentina).

Isabela Andrade do Carmo is a Bachelor in Science and Humanities at the Federal University of ABC (São Bernardo do Campo, Brazil).

José Luís Oreiro is an Associate Professor at the University of Brasília (Brasília, Brazil), and a researcher in the Graduate Program in Economics at the University of Basque Country (Bilbao, Spain) and at the National Council for Technological and Scientific Development (CNPq) in Brazil.

Juan Matías De Lucchi is a PhD candidate at The New School for Social Research (New York City, USA) and an economist at the Central Bank of Argentina (Buenos Aires, Argentina).

Julio Fernando Costa Santos is an Adjunct Professor in the Institute of Economics and International Relations at the Federal University of Uberlândia (Uberlândia, Brazil).

Luiz Fernando de Paula is a Professor of Economics at the Federal University of Rio de Janeiro (Rio de Janeiro, Brazil), a Voluntary Professor in the Institute of Social and Political Studies at the State University of Rio de Janeiro (Rio de Janeiro, Brazil) and a researcher at the National Council for Technological and Scientific Development (CNPq) and at the Rio de Janeiro Research Foundation in Brazil.

Luiz Macahyba is a PhD candidate in Public Policies, Strategies and Development at the Federal University of Rio de Janeiro (Rio de Janeiro, Brazil).

Luiza Peruffo is an Adjunct Professor in the Department of Economics and International Relations at the Federal University of Rio Grande do Sul (Porto Alegre, Brazil).

Mateus Coelho Ferreira is a PhD candidate in the Post-Graduate Program in Economics at the Federal University of Rio de Janeiro (Rio de Janeiro, Brazil).

Mateus Ramalho Ribeiro da Fonseca is an Adjunct Professor at the Faculty of Maringá (Maringá, Brazil).

Matías Vernengo is a Professor of Economics in the Department of Economics at Bucknell University (Lewisburg, USA) and a co-editor of the *Review of Keynesian Economics* (ROKE).

Norberto Montani Martins is an Adjunct Professor in the Institute of Economics at the Federal University of Rio de Janeiro (Rio de Janeiro, Brazil).

Paulo José Saraiva is an Associate Professor in the Economics Department at the Federal Rural University of Rio de Janeiro (Rio de Janeiro, Brazil).

Pedro Perfeito da Silva is a Postdoctoral Research Fellow in the Department of Economics at the University of Leeds (Leeds, UK).

Roberto Valencia Arriaga is an Associate Professor at the Autonomous National University of Mexico (Mexico City, Mexico).

Santiago Capraro Rodríguez is an Associate Professor at the Autonomous National University of Mexico (Mexico City, Mexico).

Foreword

Louis-Philippe Rochon[1]

THE ART OF CENTRAL BANKING IN A CHANGING WORLD

In the context of central banking, the Great Financial Crisis (GFC) of 2007–2008 comes as close as it gets to a structural break – a great reckoning. Indeed, after central banks came to the realization that conventional policy is of limited use and that near zero interest rates don't necessarily invigorate aggregate demand, they came face to face with the challenge of keeping monetary policy relevant. In this quest, central banks unrolled so-called unconventional policies (UMP), which proved equally as irrelevant at stimulating the economy. Yet they had some rather important consequences: they created large distributive effects. As Saiki and Frost (2014, p. 4445) argue, "UMP widened income inequality, especially after 2008 when quantitative easing became more aggressive. This is largely due to the portfolio channel."

Since then, there has been a proliferation of articles on the topic, emanating both from central banks around the world and the academic community (see Kappes, 2022, for a review). In the end, what perhaps stood out the most was the remarkable degree to which it was easy for the central bank to intervene so massively in the economy. In Europe similarly, after denying their ability to intervene, the European Central Bank (ECB) did so, effortlessly. Was it a simple question of ideology all along?

As a result, the 'art of central banking' – as Hawtrey (1932) called it – appeared to have evolved. Indeed, central banks, or so it appears, seem to be focused a little bit less on inflation. For instance, in New Zealand, the central bank has officially adopted a dual mandate, thereby taking into consideration unemployment and labour markets when setting the rate of interest, and a number of countries are adopting a more 'flexible' approach to inflation targeting, or a wait and see approach to inflation targeting. Moreover, central banks are now openly discussing such topics as financial stability, income distribution, the environment, and gender, among others – topics that have rarely been associated with monetary policy. Clearly, there appears to be a rethinking in the face of changing conditions.

In addition, central bankers themselves appear more enlightened. For instance, in a 2021 speech, Mark Carney refers to money as a "social convention" (where have I heard that before?) and, as such,

> money is more of an art grounded in values of trust, resilience, dynamism, solidarity and sustainability. Central banks are its curator. This role of central banks is being challenged in the wake of intensifying centrifugal forces, including an increasingly multi-polar global economy, the growing weight of market-based finance, and, my primary focus today, the emergence of crypto assets and distributed finance.

Despite the appearance of progress, as the old proverb goes, the more things change, the more they remain the same. Indeed, I believe this is a smokescreen or a rhetorical facade. And, if this is the case, then why the games? On the one hand, central bankers are trying to tell working households that by either having a dual mandate or by delaying pressing on the inflation trigger, they are somehow more interested in the common interest than the vested interests, in Veblen's (1919) words, and willing to consider the ills of the working person in setting interest rates. But on the other hand, they are relentless in reassuring financial interests that they won't take their eyes off the inflation target. It is the great 'having your cake and eating it too' strategy.

CENTRAL BANKING AND SOME FUNDAMENTAL TRUTHS

Despite the appearance of some openness, in the end, I would argue, not much has changed, really. Lavoie (2006, p. 167) once referred to this as 'old wine in a new bottle', though I am not sure how new the bottle really is anymore. And more recently, Lavoie and Fiebeger (2020) have argued that much of today's thinking on monetary matters is simply left-over monetarism. Taken together, these quotes make clear that the art of central banking has not evolved much: there have been changes on the surface or in the short run, but otherwise, much remains the same. Central bankers are not innovators in any sense of the word. However, let's give credit where credit is due: they did manage to protect banks from imminent collapse during the financial crisis. They did show, if willing, they are able to do good things for those vested interests.

Indeed, the ardent belief in the long-run neutrality of money truncates any serious discussion about true progress in monetary policy. For instance, mainstream discussion over income distribution is immediately shrugged off as being limited to the short run. As such, it is inconceivable for monetary policy to have any long lasting effects on income inequality. Cœuré (2013) has argued precisely this point. For him, central banks

> should refrain from engaging in income redistribution, which should be sanctioned by parliaments. This does not imply that monetary policy actions do not have distributive consequences – in fact, they always have. But these are the side-effects of a strategy that aims to ensure price stability, which is by essence neutral as regards income distribution.

The same thinking applies to environmental consequences, i.e. that somehow monetary policy has only short-run effects. For instance, in some Keynesian Dynamic Stochastic General equilibrium (DSGE) models with financial frictions, among others, so-called green monetary policies are allowed to impact emissions in the short run but never in the long run.[2]

In a recent paper (see Ferrari and Landi, 2020, p. 3, emphasis added), the authors admit as much, after offering their version of enlightenment:

> We believe that climate change is a serious issue with effects that central banks cannot ignore. Our analysis points out what Green QE [quantitative easing] can and cannot achieve. Green QE is able to temporarily reduce detrimental emissions. Green QE is less effective in affecting the stock of pollution, which follows a slow law of motion. Nevertheless, some caveats should be kept well in mind. In our model *Green QE is neutral in the long-run*.

So whether it is in discussions over income distribution or environmental concerns, monetary policy is neutral in the long run.

This discussion then leads us into what I believe are the six core assumptions central bankers and mainstream policy analysts will never abandon:

(1) In the long run money is neutral, as is policy;
(2) Inflation is related to monetary policy;
(3) Central banks are uniquely positioned to fight inflation, and that fiscal policy simply cannot. In fact, fiscal policy is the opposite: it is considered inflationary;
(4) Central banks must be independent: anything less will destabilize the economy;
(5) Central banks will always serve the needs of financial rent – the vested interests of the financial class (Veblen, 1919; Seccareccia, 2017);
(6) A natural rate of interest exists, and it guides and informs policy.

All this suggests that central banks will never (not an exaggeration) abandon their quest for price stability, that recent changes to central banking are cosmetic, and that the ideological and fundamental beliefs in the neutrality of policy will ensure that any discussion other than inflation is given mere lip service. Even the discovery of endogenous money did not amount to a change in thinking. Those six elements listed above are still defended whether central banks consider money exogenous or endogenous. As Carney (2021) has said, "Central banks have a primordial responsibility to act as the guarantors of trust and confidence in money given of their status as monopoly issuers of currency."

Yet, all this monetary non-change has also been taking place against a backdrop of tremendous change in the real world. From one crisis to another, amid the explosive fiscal response to COVID (at least in some countries), and economic shutdowns, central bankers remained convinced in their ability to control inflation emanating from the demand side of the economy, even though more often than not inflation arises from supply considerations, which seems to be especially the case at the moment.

This suggests that if central banks deserve credit for taming the inflationary beast, they have done so not through the usual transmission mechanisms of demand-side inflation (see Rochon, 2022, for a discussion), but rather through other means. Indeed, inflation has hovered around the target in recent decades because central banks have used interest rates as a threat against the private sector, and especially against the working class, and as such have weaponized inflation by relying on the concept of fine-tuning.

In other words, what inflation targeting does is precisely tell workers to keep their wage increases within the target rate; otherwise central banks may have to increase interest rates. The governors of both the Bank of England and, more recently, the Bank of Canada have made such audacious statements. What this does is to place the fight against inflation squarely on the backs of working households. In fact, losers lose twice: they are told not to ask for wage increases, and given that inflation is usually not driven by demand forces, incremental increases in interest rates will not have the expected effects until it is too late, and unemployment increases.

THIS BOOK

The editors of this book have brought together a number of key authors to explore the art of central banking from the perspective of Latin America. To the above discussion, the various contributing authors bring another layer or dimension to the discussion pertaining to capital flows and exchange rates. As if the above discussion was not complicated enough, this book brings forth a depth of analysis that is so missing from the rhetoric. These contributions are all a cut above, and explore and extend the heterodox perspective in so many ways.

Indeed, these chapters only confirm the robustness of the heterodox tradition. The authors confirm many of the arguments around the "general ineffectiveness of monetary policy" (Rochon, 2022) by questioning the key elements and arguments of the orthodox position.

If there really is an 'art' to central banking, this book comes very close to discovering it.

NOTES

1. The author would like to thank Yannis Dafermos, Sylvio Kappes, Wesley Marshall, and Mario Seccareccia for comments on an earlier draft.
2. I want to thank Yannis Dafermos for confirming my initial suspicions.

REFERENCES

Carney, M. (2021), "The art of central banking in a centrifugal world". Andrew Crockett lecture, *Bank for International Settlement*, June 28, 2021.

Cœuré, B. (2013), "Outright monetary transactions, one year on". Speech, Centre for Economic Policy Research, the *German Institute for Economic Research and the KfW Bankengruppe*, Berlin, 2 September 2013.

Ferrari, A. and V.N. Landi (2020), "Whatever it takes to save the planet: Central banks and unconventional green policy". *European Central Bank*, no. 2500, December.

Hawtrey, R.G. (1932), *The Art of Central Banking*. London: Longmans, Green and Company.

Kappes, S. (2022), "Monetary policy and personal income distribution: a survey of the literature". *Review of Political Economy*, forthcoming.

Lavoie, M. (2006), "A Post-Keynesian amendment to the new consensus on monetary policy". *Metroeconomica*, 57(2), pp. 165–192.

Lavoie, M. and B. Fieberger (2020), "Helicopter Ben, monetarism, the New Keynesian credit view and loanable funds". *Journal of Economic Issues*, 54(1), pp. 77–96.

Rochon, L.-P. (2022), "The general ineffectiveness of monetary policy or the weaponization of inflation". In S. Kappes, L.-P. Rochon, and G. Vallet (eds), *The Future of Central Banking*. Cheltenham, UK and Northampton, MA, USA: Edward Elgar Publishing.

Saiki, A. and Frost, J. (2014), "Does unconventional monetary policy affect inequality? Evidence from Japan". *Applied Economics*, 46(36), pp. 4445–4454.

Seccareccia, M. (2017), "Which vested interests do central banks really serve? Understanding central bank policy since the global financial crisis". *Journal of Economic Issues*, 51(2), pp. 341–350.

Veblen, T. (1919), *Vested Interests and the Common Man*. New York: B.W. Huebsch.

Introduction to *Central Banks and Monetary Regimes in Emerging Countries*

Fernando Ferrari-Filho and Luiz Fernando de Paula

Since the 1990s, the current globalization process – that is, the increased international mobility of trade and, mainly due to financial liberalization, capital – has seen the world economy face several economic crises, the most notable of which was the 2007–2008 international financial crisis (IFC) that resulted in the 2009 Great Recession (GR). More recently, in 2020, the lockdown restrictions due to the COVID-19 pandemic initiated the largest economic recession in the history of world economy, with a huge negative impact on GDP growth.

The effects of these crises were not neutral in economic and social terms, mainly because the crises have substantially altered the dynamic process of the international economy and have represented a major turning point. Governments of both the G7 countries and the emerging countries have responded to the IFC, and mainly the COVID-19 crisis with massive countercyclical fiscal and monetary policies.

As is well known, in *The General Theory of Employment, Interest and Money*, Keynes shows that in monetary economics, fluctuations in effective demand and in the level of employment occur because, in a world where the future is uncertain and unknown, economic agents prefer to withdraw currency. Consequently, their decisions to spend, whether on consumption or investment, are deferred. In other words, economic agents withhold currency as a kind of safeguard against the uncertainty that comes with their precarious knowledge about expected yields from their production plans. This situation occurred during the IFC and, partially, in the COVID-19 crisis, and for this reason Keynesian macroeconomic policies, in both conception and practice, were implemented, aiming to recover levels of effective demand for the purpose of mitigating the impacts of both crises. Thus, for that purpose, in 2008 and 2009, and in 2020, policymakers adopted countercyclical macroeconomic policies in such a way as to (i) operationalize fiscal policies designed to stimulate effective demand and reduce social inequalities; (ii) make for more flexible monetary policy so as to galvanize levels of consumption and investment; and (iii) coordinate and regulate financial and foreign-exchange markets in order to stabilize capital flows and exchange rates.

In line with this analysis, in Brazil and other Latin American countries, State intervention and central banks' actions, which involved important monetary, credit, financial and exchange rate measures, in the two recent crises – IFC and GR, and COVID-19 – have sparked a timely debate about which policies should be prioritized and why.

Given the above, the objective of this book, *Central Banks and Monetary Regimes in Emerging Countries: Theoretical and Empirical Analysis of Latin America*, is to analyse how the central banks' actions and the monetary regimes of the emerging countries, with a special focus on Latin America, have affected the economic performance of these countries, mainly in response to the IFC, and COVID-19 crisis.

To achieve this aim, the book has 10 chapters that analyse, theoretically and empirically, the central banks' actions and the monetary regimes of the most important Latin American countries, including, amongst others, Argentina, Brazil and Mexico. As most big Latin American economies have implemented an inflation targeting regime since the 1990s and 2000s, a special focus will be given on these experiences and how central banks dealt with IFC and COVID-19 crisis.

The opening chapter, 'Costs and benefits of currency internationalisation: Theory and the experience of emerging countries', by Bianca Orsi, Antonio José Alves Junior, and André de Melo Modenesi analyses the currency internationalization process, with a special focus on emerging economies. According to the authors, in the context of financial globalization, the increasing foreign demand for an international currency is, on the one hand, subjected to excessive exchange rate volatility and, thus, increasing uncertainty, and on the other hand it is related to external constraints whose main result is the loss of monetary policy autonomy. Given that, the chapter aims at discussing whether the actual costs outweigh the benefits of currency internationalization, mainly in emerging economies.

In the second chapter, 'Monetary institutions and economic performance in Latin America: the experience with an inflation targeting regime in the period 2000–2020', Eliane Araujo, Elisangela Araujo and Mateus Ramalho Ribeiro da Fonseca analyse, theoretically and empirically, the Inflation Targeting Regime (ITR) and the monetary policy operation for six Latin American economies: Brazil, Chile, Colombia, Guatemala, Mexico, and Peru. In the empirical part of the chapter, an econometric exercise was carried out for six of the eight countries that adopted ITR in the region. This evidenced, among other aspects, that, despite the relative price stability, the countries which adopted ITR experienced a worsening of external insertion and prolonged economic stagnation, which has the conduct of monetary policy as one of its relevant explanations.

The third chapter, 'Monetary policy in Brazil under the inflation targeting regime from a Contested Terrain Approach', by Assilio Araujo and Fernando Ferrari-Filho, shows that, based on the Contested Terrain Approach, the central bank is not a neutral institution because its actions are guided by a concern with the 'general interests'. Considering this idea, the chapter aims at explaining why the Central Bank of Brazil has presented, since at the least the *Real Plan*, a well-marked 'conservative bias', reacting much more strongly to inflationary expectations than to the level of economic activity, beyond the constraints imposed by the ITR.

In the subsequent chapter, 'The unfinished stabilization of the *Real Plan*: An analysis of the indexation of the Brazilian economy', José Luis Oreiro and Julio Fernando Costa Santos show the historical context of the emergence and evolution of the indexation of prices, wages and contracts in the Brazilian economy, as well as discuss the economic impacts of a possible full de-indexation of the Brazilian economy. According to the authors, the *Real Plan*, the Brazilian stabilization process, implemented in the middle of the 1990s, is an incomplete price stabilization of the Brazilian economy due to the fact that it did not fully eliminate the wage and price indexation in Brazil. In order to argue that, the authors formulate four econometric models that capture the relationship between the main variables (exchange rate, real interest rate, inflation expectations, inertia) and the four main price indexes (IPCA, IGP-M, IPA, IPC). Their conclusion is that there is strong evidence to suggest the implementation of a monetary reform in Brazil to eliminate any remaining price and wage indexation.

Chapter 5, 'The role of capital flow management measures when the bubble bursts: The Brazilian experience in the global financial crisis and in the COVID-19 Pandemic', by Luiza Peruffo, Pedro Perfeito da Silva and André Moreira Cunha, shows that there is a striking difference between the performance of the Brazilian economy during the 2007–2008 Global Financial Crisis (GFC) and during the ongoing COVID-19 pandemic. The objective is to discuss the role of capital flow management measures (CFMs) to (i) manage the global financial cycle in developing and emerging economies (DEEs) and (ii) create policy space for them to fight crises. In particular, it investigates the relationship between the degree of financial integration and macroeconomic performance by looking at CFMs put forward by Brazil before, during and after the two global crises of the 21st century. Empirically, the authors develop a vector autoregressive model with error correction to evaluate the relationship between Brazil's degree of financial integration and its macroeconomic performance. The chapter argues that the contrasting performance of Brazil in these two crises can be attributed both to a structural component of the international monetary and financial system, in which Brazil and other DEEs occupy an unprivileged position, and to Brazil's domestic policy decisions which have shaped the profile of its integration into global markets.

In the sixth chapter, 'Back to a high-inflation regime? The Argentine economy from the 2000s to the COVID-19 crisis', written by Hernán E. Neyra and Andrés Ferrari Haines, it is shown that, since the 1989 hyperinflation in Argentina, anti-inflationary views and policies have been dominated by an orthodox outlook. Hence, different forms of 'excess of money supply' controls have been followed. Thus, the Central Bank of Argentina's (CBA's) role in the economy has been mainly relegated to achieve the end of inflation. Matters concerning economic growth and full-employment have been delegated to the 'market'. This has meant that output became fundamentally an outcome of external trade. The chapter also argues that such a limited scope for CBA behaviour has resulted in inflationary pressures, even under a 'bonanza', because of the erratic and unstable economic context. As a result, agents push for a review of their prices and incomes as fluctuations are taken merely as an unjustified loss of purchasing power. Over time, an indexation mechanism gradually reappeared in a rather disorganized manner, which meant the CBA ended validation because of political and social pressures.

Chapter 7, 'The new foreign debt trap and its long run consequences: The persistence of Monetarism as a social doctrine in Argentina', by Juan Matías De Lucchi and Matías Vernengo, offers a detailed analysis of the problem of the current crisis of the external sector that the Argentine economy has been going through, starting with the election of the Mauricio Macri administration at the end of 2015. The focus of this analysis is placed on the errors of the previous national government, both diagnostic, theoretical and operational, which has led to a situation of complex sustainability in terms of indebtedness, which puts future possibilities of economic growth at risk. The return of Monetarism in Argentina led to a new foreign debt cycle, and the current pandemic has only aggravated the instability of the economy and the possibilities of default.

Chapter 8, 'The monetary circuit and the credit channel in Mexico', by Roberto Valencia Arriaga and Santiago Capraro Rodríguez, aims at demonstrating that, in Mexico, the credit transmission channel of the monetary policy does not work efficiently, so the Central Bank of Mexico's (CBM's) interest rate cannot be used as the only instrument to achieve the inflation target as asserted in the traditional ITR. Moreover, the chapter adheres to the Monetary Theory of Production, so it seeks to account for this hypothesis with a theoretical outline using the Stock-Flow methodology, and subsequently through a VAR model. The main result of the empirical analysis is that credit is found to be inelastic to the interest rate charged by commercial banks, while it does respond to changes in investment, so the monetary circuit hypothesis is validated, so it can explain the stagnation process of the Mexican economy.

Finally, the chapter claims that, in economies such as Mexico's, the control of inflation needs more than one instrument.

Chapter 9, 'Monetary policy in Latin America during the COVID-19 crisis: Was this time different?', by Luiz Fernando de Paula, Paulo Saraiva and Mateus Coelho Ferreira, analyses the behaviour of some emerging economies' central banks, specifically the central banks of Argentina, Brazil, Chile, Colombia, Mexico and Peru, during the COVID-19 crisis. The chapter shows that the reaction of the central banks of these South American economies was different from the central banks' response during the subprime financial crisis of 2007–2008. According to the authors, at this time, the central banks implemented and eased monetary policy aggressively, by cutting policy rates and introducing some non-conventional monetary policy. They conclude that there are, at least, three reasons for such behaviour: (i) the quick swift monetary policy easing by the Federal Reserve Bank and other advanced economy central banks that calmed global financial conditions; (ii) South American economies' cyclical position at the time of the COVID-19 shock opened up more room for easing monetary policy compared with other crises; and (iii) the sharp drop in output and inflation that followed the COVID-19 shock compounded the depressed business cycle positions and opened up space for monetary policy easing.

Chapter 10, 'The Central Bank of Brazil in the face of the COVID-19 economic crisis', by Isabela Andrade do Carmo and Fábio Henrique Bittes Terra, presents and analyses the measures undertaken by the Central Bank of Brazil (CBB) to offset the economic effects of the COVID-19 crisis. Given the huge impacts coming from the pandemic, the actions of the CBB, in terms of both the number of measures seeking financial stability and the volume of resources employed, were greater than that of the 2007–2008 subprime crisis. This gives special importance to the analysis of the behaviour of the CBB during the COVID-19 pandemic. The authors argue that the monetary policy framework available to the CBB in this crisis was bigger than in any other crisis, whether domestic or external. While in the 2008 Great Financial Crisis the CBB implemented measures to provide liquidity equal to 3.5 percent of the GDP, in the measures throughout the COVID-19 crisis, with some of them going until 2022, the total liquidity provision was 17.5 percent of the GDP. Capital relief measures were not even made in 2008, but in the COVID-19 crisis they totalled 15.8 percent of the GDP.

Finally, in Chapter 11, 'The financial aspects of the COVID-19 crisis in Brazil: A Minskyan approach', by Norberto Montani Martins, Ernani Teixeira Torres Filho and Luiz Macahyba, the theoretical framework developed by Hyman Minsky is adapted to understand the financial aspects of the COVID-19 economic crisis in Brazil. Taking the financial instability hypothesis and the concept of survival constraint as starting points, the authors analyse the

COVID-19 crisis and the responses of the Brazilian government from the perspective of three distinct, though interconnected, processes. The first process is characterized by the liquidity squeeze in financial markets and its consequences on prices and the tradability of assets. The second, which will last as long as the pandemic is not overcome, refers to the interruption of cash inflows to firms and households and the resulting disequilibria from the persistence of financial obligations and essential expenditures. Finally, the third process is associated with the deterioration of economic units' balance sheets, which can lead to failures even after the health emergency is resolved. The authors conclude that liquidity measures adopted by the CBB contributed to avoiding the liquidity squeeze morphing into financial instability. However, the erratic support to business and families was not sufficient to avoid a massive increase in financial fragility.

We would like to thank all contributors for writing and revising their contributions to satisfy our demands and those of the publishers. We also wish to thank our friend Louis-Philippe Rochon for stimulating us to edit this book, introducing us to Edward Elgar Publishing and, mainly, writing the preface of this book. Alan Sturmer from Edward Elgar and his staff were extremely helpful during this project. Finally, we are grateful all these people for making this book possible.

1. Costs and benefits of currency internationalisation: theory and the experience of emerging countries

Bianca Orsi, Antonio José Alves Junior and André de Melo Modenesi

INTRODUCTION

The international use of currencies, i.e. currency internationalisation, is a topic that has been discussed by many researchers over the years, from the monetary regime of the Gold Standard, to Bretton Woods and to the current regime dominated by the US dollar, the *floating dollar standard* (Medeiros and Serrano, 2003). The International Monetary System is, however, marked by an acute asymmetry between national currencies, which can be illustrated in the form of a currency hierarchy. While the US dollar and other central currencies from developed economies are positioned at the top of the hierarchy (the so-called central currencies), many other currencies from emerging and developing economies (the peripheral currencies) are placed at an inferior level.

The competition among currencies can be viewed as a 'natural' result of a complex political and economic struggle between countries. As some economies gain international relevance, new international currencies would arise, although they play different roles in the International Monetary System, i.e. across various types of currency internationalisation. In this mainstream perspective, the internationalisation of currencies mainly reflects market forces, such as the relative weight of central countries on international trade as well as the development of their financial markets. Notwithstanding, this process also requires institutional support and innovation from national governments – the 'political willingness' to promote the internationalisation of their currencies (De Conti, 2011). The political decision is a necessary, yet not sufficient, condition for greater use of a domestic currency beyond its national frontier, such as less restrictive regulations of the foreign exchange market to allow non-residents to operate, openness of capital account and currency convertibility. Given the complexity of the possible consequences involved in each of these policy decisions, it becomes particularly difficult to work out the balance between costs and benefits of currency internationalisation and their respective consequences over the economy.

This asymmetric feature of the International Monetary System raises, therefore, many policy questions. Should developing and emerging countries try to internationalise their currencies to overcome the subordinate position in the currency hierarchy? Should we aim for a multipolar monetary system? For instance, would the benefits of having a dominant and single international currency, such as advantages in transaction costs, outweigh the gains of having a plethora of currencies to choose from? Policymakers must take these questions into account as they consider whether a currency internationalisation strategy should be put forward.

There is an extensive literature on the costs and benefits of currency internationalisation, which are mainly summarised in the work of Cohen (2011), a distinguished International Political Economy scholar in the field of currency internationalisation. This literature, however, seems to focus on the costs and benefits of issuing a currency that stands on the highest positions of the currency hierarchy. This approach overlooks the recent internationalisation of peripheral currencies as it overestimates the advantages of this process for emerging and developing countries and it fails to account for the main disadvantages of the international use of these currencies. The current chapter addresses the research questions mentioned above by analysing each of the costs and benefits discussed in the literature on the perspective of the internationalisation of peripheral currencies.

Some strategies of currency internationalisation, generally advocated by mainstream economists, propose the full convertibility of national currency and the authorisation of residents to hold deposits in foreign currencies. In this view, as the full convertibility increases the international liquidity of a national currency, and the deposits in foreign currencies reduce transaction costs, the internationalisation of the national currency would be easier and stronger. However, as we argue in this chapter, some economists fear that such a policy strategy would also expose a domestic economy to financial crises and cause further destabilisation, which would, in turn, compromise the internationalisation process. Moreover, it could open doors to the possibility of partial currency substitution or, in the extreme, full dollarisation. Accordingly, instead of helping a currency to improve its position in the hierarchy, internationalisation could cement its subordinate role in the International Monetary System.

This chapter is organised as follows. After this introduction, the second section reviews the existing literature on currency internationalisation, which is focused on developed economies – issuers of central currencies. Special attention will be given to Cohen's contribution. The third section presents an analysis of the benefits and costs of currency internationalisation, which takes into account the case of emerging and developing economies – issuers of peripheral currencies. The final section summarises the main conclusions of this chapter: the actual costs seem to outweigh the benefits of the (partial) internationalisation of peripheral currencies.

CURRENCY INTERNATIONALISATION AND THE HIERARCHICAL INTERNATIONAL MONETARY SYSTEM

The Functional Analysis of Currency Internationalisation

Currency internationalisation is generally conceptualised as the process whereby a domestic currency is used beyond its national frontier. This topic is widely discussed in the fields of economics and International Political Economy, and it is a topic that builds a bridge between international relations and international economics (Cohen, 2008). To understand the role of different currencies in the international monetary system, Cohen (1971), an International Political Economy scholar, was the pioneer in proposing the analysis of this process through the lenses of the traditional functions of money, i.e. the medium of exchange, the unit of account and the store of value.

Table 1.1 summarises these three functions of international money, which are analysed in both private and public (or official) sectors. The private sector considers the functions of money in terms of the choices of individuals to use one currency or another, while the official sector focuses on the monetary authority decisions regarding foreign currencies. In the analysis of Cohen (1971), a currency is fully internationalised when it performs all the three functions of money outside the domestic economy.

Table 1.1   The roles of international money

Functions of money	Private	Official
Medium of exchange	Vehicle currency, trade settlement	Intervention currency
Unit of account	Trade invoicing currency	Exchange rate anchor
Store of value	Investment currency	Reserve currency

Source: Cohen and Benney (2013).

The medium of exchange refers to the ability of money to facilitate trade by serving as a general method of payment in the international market. Without an international currency that emerges as a medium of exchange, a transaction between two countries would only happen if one of these countries is willing to hold the currency of the other, similar to a barter economy. Therefore, a fully developed international money arises as the method to circumvent the double coincidence of wants (Cohen, 1971).

In the private sector, a currency is an international medium of exchange when it is used as a vehicle for foreign exchange operations and/or an instrument for trade settlement. Although these two roles are closely related, they are not synonyms (Cohen, 2013). The vehicle currency serves as an intermediary to triangulate the currency pairs that are not traded directly (Goldberg and Tille, 2005). The trade settlement currency is the one used as a medium of exchange for international transactions of goods and services. In the official sector, central banks use an international medium of exchange for interventions in the foreign exchange market.

The second function of international money measures the relative value of assets, goods and services in the international market – the unit of account. In the private sector, a currency is internationalised as a unit of account when foreign investors use it to invoice trade operations. Although the currency used as trade settlement may differ from the currency used as trade invoicing, empirical evidence suggests that they are normally the same (Friberg and Wilander, 2008; Ito and Chinn, 2014). Regardless of the trade settlement currency, an international unit of account is used whenever there is a foreign transaction, as contracts must be denominated in a single currency (Cohen, 1971). A currency is also an international unit of account when the monetary authority of other countries adopt it as an exchange rate anchor, i.e. when the central bank pegs the domestic currency to an international unit of account.

The last function of money, the store of value, represents the ability of a currency to preserve its value through time. Economic agents store their wealth by investing in assets denominated in a currency that they believe to have a stable value, both with regards to exchange rate stability and inflation. This role of international money is often called 'investment currency' (Cohen and Benney, 2013). In the official sector, central banks also hold stable international currencies that are able to preserve their reserves.

Cohen (2011) distinguishes between two purposes of international currencies: the use for transactions between countries and within a single country. While the former refers to the process of currency internationalisation per se, the latter is called 'currency substitution'. The most internationalised currencies are usually the ones with the highest potential of substituting those national currencies that do not perform the functions of money in the domestic market. The substitution process of the domestic currency for an international currency was coined 'dollarisation' because of the strong and frequent presence of the US dollar in many countries whose currencies have no role in both the international and domestic markets.

It is important to notice, however, that these countries may adopt different degrees of dollarisation (that is, currency substitution). Currently, only a few countries have completely relinquished their domestic currency for an international currency, such as El Salvador and Ecuador. Most countries that have experienced some degree of dollarisation have adopted only a partial use of the US dollar, such as Panama and Argentina. Despite the term 'dollarisation', other currencies are also used beyond their national frontier. The euro, for instance, is also adopted by other European countries that are not members of the Eurozone, such as Montenegro and Kosovo. Curiously, less internationalised currencies are also adopted in other countries. This is the case of the South African Rand, which is used in countries with political and geographical proximity with South Africa, e.g. Namibia and Eswatini.

Although currency internationalisation and currency substitution are two different concepts, they are intrinsically linked. The foreign currency chosen to substitute a national currency is, in most cases, highly internationalised, i.e. it is a currency that performs the functions of international money. Thus, the process of currency substitution is a consequence of the national currency's poor performance of the functions of money, while it evidences the internationalisation of the foreign currency. Therefore, the episode of dollarisation experienced in Latin America reinforces the power of the US dollar, but it is not the foundation of its internationalisation.

Financial Liberalisation or Currency Internationalisation?

Although the functional definition of currency internationalisation is widely adopted in the literature (Krugman, 1980; Kenen, 1983; De Paula et al., 2015; De Conti and Prates, 2018), in which the more functions of international money a currency performs, the more internationalised it is, researchers in this literature often take on different perspectives to analyse this phenomenon.

Kenen (1983) complements this functional approach by focusing on the type of actor that demands the currency – residents or non-residents. He argues that a currency may be internationalised when traded between a resident and a non-resident, but a currency shows strong internationalisation when it is used in transactions between non-residents. For instance, in the bond market, the internationalisation of the US dollar is evidenced by the demand of non-residents not only to hold but also to issue bonds denominated in this currency. However, a stronger indication of currency internationalisation is observed when a US dollar bond issued by a non-resident is negotiated offshore with other non-resident investors (Lim, 2006; McCauley, 2006).

The distinction between weaker and stronger forms of currency internationalisation can be important when assessing the international status of a currency. While central currencies (issued by developed economies) are generally internationalised and traded between non-residents, some peripheral currencies (issued by emerging and developing economies) have recently become more internationalised, but in the weaker form of internationalisation. Essentially, these currencies are only internationalised across a few functions of international money, and mostly traded between a resident and a non-resident. The current foreign exchange regulation in Brazil, for instance, hinders the trade of Brazilian Real (BRL) between non-residents. In practice, this means that the BRL offshore market does not exist, which, in turn, prevents the BRL from achieving a stronger form of internationalisation.

Another perspective taken in the literature refers to a regulatory analysis of currency internationalisation, i.e. currency convertibility. McCauley (2006) and many other researchers in this field (Cohen, 1998; Arida, 2003) follow the approach that defines an internationalised currency as one that can be freely traded between residents and non-residents of a country for several different purposes, as described in the functions of international money conceptualised by Cohen (1971). The Chinese Renminbi is a good example of the impact of regulatory restrictions on currency convertibility, which is often dependent on the type of actor involved in the transaction. Transactions between residents and non-residents (onshore) are highly regulated and controlled by the monetary authority. For this reason, the Renminbi traded on mainland China (CNY) is mostly non-convertible. In contrast, transactions between non-residents (offshore), traded in other foreign exchange markets such as in Hong Kong, are not subjected to strict regulation. The Renminbi traded offshore from mainland China (CNH) is fully convertible.

This regulatory understanding of currency internationalisation often relies on the argument that the free convertibility of a currency, granted by the lack of regulatory restrictions or interventions on the foreign exchange market, assures international agents and promotes the internationalisation of the domestic currency. For this reason, some economists promote the liberalisation of capital movements as the solution to the problem of currency convertibility (Arida, 2003). Indeed, regulatory restrictions may curb currency internationalisation, as the instruments used by the central banks can prevent or discourage international agents from accessing the domestic currency. This argument, however, overlooks the fact that currencies are qualitatively different: removing regulatory restrictions on the currency movements (*de jure* convertibility) does not imply or lead to a greater demand for the domestic currency in the international market (*de facto* convertibility) (Prates, 2002; Carneiro, 2008). Taking the Chinese Renminbi as an example, the full convertibility (*de jure*) of the CNH alone is not enough to guarantee its internationalisation (*de facto*), but it is a pre-condition to currency internationalisation.

In parallel to the literature on currency internationalisation,[1] Post-Keynesian economists have been the pioneers in developing another approach to understand the international demand for currencies – the currency hierarchy literature (Andrade and Prates, 2013; De Paula et al., 2015, 2017; Kaltenbrunner,

2015, 2018; Fritz et al., 2018). These authors mostly use Keynes' liquidity premium theory (1936) to characterise the position of a currency in the hierarchy. The US dollar, the most liquid currency of the International Monetary System, is positioned at the top of this hierarchy, followed by other central currencies, with some degree of liquidity. The central currencies are marked by their ability to perform several functions of money at the international level. At the bottom of this hierarchy, in a subordinate position, are positioned the peripheral currencies, with a very low liquidity premium and limited ability to perform any functions of international money.

THE BENEFITS AND COSTS OF CURRENCY INTERNATIONALISATION: ARE WE GETTING THE CALCULUS RIGHT?

The Benefits of Issuing an International Currency

Currency internationalisation is often understood as a natural consequence of the expansion process of issuing countries, which would spill over its economic and political strength in a favourable international context. Kim and Suh (2011), Gao and Yu (2011) and Cohen (2011), among others, criticised this idea for neglecting the strategic dimension of this process. Essentially, if the economic and political conditions define the possibilities of currency internationalisation, its nature and speed will depend on policy decisions that will guide the necessary institutional innovations that need to take place. The strategy of currency internationalisation should also consider that the logic of interstate competition guides international relations. A country that ventures into the internationalisation of its currency seeks to obtain a more favourable position in trade, finance, and international relations. However, one should expect other countries and the market to react, which can range from adapting to the new international money, to policies to hinder its use by the domestic actors. Thus, the benefits that motivate the decision to internationalise a currency must be carefully analysed, and then contrasted with the possible costs.

One advantage of currency internationalisation as a trade intermediary is directly related to reduction of transaction costs, i.e. cutting off costs of international payments in commercial and financial operations, such as bid-ask spreads, commissions, hedging, fees, and taxes. This approach suggests that transactions between economic agents in two different countries using a third currency as a means of payments face more costs than using the currency of one of them to settle the transactions. In the former case, where a third (vehicle) currency is involved, it is necessary to carry out at least two foreign exchange transactions. In the latter case, transaction costs are likely to reduce as there are fewer foreign exchange transactions.

It is important to emphasise that the distribution of these benefits among the economic agents of the issuing country is not uniform. Banks usually benefit the most from the internationalisation of the domestic currency, mainly because they have more manageable access to monetary authorities, enabling them to create liabilities denominated in the domestic currency. Banks may also benefit from gaining access to other markets as the domestic currency becomes more accepted for international transactions, facilitating the process of currency internationalisation.

For example, one can speculate that one of the largest private banks in Brazil, Itaú, is a candidate to reap good advantages if the Real, the Brazilian currency, were to become accepted for the settlement of Latin American inner transactions. This bank has been accumulating know-how in regional financial activities, from which it already extracts a relevant fraction of its income. According to the report entitled 'Management discussion & analysis and complete financial statements', Itaú (2021) obtained, in the first half of 2021, approximately R$12.8 billion in net income. Of this total, R$4 billion came from its activities abroad, of which just over R$1 billion came from Latin America corporate and investments finance, retail and private banking, and asset management activities. The internationalisation of the Real in this continent would possibly boost its business due to the bank's ability to expand its loans with lower liquidity risk due to access to reserves in Real with the Central Bank of Brazil. At the same time, if Brazilian banks increase their activities in the region, the Real would be more acceptable.

Non-financial companies could also benefit from this reduction in the transaction costs internationalisation granted so that they could explore business opportunities abroad. The main advantage stems from reducing their exposition to risks of currency mismatch between their assets (revenue) and liabilities (costs), and the associated hedging costs. Once again, currency internationalisation benefits the economic agents asymmetrically. Companies that are closer to international trade and finance are able to benefit more from the reduction of international transaction costs than others. Although there is no absolute loss for other residents in terms of transaction costs, currency internationalisation promotes changes in relative economic and political positions among resident agents. The analysis of this unbalance is, however, out of the scope of this chapter.

One should ask how emerging countries can internationalise their money as a means of payment to achieve benefits from reducing transaction costs in international trade and finance. According to the Post-Keynesian approach, an international currency is more likely to be used as a means of payment if it becomes desired as a store of value (Orsi, 2019). As there are other currencies that are already established as a store of value, such as the dollar and the euro, the new money has to show differential attributes to be seen as a diversification opportunity for private investors and foreign governments. However, as this attribute can represent costs to issuing countries, one has to ask if it would be outweighed by benefits.

Another benefit generally discussed in this literature is the seigniorage gains obtained by the country issuer of an international currency. The narrowest definition of seigniorage gains, in the context of a closed economy, refers to the difference between the nominal value of money and its cost of production. At the international level, in a broader definition, the seigniorage gains would arise from the acceptance of the domestic currency by foreign agents in exchange for exported goods and services, representing a benefit in terms of real resources for the economy. The accumulation of domestic money by foreigners would, therefore, be equivalent to an interest-free financing for the issuing country. Cohen (2011) estimates that the United States, in 2005, earned around US$18 billion in seigniorage *stricto sensu*, as a result of an average interest rate of 4 percent per year applied to around US$450 billion in cash, which was held by foreigners.

A second component of the seigniorage comes from the accumulation of financial assets denominated in the internationalised currency by non-residents. This component will supplant the *stricto sensu* seigniorage as the non-residents' accumulation of foreign currency would be a worse financial option than maintaining the reserves invested in bonds denominated in the issuing country's currency, as the amounts of these financial assets in their hands are supposed to be greater than this currency.

This is the case of the maintenance of international reserves, by the Central Banks, in American government bonds, and the cash balances of companies and individuals in government bonds and other financial assets, which would reflect the preference for international liquidity. As this demand would represent an additional demand to that of residents, US asset prices would tend to be higher than in the absence of such demand, or, to put it another way, funding costs in the USA would be lower. Warnock and Warnock (2009) estimated this annual liquidity premium for the USA at 80 basis points, representing an even larger 'subsidy' of around US$150 billion in 2008. Gourichas and Rey (2005) calculated the benefit of financial accumulation as the difference between the costs of raising dollars for Americans and the return on assets abroad. The excess return would be in the order of 300 basis points per year.

Despite the relevance of international seigniorage gains, the main question is how could emerging economies develop strategies to capture any seigniorage gain? One can state that as long as emergent countries can sell debt denominated in their currency to foreigners, they can benefit from a cut in interest rates as developing countries do. However, foreign governments and corporations demanded international money at the top of the currency hierarchy as a reserve-of-value, reflecting a global preference for liquidity. In the case of emergent currency, foreign investors do not demand it as reserve-of-value but as a short-term investment asset. These investors do not demand safety but make speculative gains during phases of low liquidity preference.

This difference is capital. Even considering that emergent issuers can obtain gains of seigniorage issuing debts denominated in their currency, the costs of this option are higher. While the demand for top currencies grows every time international liquidity preference increases, the demand for emergent currency-denominated debt tends to vanish, bringing high costs to emergent economies.

Another advantage of currency internationalisation is that it would provide gains to the issuing country in terms of macroeconomic flexibility, as the currency itself could be used to cover the balance of payments deficits. Since the Second World War, only the USA has thoroughly enjoyed the benefit of the continuous generation of a balance of payments deficit without reducing imports and raising interest rates to attract foreign capital. The USA has an exorbitant privilege, as Valéry Giscard D'Estaigne, the French minister of Finance, said in the 1960s.

While the USA used its exorbitant privilege to increase its economic and political power since the Second World War, at the opposite pole was the Latin American countries, who faced, from time to time, hard external growth constraints that limited their policy space.

These countries could not use their currencies to compensate for deficits in their balance of payments. That is why they had to change their development policies, sometimes promoting non-orthodox institutional innovation, to deal with dollar scarcity while trying to sustain some level of growth.

However, since the 1990s, Latin American countries liberalised their capital account to attract financial investors to increase their macroeconomic performance and fight inflation with stabilisation plans based on an exchange rate anchor. So, in the wake of liberal economic policies and low international liquidity preference, they increased their interest rates to attract the capital flow. As the exchange rates became valued, domestic currencies became internationalised as 'short-term investment assets'.

However, the macroeconomic policy of Latin American countries did not gain structural flexibility. As the balance of payment dynamics became more influenced by massive and volatile capital movements, the monetary policy had to sustain interest rates at high levels to avoid speculative attacks and capital flight. Every time international liquidity preference increases, local interest rates must go up to avoid both the ghost of dollar devaluation and the fear of inflation pass-through.

So, even considering that currency internationalisation can bring flexibility to emerging countries, transforming domestic currencies into short-term investment assets is not the answer.

Political science introduces another perspective on the effects of the greater degree of freedom that the internationalised currency allows, emphasising the gains in power. Power would manifest itself through the capacity of a country to influence, to its advantage, the actions of other countries. Alternatively, power would also manifest itself through autonomy, i.e., the ability to act without being influenced or restricted by others.

Autonomy allows the issuing country of the international currency to increase its international leverage. The more foreigners depend on the internationalised currency, the more the issuing country has an advantage. This power will be exercised either directly, when the issuing country imposes its will to control the resources, or indirectly, by virtue of the institutional infrastructure created as the internationalisation process progresses. Without the need to demand it, countries dependent on the international currency must adjust their behaviour to the requirements of the issuing country.

An issuer of an internationally accepted currency also benefits from increasing reputation. As long as the international currency is a symbol of economic and political strength, it is a source of prestige in the community of countries. The case of the USA is exceptional, as the dollar is the top currency in the currency hierarchy. Therefore, the country has an enormous capacity to mobilise real and financial resources and great control over international financial markets through its monetary policies and the administration of payment system.

Other countries also benefit from the internationalisation of their domestic money to increase their international influence. The example of the euro is self-evident. Countries that adopt the euro have more international prestige. This can also influence countries whose currencies are low in the money hierarchy and give some autonomy in the face of the USA. In this sense, should emerging countries try to issue international currencies to achieve leverage and improve their reputation? It depends. The experience that Latin Americans had with its currency internationalisation as short-term investment assets suggests the opposite. Indeed, its reputation as a safe and promising economy during periods of low international liquidity preference vanished with the emergence of high international liquidity preference. It did not increase its autonomy or its power to influence internationalisation. This strategy was a failure.

Alternatively, a country that issues a currency with regional strength can increase its political power to the extent that it can pay a relevant part of its imports and financial expenses with its currency. Its regional projection would naturally increase, and it becomes easier to impose regional institutions in accord with its interests. The Chinese case, at present, seems to fit well into this category.

Eichengreen and Lombardi (2015) highlight the regional presence of China in Asia as an obvious way to renminbi internationalisation, even considering that renminbi is a candidate for a global currency. China is the most relevant supporter of the Asian Bond Market Initiative, Asian Bond Forum, Asian Bond Fund, Chiang Mai Initiative Multilateralisation and ASEAN-China Free Trade Agreement. All of which work to further deepen economic and financial integration in the region.

Recently, the Belt and Road Initiative (BRI) gave new impulse to this movement of integration. It envisages investments in transport and energy infrastructure primarily concentrated in Asia and secondarily in Africa, of the order of US$1 trillion. The expectation is that the BRI will develop the regional economy in line with Chinese interests. One of the components of this project is the advancement of the renminbi's internationalisation, the currency of denomination for most of the financing to be carried out through Chinese banks and capital markets for companies and governments of countries directly affected by BRI (Chatzky and McBride, 2020). The Chinese case reinforces the notion that currency internationalisation strategy should be coherent with the country's development strategy to increase its international reputation and leverage.

The Costs of Currency Internationalisation

The costs and benefits of currency internationalisation have been widely discussed in the literature. While mainstream economists mostly present an economic analysis of the potential benefits of issuing the key currency of the system (Tavlas, 1997), such as transactional costs, international seigniorage and flexibility of macroeconomic policy, the costs of the internationalisation of a currency seem to be underestimated. Driven by the lack of a political analysis of currency internationalisation, International Political Economy scholars presented further benefits of this process. However, once again, both the economic and political costs considered are from the standpoint of issuing a central currency or the key-currency of the international monetary system.

In this literature, both mainstream economists and International Political Economy scholars failed to account for the costs of internationalising a currency issued by an emerging or developing economies (i.e. peripheral currencies), which, by definition, are located in the lowest positions of the currency hierarchy. Post-Keynesian economists, who have been more recently contributing to this literature, have emphasised other risks involved in this process, such as exchange rate volatility, loss of monetary policy autonomy and financial fragility (Fritz et al., 2018; Kaltenbrunner, 2018). So the question that needs to be raised is: are we actually 'getting the calculus right', as suggested by Cohen (2012)? Currency internationalisation is seen as a positive phenomenon that mostly brings economic and political prosperity, with a few minor costs incurred in this process. Although this may be true for those currencies positioned at the top of the currency hierarchy, peripheral currencies, which arguably have become more internationalised in the recent years, may not experience any of the benefits discussed in the previous session. In fact, these currencies have to endure further severe costs that are mostly disregarded in the literature.

De Conti (2011) brings a new factor to explain an additional determinant of currency internationalisation: political willingness. Although he recognises this factor per se is not enough to internationalise a currency, as this process is also a result of market forces, political strength and domestic regulation, it can still be a decisive factor in this process. Essentially, policymakers cannot force a currency to become more internationalised, but they have the tools to prevent it. In evaluating whether or not currency internationalisation should be promoted or avoided through policymaking, a thorough analysis of the costs of currency internationalisation needs to be taken into consideration.

The first cost discussed in the literature is the loss of control of domestic monetary policy (Tavlas, 1997). This cost refers to the fact that a highly internationalised currency, or the key currency of the system must have its liabilities held by foreigners, which is currently the case of the USA. However, this cost of currency internationalisation presents two main flaws. First, the loss of control of monetary policy would be an issue of the key-currency of the international system, and it would probably not present a threat to other currencies that are also internationalised. Thus, this is not a disadvantage of internationalising a currency, but a cost of issuing the most internationalised currency of the system. In fact, the cost of depending on an international currency is probably much higher than the cost of the responsibility to provide liquidity to the international monetary system. Second, inflation is not merely a monetary phenomenon, as argued by monetarists and other mainstream economists (Friedman, 1971). In that sense, despite the fact that controlling money supply may be more complicated with the presence of foreign actors, it does not mean that inflation will be harder to be tamed.

It is interesting to notice that the loss of control of monetary policy would be caused by another cost of currency internationalisation – policy responsibility. As the issuer of the key-currency of the international monetary system, the US must provide liquidity to the rest of the world. In fact, it was precisely the liquidity provision after the Second World War in the form of credit to support the European economic recovery, and later reinforced in the Bretton Woods system, that reinforced the current international currency status of the US dollar. Although having the domestic currency under the possession of non-residents increases the difficulty of controlling monetary conditions in the domestic country, it also gives the country the power (benefits) of seigniorage and macroeconomic flexibility.

The third cost of currency internationalisation, discussed by Cohen (2012), is the risk of exchange rate appreciation. Indeed, as the US dollar stands at the highest position of the currency hierarchy, it is considered the most liquid currency of the International Monetary System. De Conti et al. (2013) uses a Minskyan framework to explain the cyclical demand for currencies in the international market. In times of economic prosperity, when agents are less risk averse, investors are 'searching for yield' and capital flows move towards emerging countries. While this may cause an appreciation pressure on peripheral currencies, the demand for the key-currency of the system is still relatively stable. That is because the US dollar is not only used as a store of value ('investment currency'), but also as a means of payment and unit of account, both in the private and public sectors. So even though part of this international demand may shift towards emerging market economies (EMEs), there is a stable, inertial factor that maintains the stability of the US dollar. Conversely, in times of economic recession or a general deterioration of international agents' expectations about international assets, there is a reversion of the capital flows towards a 'safe heaven' – the US dollar. That explains the reason why the key currency of the system may face constant appreciation pressures.

In terms of managing exchange rates in the US, it may be more difficult to devalue the US dollar. Even in times of economic crisis, such as the 2008 financial crisis, in which the USA was the centre of the crisis, there were large capital flows towards this country. On the other hand, the US has the privilege of greater policy autonomy: it is a 'policymaker' as opposed to a 'policy-taker' (Ocampo, 2001; Prates, 2020). In that sense, small changes in the interest rates attract large capital inflows, as dollar-denominated assets are extremely liquid. Consequently, the issuer of the key-currency of the International Monetary System may face exchange rate appreciation pressures, which can lead to deficits in the current account and have a negative effect on producers, as both exporters and importers will lose competitiveness (Cohen, 2012).

The fourth cost of issuing an international currency identified by Cohen (2012) is external constraint. This cost refers to the disadvantage of issuing a much internationalised currency as it creates international liabilities issues in the domestic currency. According to this literature, this cost may undermine the benefit of 'macroeconomic flexibility'; given that these liabilities are very liquid, as they are denominated in an internationalised currency, it can increase the volatility of the exchange rate, as the demand for this money may change in the short term. Another risk is that this country becomes more exposed to changes in the international market.

Although many peripheral currencies generally do not denominate international liabilities (the financial side of the unit of account), the type of currency internationalisation that emerging countries experience may lead to much heavier external constraints – the speculative currency internationalisation

(Orsi, 2019). In periods of economic prosperity, when there is an excess of liquidity in the international market, there is an increasing demand for assets denominated in peripheral currencies, which generally offer higher returns, i.e. higher interest rates. Conversely, with changes in the international liquidity preference in times of greater economic and financial distress, such as in the Global Financial Crisis or at the beginning of the pandemic, these capital flows are quickly reversed towards a 'safe heaven' (De Conti et al., 2013; De Paula et al., 2017). Therefore, as peripheral currencies become more internationalised in a broader sense, i.e. they are held by non-residents, these countries may experience greater exchange rate volatility and higher vulnerability to external factors, such as sudden changes in the international liquidity preference.

CONCLUSION

The existing literature focuses on internationalised currencies that belong to the top of the currency hierarchy. Little attention has been paid to those inter-nationalised currencies that belong to the base of the currency hierarchy. We have addressed this literature gap. Accordingly, we re-evaluate benefits and costs of emerging economies currency internationalisation.

On the one hand, the benefits of currency internationalisation – that belongs to the top of money hierarchy – does not fully apply to emerging economies' currencies. For example, one should *not* hope that an emerging country cur-rency – such as the Brazilian Real – will benefit from seigniorage gains. This will happen, in the best scenario, only very partially or marginally. The same may be said of other benefits of currency internationalisation.

On the other hand, the costs of internationalisation seem to be more rele-vant for emerging economies' currencies. We are especially concerned with the dependence of those economies on a 'speculative investment currency' or the so-called carry trade capital. This concern is particularly relevant for Post-Keynesians since the volatility of those capital flows enhances uncertainty.

Summing up, the actual costs seem to outweigh the benefits of a partial currency internationalisation. Given the complexity and relevance of the topic, further research must be done. A natural further step is to analyse a specific case of currency internationalisation, such as the Brazilian Real.

NOTE

1. Currency internationalisation (and currency convertibility) may also be analysed in terms of the capacity of domestic actors to issue debt in local currency. This limitation of emerging and developing countries to borrow in local currency was coined by Eichengreen et al. (2005) as the 'original sin'.

REFERENCES

Andrade, R. P. and Prates, D. M. (2013), 'Exchange rate dynamics in a peripheral monetary economy: A Keynesian perspective'. *Journal of Post Keynesian Economics*, 35, 399–424.

Arida, P. (2003), 'Por uma moeda plenamente conversível'. *Brazilian Journal of Political Economy*, 23, 497–501.

Carneiro, R. (2008), 'Globalização e inconversibilidade monetária'. *Revista de Economia Política*, 28(4), 539–556.

Chatzky, A. and McBride, J. (2020), 'China's massive road and belt initiative'. *Council of Foreign Relations Newsletter*. Available at: https://www.cfr.org/backgrounder/chinas-massive-belt-and-road-initiative, accessed 15 October 2021.

Cohen, B. J. (1971), *The Future of Sterling as an International Currency*. London: Macmillan.

Cohen, B. J. (1998), *The Geography of Money*. New York: Cornell University Press.

Cohen, B. J. (2008), *International Political Economy: An Intellectual History*. Princeton: Princeton University Press.

Cohen, B. J. (2011), *The Future of Global Currency: The Euro Versus the Dollar*. Abingdon: Routledge University Press.

Cohen, B. J. (2012), 'The benefits and costs of an international currency: Getting the calculus right'. *Open Economic Review*, 23, 13–31.

Cohen, B. J. (2013), 'Currency and state power'. In M. Finnemore and J. Goldstein (eds), *Back to Basics: State Power in a Contemporary World*. Oxford: Oxford University Press.

Cohen, B. J. and Benney, T. M. (2013), 'What does the international currency system really look like?' *Review of International Political Economy*, 21(5), 1017–1041.

De Conti, B. M. (2011), 'Políticas cambial e monetária: Os dilemas enfrentados por países emissores de moedas periféricas'. PhD thesis, Universidade Estadual de Campinas (UNICAMP).

De Conti, B. and Prates, D. M. (2018), 'The International Monetary System hierarchy: current configuration and determinants'. *Texto Para Discussão*. Campinas: Unicamp.

De Conti, B. M., Bainacarelli, A. and Rossi, P. (2013), 'Currency hierarchy, liquidity preference and exchange rates: A Keynesian/Minskyan approach'. *Congrès de l'Association Française d'Économie Politique*. Université Montesquieu Bordeaux IV, France.

De Paula, L. F., Fritza, B. and Prates, D. M. (2015), 'Center and periphery in international monetary relations implications for macroeconomic policies in emerging economies'. *Desigualdades Working Paper Series*.

De Paula, L. F., Fritz, B. and Prates, D. M. (2017), 'Keynes at the periphery: Currency hierarchy and challenges for economic policy in emerging economies'. *Journal of Post Keynesian Economics*, 40, 183–202.

Eichengreen, B. and Lombardi, D. (2015), 'Rmbi or Rmbr: Is the renminbi destined to become a global or regional currency?' *Working Paper 21716*. Available at: http://www.nber.org/papers/w21716, accessed 15 October 2021.

Eichengreen, B., Hausmann, R. and Panizza, U. (2005), 'The pain of original sin'. In B. Eichengreen and R. Hausmann (eds), *Other People's Money: Debt Denomination and Financial Instability in Emerging Market Economies*. Chicago: The University of Chicago Press, 1–49.

Friberg, R. and Wilander, F. (2008), 'The currency denomination of exports: A questionnaire study'. *Journal of International Economics*, 75, 54–69.

Friedman, M. (1971), *A Theoretical Framework for Monetary Analysis*. Cambridge: NBER Books.

Fritz, B., De Paula, L. F. and Prates, D. M. (2018), 'Global currency hierarchy and national policy space: a framework for peripheral economies'. *European Journal of Economics and Economic Policies: Intervention*, 15, 208–218.

Gao, H. and Yu, Y. (2011), 'Internationalisation of the renminbi'. In Bank for International Settlements (ed.), *Currency Internationalisation: Lessons from the Global Financial Crisis and Prospects for the Future in Asia and the Pacific*, vol. 61, pp. 105–124. Bank for International Settlements.

Goldberg, L. S. and Tille, C. (2005), 'Vehicle currency use in international trade'. *Staff Reports*. Federal Reserve Bank of New York.

Gourichas, P. and Rey, H. (2005), 'International financial adjustment'. *Journal of Political Economy*, 115, 665–703.

Itaú (2021), *Management Discussion and Analysis and Complete Financial Statements of the Second Quarter of 2021*. Available at: https://www.itau.com.br/relacoes -com-investidores/listresultados.aspx?idCanal=lyyjtVJ4BExsF2fi1Kfy0Q==& linguagem=en#, accessed 15 October 2021.

Ito, H. and Chinn, M. D. (2014), 'The rise of the "redback" and the People's Republic of China's capital account liberalization: An empirical analysis of the determinants of invoicing currencies'. *ADBI Working Paper 473*.

Kaltenbrunner, A. (2015), 'A Post Keynesian framework of exchange rate determination: A Minskyan approach'. *Journal of Post Keynesian Economics*, 38, 426–448.

Kaltenbrunner, A. (2018), 'Financialised internationalisation and structural hierarchies: A mixed-method study of exchange rate determination in emerging economies'. *Cambridge Journal of Economics*, 42, 1315–1341.

Kenen, P. B. (1983), *The Role of the Dollar as an International Currency*. New York: Group of Thirty.

Keynes, J. M. (1936), *The General Theory of Employment, Interest and Money*. London: Macmillan.

Kim, K. and Suh, Y (2011), 'Dealing with the benefits and costs of internationalisation of the Korean won'. In Bank for International Settlements (ed.), *Currency Internationalisation: Lessons from the Global Financial Crisis and Prospects for the Future in Asia and the Pacific*, vol. 61, pp. 151–171. Bank for International Settlements.

Krugman, P. R. (1980), 'Vehicle currencies and the structure of international exchange'. *Journal of Money, Credit and Banking*, 12, 513–526.

Lim, E.-G. (2006), 'The Euro's challenge to the dollar: Different views from economists and evidence from COFER (Currency Composition of Foreign Exchange Reserves) and other data'. *International Monetary Fund Working Papers 153*.

Medeiros, C. and Serrano, F. (2003), 'Capital flows to emerging markets under the floating dollar standard: A critical view based on the Brazilian experience'. In L. R. M. Vernengo (ed.), *Monetary and Financial Integration*, pp. 218–242. Cheltenham, UK and Northampton, MA, USA: Edward Elgar.

McCauley, R. (2006), 'Internationalising a currency: The case of the Australian dollar'. *BIS Quarterly Review*, 41–54.

Ocampo, J.A. (2001), 'International asymmetries and the design of the international financial system'. *CEPAL Serie Temas de Coyuntura*, 15.

Orsi, B. (2019), *Currency Internationalisation and Currency Hierarchy in Emerging Economies: The Role of the Brazilian Real.* Leeds: University of Leeds.

Prates, D. M. (2002), 'Crises financeiras dos paises "emergentes": Uma interpretação heterodoxa'. PhD Thesis, Campinas: Universidade Estadual de Campinas.

Prates, D. M. (2020), 'Beyond modern money theory: A Post-Keynesian approach to the currency hierarchy, monetary sovereignty, and policy space'. *Review of Keynesian Economics*, 8(4), 494–511.

Tavlas, G. S. (1997), 'Internationalization of currencies: The case of the US dollar and its challenger euro'. *The International Executive*, 39, 581–597.

Warnock, F. E. and Warnock, V. C. (2009), 'International capital flows and US interest rates'. *Journal of International Money and Finance*, 28, 903–919.

2. Monetary institutions and economic performance in Latin America: the experience with an inflation targeting regime in the period 2000–2020

Eliane Araujo, Elisangela Araujo and Mateus Ramalho Ribeiro da Fonseca

INTRODUCTION

The Inflation Targeting (IT) regime was first introduced in New Zealand in 1990 and has since been adopted by many emerging economies. Some countries in Latin America (LA), a region that experienced episodes of runaway inflation throughout the 1980s crisis, did not shirk the rule, implementing such a strategy as well. Brazil was the first country to do so in mid-1999. Currently, eight Latin American countries conduct their monetary policy through the IT regime, namely: Brazil, Chile, Colombia, Guatemala, Mexico, Paraguay, Peru and Uruguay.

IT is part of the New Consensus Macroeconomic (NCM) theoretical framework. It is considered a state-of-the-art conduct of monetary policy and postulates that the inflation rate must be low and stable for long-term growth. Supported by theoretical and empirical elements from mainstream schools of thought, it suggests that the short-term interest rate allows inflation to be driven to the center of the given target: it is high whenever inflation or the economy's potential GDP is close to the target set for inflation or vice versa.

Regarding the positive aspects that accompany these Latin American economies since the adoption of the IT regime, is the fact that they managed to reduce inflation levels and keep them relatively under control. At the same time, it should be mentioned that this region also followed a liberalizing reform agenda throughout the 1990s. The targeted economic growth, however, has decelerated considerably since then, either relative to LA's own historical trend or in comparison with other developing economies.

Therefore, it is clear that, in practice, the strategies adopted by Latin American countries, including IT, instead of contributing to the stabilization and growth of the region, left structural weaknesses exposed, perpetuating the social and economic gap historically present in these countries. As particular facts of these economies, it is important to highlight the increase in interest rates and the tendency of chronic overvaluation of the exchange rate, which represent a competitive disadvantage for these economies, compromise their catching up process and consolidate this region as being one of the least promising in terms of growth in the world in recent decades. In fact, the region's international integration has been extremely fragile, relying primarily on some commodities of global interest, subject to the volatility of global financial cycles and the restrictions of the international monetary hierarchy.

In this context, the aim of this chapter is to analyze theoretically and empirically the Latin American experience with IT, emphasizing its effects on inflation and economic performance in the region. The central idea is to relate the institutional aspects of the price control policy with the development trajectories experienced by Latin American countries that adopted IT, discussing its implications and listing possible paths for an agenda based on growth and improvement in external insertion.

Therefore, the research is divided into three sections, in addition to the introduction and final considerations. After the introduction, the second section discusses the basic characteristics of the institutional aspects of IT in Latin America. The third section investigates the performance of countries in terms of inflation and economic growth. Then, in the fourth section, an empirical analysis is carried out – for six of the eight countries who adopted the IT (Brazil, Chile, Colombia, Guatemala, Mexico and Peru owing to data availability) – on the transmission of the monetary policy for each of the countries. The analysis aimed at investigating the main effects of the monetary policy on domestic macroeconomic variables: price, exchange rate and economic growth, with a discussion of the main results. Finally, the concluding comments of the research are presented, adding that the monetary policy conducted under IT showed effectiveness in controlling prices. However, it implied high interest rates and, with this, influenced the appreciation of the domestic currency, with erratic effects on the product in the region.

INFLATION TARGETING: THEORETICAL-CONCEPTUAL AND INSTITUTIONAL ASPECTS

According to the New Classic school, the fact that economic agents anticipate policymakers' decisions implies that it is not possible to conduct monetary policy in a discretionary manner. Monetary policy rules, on the other hand, can be used to fight inflation without the short-term recessive costs present in the monetarist model. As a result, several models emerge in an attempt to outline an optimal conduct for central banks, with an emphasis on the independent central bank and inflation targeting regime models, which are based on the credibility–reputation–delegation triad.

According to the NCM, IT is considered state-of-the-art and postulates that the inflation rate must be low and stable in order to sustain long-term growth. Supported by theoretical and empirical elements from various positions of thought, notably in the new classical economics – which includes the hypothesis of rational expectations, the temporal inconsistency of monetary policy and the inflation bias – the NCM implicitly brings old ideas from macroeconomics, such as the existence of a natural rate of unemployment and currency neutrality in the long term (but not in the short run, due to the rigidity of prices and wages, as suggested by the New Keynesians).

The IT model is characterized by three equations, namely: the IS, in equation (2.1), representing the demand side; the Phillips curve (PC), in equation (2.2), representing the supply side; and the monetary policy rule in equation (2.3), derived from the government or central bank trade-off between output and inflation (Arestis and Sawyer, 2008; Fontana, 2009). Analytically:

$$\pi_t = (y_t - y^*_t), s_t) \tag{2.1}$$

$$(y_t - y^*_t) = h(X_t, R_t, Z_t) \tag{2.2}$$

$$r_t = r_t^* + \alpha\left(\pi_t - \pi_t^*\right) + \beta(y_t - \overline{y}_t) \tag{2.3}$$

Equations (2.1) and (2.2) relate the output gap respectively to the inflation rate (π_t) and to a vector of exogenous variables (X_t) and (R_t), which are, respectively, net exports and primary surplus. The variable (Z_t) is an error term. Equation (2.3), in turn, shows a simple rule for the conduct of policy by the Central Bank, in which the nominal interest rate (r_t^*) is a function of the real effective interest rate (r_t^*) and the difference between real inflation (π_t) and the inflation target (π_t^*) and the output gap (Fontana, 2009).

According to Arestis, Ferrari-Filho and Paula (2011), the main theoretical characteristics of the Central Bank of Brazil (CBB) macroeconomic model, closely based on the NCM model, can be summarized as follows:

(i)   Price stability is the main long-term objective of monetary policy. Furthermore, the price stability target can be accompanied by output stabilization, as long as price stability is not violated;

(ii)   IT is a monetary policy framework in which public announcement of official inflation targeting is required. In this approach, 'expected inflation' and transparency of inflation forecasts are an important element of the policy;

(iii)   Monetary policy is the main instrument of macroeconomic policy, and should not be operated by politicians, but by specialists: so-called independent central banks;

(iv)   Fiscal policy is no longer seen as a powerful macroeconomic instrument to stabilize the economy. Thus, economic authorities should adopt a fiscal target in terms of primary surplus;

(v)   The level of economic activity oscillates around an equilibrium on the supply side. This means that the level of effective demand does not play an independent role in the long-term economic activity;

(vi)   Finally, considering the context of open emerging economies and with a long history of external imbalances and crises, the exchange rate is a crucially important variable as it transmits certain external effects on the interest rate and the inflation rate, among others. Given that, IT can lead to a more stable currency, as it signals a clear commitment to price stability, in a floating exchange rate system.

The proposal for central bank independence consists of delegating the conduct of monetary policy to an independent agent, with the objective of controlling inflation, thus maintaining the credibility of the monetary policy and the reputation of the monetary authority. On the other hand, IT can be defined as a regime for conducting the monetary policy, based on the announcement of a medium-term target for inflation. In other words, there is an anchorage via agents' expectations about future inflation, through which the transparency of monetary policy, which must communicate the plans, objectives and decisions to the public, plays a fundamental role.

In addition, the monetary authority commits to price stability, to which the other objectives are subordinated, so that the independence of the central bank is also a desirable aspect for this school. The use of available information on many variables serves as a basis for adjusting the instrument of monetary policy performance – the short-term interest rate – whose level allows for driving inflation to the center of the stipulated target: it is high whenever inflation or the economy's potential GDP is close to the inflation target.

The set of central banks currently adopting the IT regimes is very heterogeneous, including nine developed countries and 18 developing and emerging market economies on all continents. The first country to adopt IT was New Zealand in December 1989 and the most recent was Serbia in 2009.

The implementation of IT resulted basically from two circumstances. The first is the inefficiency of existing nominal anchors, such as exchange rate targets and monetary targets, which have failed to control inflation. Second, there is the advance of the ideas of the NCM, whose rise from the 1990s onwards decisively influenced policymakers around the world, particularly due to the idea of the impossibility of monetary policy to affect real variables, such as output and the permanent employment, following the recommendation that this should not be conducted in a discretionary manner, but in accordance with a rule of conduct.

In developing countries, the context for implementing IT was similar. Mostly, it took place during the 1990s and 2000, in a context of high inflation rates, finding in this framework an alternative for macroeconomic stabilization. In some cases, such as South Korea and Chile, the prevailing context was related to growth, which continued after the introduction of the regime (Fonseca et al., 2016).

In other cases, such as Mexico and even Brazil, high inflation rates were driven by economic crises, but deep down they had complex, structural and institutional characteristics which governments had difficulties fighting. Thus, the economic authorities began to strive to use monetary controls and the Central Banks began to monitor credit, exchange rates, interest rates and foreign currency reserves. In most countries, however, an informal containment of these variables was used and, only after obtaining some results, was IT rigorously adopted. This was the case in Mexico, South Africa and Chile.

Currently, eight Latin American countries conduct their monetary policy through IT: Brazil, Chile, Colombia, Guatemala, Mexico, Paraguay, Peru and Uruguay. However, this research analyzed six countries in the empirical part (Brazil, Chile, Colombia, Guatemala, Mexico and Peru). Therefore, the following data refer only to these selected countries. Table 2.1 shows the period of adoption and the characteristics of the IT in these countries.

Initially, Table 2.1 shows a certain convergence in the legal mandates of central banks, making it possible to apprehend that central banks that adopt IT establish price stability as the main objective of monetary policy, a fact that clashes with most central banks from the rest of the world, in which there are multiple objectives for the performance of monetary policy, such as pursuing economic growth, well-being, low unemployment and financial stability (Niedźwiedzińska, 2018).

With regard to central bank independence, in terms of autonomy to define the objective of monetary policy, Hammond (2012) highlights that, as the objective of a monetary policy of price stability is generally established by law, the independence of the objective, in the terms suggested by Rogoff (1985), becomes a second-order issue in the definition of inflation targeting regimes. However, it is worth noting that the central banks of countries that adopt IT have operational independence: that is, as monetary policy managers, they are free to choose the instruments necessary to reach the previously established

Table 2.1   *Institutional aspects of the IT in Latin American countries*

Country and date of adoption of the IT regime	Legal mandate	Target horizon	Operational independence of the CB	Type of target and measurement	IT target specified by band	Index or inflation core
Brazil, Jun. 1999	Price stability	Yearly target	Yes	Target + band; target core	Government and Central Bank	IPCA
Chile, Sep. 1999	Currency stability and regular functioning of domestic and foreign payments	Around two years	Yes	Target + band; target core	Central Bank	IPC
Colombia, Oct. 1999	Maintain the currency's purchasing power	Mid-term	Yes	Band; target core	Central Bank	IPC
Guatemala, 2005	Price stability	End of the year	Yes	Target + band; target core	Central Bank	IPC
Mexico, 2001	Maintain the purchasing power of the Mexican currency	Mid-term	Yes	Target + band; target core	Central Bank	IPC
Peru, Jan. 2002	Reserves for monetary stability	At anytime	Yes	Target + band; target core	Central Bank	IPC

Source: Authors' elaboration based on Hammond (2012), Central Bank of Brazil (2021), Central Bank of Chile (2021), Central Bank of Colombia (2021), Central Bank of Guatemala (2021), Central Bank of Mexico (2021) and Central Reserve Bank of Peru (2021).

inflation target. In theoretical terms, this is what Walsh (1995) suggests with regards to the independence of the central bank economic policy instruments.

Regarding the convergence horizon, there is a clear division: three countries adopt a medium-term convergence period of two years (Chile, Colombia and Mexico) and the others have a shorter term, formally defined as: one year, at end of the year or at any time (Brazil, Guatemala and Peru). It should be noted that medium-term horizons provide greater flexibility to the inflation targeting regime, as they anchor inflation expectations while allowing for short-term divergences from the stipulated target. It should be noted that an important aspect in choosing the time horizon for the convergence of inflation targeting is the extension of the transmission mechanisms of the monetary policy: that is, if the process through which monetary policy decisions are transmitted to real output and inflation is slow, the central bank is not able to influence inflation in the short term.

Another relevant feature of the IT regime is the definition of a point target or a tolerance band. The point target implies a stricter regime and can also be more difficult to be achieved. The target established in the form of tolerance bands, on the other hand, gives greater flexibility to the regime, facilitating its achievement. Table 2.1 shows that, in general, countries opt for both, that is, a point target with top and bottom tolerance limits for inflation.

The definition of the price index is also an important IT issue, as the adopted index can be a full index or a core inflation measure. Considering all countries that adopt IT in the world, these use the consumer price index (CPI) as a measure of inflation, especially due to its monthly frequency. However, despite using the full index, many central banks also look at core inflation measures as an indicator of inflationary pressures in the economy. Hammond (2012) highlights that in several other countries, such as Australia, Canada, the Czech Republic, Ghana, Hungary, Norway, Poland, Sweden and Turkey, they also publish core inflation forecasts and not just global inflation. These core inflation measures are characterized by excluding components that are more sensitive to different types of shocks in the inflation computation. The use of core inflation aims to reduce the volatility of the price index and, therefore, avoid excessive use of monetary policy in the event of supply shocks. In this respect, in relation to the Latin American countries, it is worth noting that none of them uses any measure of core inflation, but only the full index (CPI).

Finally, regarding the establishment of the target, in most countries that have adopted IT worldwide, according to Hammond (2012) and Niedźwiedzińska (2018), the inflation target is established jointly between the government and the Central Bank. In only three cases is the target established exclusively by the government. In this issue, the Latin American countries also differ from the majority, as the target is set solely by the central bank. Brazil is the only exception, where the target is defined by the government.

In short, the observation of the institutional aspects of IT in Latin America makes it clear that questions relating to the objective of monetary policy and the horizon of convergence of inflation to the target are focused on price stability and in the short term. This fact shows that monetary policy is underused in terms of achieving broader economic objectives, as is done in other countries under the same institutional framework as IT. Thus, when the economy suffers shocks, central banks need to respond quickly to shocks in order to meet the inflation target within the established horizon.

This implies that price stability is the essence of monetary policy and that inflation must be fought, even to the detriment of other central economic variables, such as output and employment. In addition, given the short horizon of inflation targeting convergence, there are difficulties for the economy to adjust to the occurrence of supply shocks, which are aggravated by the fact that they are not considered an inflation core, or for the transmission mechanisms of monetary policy to have the desired effects on final targets.

The next section provides a contextualization of monetary policy and its results in Latin America in recent decades.

MONETARY POLICY AND ECONOMIC PERFORMANCE IN LATIN AMERICA UNDER IT

The last few decades have been marked by a relative price stability in several countries in LA, indicating a certain convergence between the inflation rates verified in the region and the world rates. In fact, according to IMF data (2021b), the average inflation rate in countries that adopt IT in Latin America was 6.07 percent between 1999 and 2020, higher than the world average, which was 3.94 percent in the same period. When compared with the group of emerging economies, however, this rate was closer (6.38 percent).

In this sense, as positive aspects of the policy conducted through IT, it is worth highlighting the fact that these countries managed to reduce the uncontrolled inflation levels that characterized the region throughout the 1980s and 1990s and kept it relatively under control, at levels similar to their peers and, even acceptable, by the world standard. Table 2.2 shows the inflation rates and basic interest rate in Latin American countries that have adopted IT.

Note in Table 2.2 that there was a clear downward trend in inflation after the early 2000s. Nevertheless, price volatility can also be seen in times of greater global instability, such as in the international financial crisis of 2007/2008. Another interesting detail refers to the fact that, among the countries analyzed, two had an average inflation below 3.5 percent p.a. – Chile and Peru – while the other four had an average inflation above 5 percent p.a., with Brazil standing out for having the highest average inflation rate: 6.14 percent p.a. between 1999–2020.

Regarding the interest rates established by the Latin American central banks, the so-called 'policy rate', it is worth noting that there is again a considerable volatility component, associated at times to events related to the external sector, but also to their own domestic dynamics. With respect to the levels of basic interest rates, it can be seen that, on average, between 2002 and 2020 the rate established by most countries was between 3.5 percent and 6.0 percent p.a., on average, with the exception being Brazil, where this rate was almost twofold: 11.7 percent per year, in the same period.

With these inflation and interest rates highlighted, it should be clarified that, alongside the IT regime, several other liberalizing institutional reforms were adopted in Latin America from the 1990s onwards. Despite contributing to promote price stabilization, the fact is that the region has been characterized

Table 2.2   *Inflation rate and basic interest rate* in Latin American countries that have adopted IT (1999–2020)*

	Brazil		Chile		Colombia		Guatemala		Mexico		Peru	
Year	Inflation	Interest Rate	Inflation	Interest Rate	Inflation	Interest Rate	Inflation	Interest Rate	Inflation	Interest Rate	Inflation	Interest Rate
1999	4.86	–	3.34	–	10.87	–	5.21	–	16.59	–	3.47	–
2000	7.04	–	3.84	–	9.22	–	5.98	–	9.49	–	3.76	–
2001	6.84	–	3.57	–	7.97	–	7.29	–	6.37	–	1.98	–
2002	8.45	25.00	2.49	3.00	6.35	5.25	8.13	–	5.03	8.25	0.19	–
2003	14.71	16.50	2.81	2.25	7.13	7.25	5.60	–	4.55	6.12	2.26	–
2004	6.60	17.75	1.05	2.25	5.90	6.50	7.58	–	4.69	8.75	3.66	3.00
2005	6.87	18.00	3.05	4.50	5.05	6.00	9.11	4.25	3.99	8.27	1.62	3.25
2006	4.18	13.25	3.39	5.25	4.29	7.50	6.56	5.00	3.63	7.02	2.00	4.50
2007	3.64	11.25	4.41	6.00	5.55	9.50	6.82	6.50	3.97	7.57	1.78	5.00
2008	5.68	13.75	8.72	8.25	7.00	9.50	11.36	7.25	5.12	8.25	5.79	6.50
2009	4.89	8.75	0.35	0.50	4.20	3.50	1.86	4.50	5.30	4.50	2.94	1.25
2010	5.04	10.75	1.41	3.25	2.27	3.00	3.86	4.50	4.16	4.50	1.53	3.00
2011	6.64	11.00	3.34	5.25	3.42	4.75	6.21	5.50	3.41	4.50	3.37	4.25
2012	5.40	7.25	3.01	5.00	3.17	4.25	3.78	5.00	4.11	4.50	3.66	4.25
2013	6.20	10.00	1.79	4.50	2.02	3.25	4.34	5.00	3.81	3.50	2.81	4.00
2014	6.33	11.75	4.72	3.00	2.90	4.50	3.42	4.00	4.02	3.00	3.24	3.50
2015	9.03	14.25	4.35	3.50	4.99	5.75	2.39	3.00	2.72	3.25	3.55	3.75
2016	8.74	13.75	3.79	3.50	7.51	7.50	4.45	3.00	2.82	5.75	3.59	4.25
2017	3.45	7.00	2.18	2.50	4.31	4.75	4.42	2.75	6.04	7.25	2.80	3.25
2018	3.66	6.50	2.43	2.75	3.24	4.25	3.75	2.75	4.90	8.25	1.32	2.75
2019	3.73	4.50	2.56	1.75	3.53	4.25	3.70	2.75	3.64	7.25	2.14	2.25
2020	3.21	2.00	3.05	0.50	2.52	1.75	3.21	1.75	3.40	4.25	1.83	0.25

Note: (*) Refers to the central bank policy rate – the central bank policy rate (CBPR) – which is the rate used by the Central Bank to implement or signal its actions within the scope of monetary policy.
Source: World Bank (2021) and IMF (International Financial Statistics, 2021a).

in recent decades by the persistent trend of stagnation in productivity and poor economic performance compared with other emerging economies (Palma, 2010).

As particular facts in these Latin American countries, it is worth noting the increase in the interest rate, the tendency to chronic overvaluation of the exchange rate, which represents a competitive disadvantage for these economies, compromising their catching up process. As shown by the IMF (2021b) data, the real effective exchange rate (REER), which is an important measure of the competitiveness of countries, was appreciated in several Latin American countries. By way of illustration, between 1999 and 2020, in Brazil, the index that demonstrates the trajectory of the aforementioned variable, went from 71.0 to 55.3, in Chile, from 107.3 to 84.8, in Colombia, from 89.9 to 67.0 and in Mexico from 106.7 to 77.3, indicating an unfavorable evolution to the foreign trade of these countries.[1]

The region's external insertion, in this context, has proved to be extremely fragile, based on a few commodities of world interest, subject to the volatility of global financial cycles and the constraints of the international currency hierarchy. As highlighted by Araujo et al. (2020), these developing economies, located at the base of the global monetary hierarchy, under external financial liberalization, are favored by the increase in capital inflows at times of expansion of global liquidity, when they finance the payments balance without major problems (meaning recurring current account deficits and capital account surpluses). And so, while the global bonanza lasts, capital inflows fuel the currency's overvaluation, forcing the expansion of consumption at the expense of external competitiveness. However, when global or country-specific shocks occur, which lead to a change in the risk perception of foreign investors, these economies start to face financial fragility, with the devaluation of the domestic currency, growth stagnation and even a financial crisis.

Therefore, there is a great impasse for the autonomy of economic policies in developing countries subject to cyclical fluctuations. Since the monetary policy is rigid in its conduct, moments of reversal in the financial and commodities cycle have strong effects, such as increases in exchange rates, interest rates, debt and reversal of possible ongoing growth trajectories.

This can be seen in Figure 2.1, which illustrates the behavior of terms of trade and GDP, for LA as a whole, between 1999 and 2020.

Figure 2.1 shows the existence of a direct relationship between the behavior of the terms of trade and the economic performance in Latin America is evident, so that when they improve, for example in the period from 2001 to the financial crisis in 2007/2008, the region's product follows the same trajectory. In times of global crisis, such as the aforementioned financial crisis and also in the post-2011 period, when the weakening of the commodity price boom is observed, the region returns to meager growth rates, being strongly affected in the context of the current crisis in 2020.

In short, despite its success in achieving price stability, Latin America was unable to turn this achievement into an ally of growth. Quite the opposite: the analysis of these data suggests that the institutional rigidity of IT in Latin America exacerbates the recessive effects of the financial and commodity cycle, so that there is room for improvement and use for the purpose of economic growth and improving the well-being of its population. In this sense, special attention to important variables such as the exchange rate is required, to improve the insertion of these countries in the world economy.

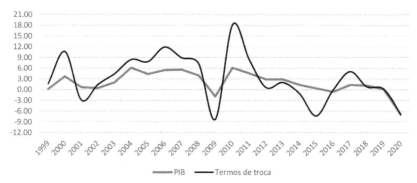

Source: IMF/WEO (2021a).

Figure 2.1   Percentage change in terms of trade and gross domestic product in Latin America, 1999–2020

AN EMPIRICAL ANALYSIS OF THE EFFECTS OF MONETARY SHOCKS IN COUNTRIES THAT ADOPT INFLATION TARGETING IN LATIN AMERICA

The objective of this section is to analyze the effects of shocks on monetary policies in Latin American countries (Brazil, Chile, Colombia, Guatemala, Mexico and Peru) that adopt the inflation targeting regime, investigating the response of some variables such as inflation, growth and exchange rate to a change in interest rate. The empirical exercise is inspired by articles that investigated the possibility of different economic policy outcomes, when considering regime change, that is, the distinction between periods of longer (regime 1) and lower interest rate volatility (regime 2). Some examples of articles dealing with the possible non-linearity of the effects of shocks on monetary policy are Artis et al. (2003) and Krolzig (2003).

The empirical research strategy consists, therefore, in estimating a Markov-Switching vector autoregressive (MS-VAR) model, which is generally used to capture the effects of monetary and fiscal shocks in the economy, considering the possibility of regime changes. For a set K of time series variables, $y_t = (y_1, ..., y_{kt})$, a VAR model captures the dynamic interactions between these variables. Its basic form with an order $p(\text{VAR}(p))$ can be represented as follows:

$$y_t = A_1 y_{t-1} + \cdots + A_p y_{t-p} + u_t \tag{2.4}$$

in which A_1 are matrices of coefficients $(K \times K)$ and $u_t = (u_{1t},\ldots,u_{kt})$ are the error terms, supposedly zero-meaning and independent.

There are several advantages to using VAR templates. First, the approach allows estimation of models with many parameters and does not impose restrictions on the form of impulse-response functions. Second, these models can be easily extended to estimate the effects of potential nonlinearities of shocks, as is the case in this research. Third, the model is well suited to dealing with error terms correlated over time.

The empirical analysis was developed for Latin American countries (Brazil, Chile, Colombia, Guatemala, Mexico and Peru) that adopted the inflation targeting regime, between 2000 and 2020, with monthly data. The variables used in the econometric analysis are the following: *IR* is the effective interest rate (annualized); *CPI* is inflation measured by the consumer price index; *EAI* is the economic activity index in which the industrial production variable was used as a proxy for economic activity (seasonally adjusted and deflated) and *ER* is the monthly exchange rate, measured by the national currency/US dollar ratio. Description of variables and their sources are available in the Appendix. The order of the estimated VAR starts with the economic policy shock variables, interest rate, inflation, followed by the economic activity and exchange rate variables.

Regarding the use of variables at level, instead of using the results of unit root tests, Sims (1990) emphasizes that the series should not be differentiated if the objective of the estimation is to understand the interrelationships between the variables, given that the process of differentiation leads to the loss of such relationships. Furthermore, the variables were transformed to natural logarithms to standardize the different ladders of variables and obtain the elasticities of these impulses in the Impulse-Response Functions.

Since the objective of this section is to estimate the impacts of monetary policy shocks on the economy at times of high and low interest rate volatility, the model is divided into two regimes. Regime 1 refers to moments of more volatile interest rates, and regime 2 represents moments of more stable interest rates. The model adopted for all countries was MS(2)-VAR(2), given the tests performed and in order to make the results comparable between countries.

The data were used to estimate and analyze an unrestricted MS-VAR model, with intercept, variance and parameters varying by regime. The justification for using the MS-VAR model comes from the possible non-linearity in the model's parameters, resulting from significant changes in these from one regime to another. The investigation of this hypothesis is carried out by the LR Test, under the null hypothesis that the model is linear in its parameters. Its result indicates that it is possible to reject the null hypothesis of linearity with a confidence level of 99 percent in relation to the alternative hypothesis that the

Table 2.3   *Effects of a monetary policy shock (interest) on GDP,*
exchange and inflation

		GDP	Exchange	Inflation
Brazil	Regime 1	Reduces	Appreciates +	Reduces+
	Regime 2	Increases	Appreciates	Reduces
Chile	Regime 1	Increases	Appreciates +	Reduces+
	Regime 2	Reduces	Appreciates	Reduces
Colombia	Regime 1	Increases	Appreciates	Reduces (puzzle)
	Regime 2	Increases	Depreciates	Reduces (puzzle)
Guatemala	Regime 1	Reduces+	Appreciates	Reduces
	Regime 2	Reduces	Does not change	Reduces
Mexico	Regime 1	Increases	Does not change	Reduces+
	Regime 2	Does not change	Appreciates +	Reduces (puzzle)
Peru	Regime 1	Increases	Depreciates	Reduces (puzzle)
	Regime 2	Does not change	Appreciates +	Reduces

Source: Authors' elaboration based on research data.

tested model is non-linear in Latin American countries, corroborating the use of the MS-VAR methodology.

Regarding the convergence of the EM algorithm, it took place after two interactions, with a change probability of 0.0001. This demonstrates that the model is highly convergent and stable from a statistical point of view. Figure 2.1 shows the good fit of the model in each estimated regime and indicates the occurrence of two regimes, demarcated by the GDP variable (Y).

The analysis of the results was conducted through the interpretation of impulse-response functions, which show the behavior of a certain variable in the model to shocks in the other variables included in the system. To facilitate the identification of the results, Table 2.3 summarizes the results of the impulse-response functions for regime 1, with a high interest rate, and for regime 2, with a low interest rate.

With regard to the effects of an increase in the interest rate (base interest rate set by central banks) on inflation, it is known that, under the IT regime, the objective of the central banks is to maintain inflation within the established target. In this sense, the monetary policy instrument is adjusted, that is, the base interest rate, so that current inflation converges towards the long-term inflation target. The impulse-response functions for the six Latin American economies studied show that a shock to the policy rate reduces inflation in all cases, mainly in regime 1, with more volatile interest rates for the cases of Brazil, Chile and Mexico. It is also worth noting that, in some countries such as Colombia, Mexico and Peru, it was identified that the initial effect of interest on prices was positive. Other authors have already identified this same effect, called the price puzzle, which has already been registered and investigated by several studies. Although the authors (Christiano et al., 1996; Sims, 1992; Sims and Zha, 1998) highlight the occurrence of this unexpected effect due to problems in the functional specification of the central banks' reaction function, specifically due to the omission of variables, others (Arestis, 1992; Palley, 1996) justify it by the increase in production costs resulting from an increase in the interest rate, which are quickly transmitted to prices, thus explaining the positive effects of an increase in interest rates on prices. However, after the first periods of the shock, the increase in the interest rate contributes to the reduction of inflation, as IT presupposes.

With regard to the effects of the increase in the interest rate on the exchange rate, in an environment in which financial opening implied a renunciation of capital account management and left Latin American countries subject to fluctuations in financial flows, the increase in interest rates promoted the inflow of capital into the Brazilian economy and the other Latin American economies analyzed, which contributed to the appreciation of the exchange rate, making the products of these economies more expensive in relation to foreign ones. The cumulative effect of an interest rate shock on the exchange rate is negative, as shown in the impulse-response functions for different countries. Thus, increases in the interest rate contribute to the appreciation of the exchange rate, a fact that can have important effects on the growth trajectory, especially in emerging and developing economies, as several authors point out.[2] There are some opposite effects, such as Colombia under regime 2 and Peru under regime 1. In both cases, the increase in the interest rate causes a depreciation of the exchange rate that could be explained by the fact that the monetary policy transmission mechanism of these countries is different from the other countries analyzed.

About the interest, exchange rate and stability relationship, two points can be highlighted regarding the Latin American countries. The first is that trade and financial liberalization policies have changed the profile of these economies' external insertion, with important consequences for the country's monetary stability conditions. Greater trade liberalization has made the inflation of these economies more dependent on the inflation of their trading partners. In addition, inflation is also being more influenced by commodity prices in the international market. Greater financial opening, on the other hand, increases capital flows between countries, as well as their volatility, becoming a factor of frequent pressure on exchange rates and, by extension, on inflation and interest rate policies.

Bresser-Pereira et al. (2020) critically investigated this issue, and found evidence that liberalizing reforms had pronounced effects on Latin American countries. The authors explain the low economic growth observed in Latin America since the 1980s. This has occurred essentially because these reforms caused an increase in the interest rate and an appreciation of the exchange rate. Since then, this factor constitutes a great competitive disadvantage for the manufacturing industry of these countries, with important ramifications for national production and foreign trade.

The second interesting point to be noted concerns the emphasis given by Latin American economies to the use of exchange rate anchors for price sta-bility. In this regard, Frenkel (2004), when analyzing the relationship between real exchange rates and employment in Argentina, Brazil, Chile and Mexico, highlights that, although there are several experiences with exchange rate policies in the period after liberalization, most of these economies use the exchange rate as an instrument to control inflation. The author reports that exchange rates were used as anchors for stabilization in Argentina and Chile in the 1970s, in Mexico in the 1980s and 1990s, and in Argentina and Brazil in the 1990s, and, one of the results of these policies was economic crises.

Frenkel (2004) also adds that, despite the fact that these economies have adopted floating exchange rate regimes more recently, macroeconomic poli-cies continued, in most cases, to focus on the problem of inflation to the det-riment of real targets, such as growth and employment, which were excluded from the main focus of exchange rate policies. Thus, the exchange rate remains an important transmission mechanism for monetary policy.

As for the effects of the interest rate increase on GDP, this is perhaps the variable with the most erratic movements, without a very clear trend. Given a positive interest rate shock to economies, GDP can increase, decrease or remain unchanged. The movements of an increase or decrease in GDP due to interest rate shocks are perceived for Brazil and Chile, depending on the regime analyzed. In the case of Colombia and Guatemala, the first shows only an increasing movement, regardless of the analyzed regime, while for Guatemala the movement is the opposite. Finally, Mexico and Peru show an increase in regime 1 while in regime 2 there was no change. Perhaps the GDP response to monetary policy is influenced by other variables, such as commodity prices, growth in other parts of the world, occurrence of crises, among others.

FINAL COMMENTS

This chapter theoretically and empirically analyzed the Latin American experience with IT in the period between 2000 and 2020 and investigated the effects of monetary policy on inflation and economic performance.

Initially, supported by the theoretical-empirical literature on IT, the existence of a rigid institutional regime that places strong emphasis on price stability was verified, relative to experiences elsewhere worldwide. Next, the performance of IT was evidenced with regard to the behavior of interest rates and inflation rates. In this aspect, the notorious susceptibility of these indicators to the global financial and commodities cycle was verified, so that interest rates are higher and so are prices in these moments of global instability. The trend towards an appreciation of real exchange rates was also established, with a volatile and pro-cyclical behavior of the terms of trade, strongly related to GDP in countries adopting the IT regime.

In the empirical part of the research, an econometric exercise was carried out for six of the eight countries that adopted IT in the region. This evidenced, among other aspects, that, despite the relative price stability, the countries which adopted IT experienced a worsening of external insertion and prolonged economic stagnation, which has the conduct of monetary policy as one of its relevant explanations.

In this scenario, one of the main aspects that this analysis draws attention to is the fact that the rigid institutional aspects of IT in the region, combined with liberalizing reforms after the 1990s, caused an increase in the interest rate and an appreciation of the exchange rate. Since then, these aspects constitute a great competitive disadvantage for the productive structure of these economies. It is worth noting that they are currently based primarily on some commodities of global interest, subject to the volatility of global financial cycles and the restrictions of the international monetary hierarchy. This fact has made it even more difficult to consolidate an economic environment conducive to the resumption of sustained growth, so that an adequate reassessment of these adopted economic policies would be essential.

NOTES

1.   The real effective exchange rate (REER) refers to the nominal effective exchange rate (a measure of the value of a currency relative to the weighted average of several foreign currencies), divided by a price deflator or cost index. Refer to World Bank/World Development Indicators (2021).
2.   In recent years, a number of authors have defended the importance of the exchange rate as a key variable in a long-term economic growth strategy. According to them, by making a range of products with greater added value and technological intensity competitive, a competitive exchange rate can result in

greater economic growth in the long term. For example, refer to Rodrik (2008), Williamson (2003) and Bresser-Pereira et al. (2015).

REFERENCES

Araujo, E. L., Araujo, E. C., Fonseca, M. R. and Silva, P. P. (2020), 'Inflation targeting regime and the global financial cycle: An assessment for the Brazilian economy'. *PSL Quarterly Review*, 73(292), 27–49.

Arestis, P. and Sawyer, M. (2008), 'New consensus macroeconomics and inflation targeting: A Keynesian critique'. *Economia e Sociedade*, 17(Special Issue), 631–655.

Arestis, P., Ferrari-Filho, F. and Paula, L. F. (2011), 'Inflation targeting in Brazil'. *International Review of Applied Economics*, 25(2), 127–148.

Arestis, P. (1992), *The Post-Keynesian Approach to Economics: An Alternative Analysis of Economic Theory and Policy*. Cheltenham, UK and Northampton, MA, USA: Edward Elgar Publishing.

Artis, M., Canova, F., Gali, J., Giavazzi, F., Portes, R., Reichlin, L., Uhlig, H. and Weil, P. (2003), 'Business cycle dating'. *Committee of the Centre for Economic Policy Research*, CEPR.

Brazilian Institute of Geography and Statistics (IBGE) (2021), Estatísticas, available at: https://www.ibge.gov.br, accessed June 15, 2021.

Bresser-Pereira, L. C., Oreiro, J. L. and Marconi, N. (2015), *Developmental Macroeconomics*. London: Routledge.

Bresser-Pereira, L. C., Araujo, E. C. and Peres, S. C. (2020), 'An alternative to the middle-income trap'. *Structural Change and Economic Dynamics*, 52, 294–312.

Central Bank of Brazil (CBB) (2021), *Statistics*, available at: http://www.bcb.gov.br, accessed June 15, 2021.

Central Bank of Chile (CBC) (2021), *Statistics Database*, available at: http://www.bcentral.cl, accessed June 15, 2021.

Central Bank of Colombia (BANREP) (2021), *Statistics Database*, available at: http://www.banrep.gov.br, accessed June 15, 2021.

Central Bank of Guatemala (BANGUAT) (2021), *Statistics Database*, available at: http://www.banguat.gob.gt, accessed June 15, 2021.

Central Bank of Mexico (BANXICO) (2021), *Economic Information System*, available at: https://www.banxico.org.mx, accessed June 15, 2021.

Central Reserve Bank of Peru (BCRP) (2021), *Gerencia Central de Estudios Económicos*, available at: https://www.bcrp.gob.pe, accessed June 15, 2021.

Christiano, L., Eichenbaum, M. and Evans, C. L. (1996), 'The effects of monetary policy shocks: Evidence from the flow of funds'. *Review of Economics and Statistics*, 78(1), 16–34.

Fonseca, M., Peres, S. C. and Araujo, E. (2016), 'Regime de metas de inflação: Análise comparativa e evidências empíricas para países emergentes selecionados'. *Revista de Economia Contemporânea*, 20(1), 113–143.

Fontana, G. (2009), 'Whither new consensus macroeconomics? The role of government and fiscal policy in modern macroeconomics'. *Working Paper 563, The Levy Economics Institute*, 1–24, May.

Frenkel, R. (2004), 'Real exchange rate and employment in Argentina, Brazil, Chile and Mexico, Cedes, Buenos Aires'. Paper presented to the G24, available at: https://www.g24.org/wp-content/uploads/2016/01/Real-Exchange-Rate-and-Employment.pdf, accessed June 2021.

Hammond, G. (2012), *State of the Art of Inflation Targeting*. Bank of England: CBCS Handbook n. 29, February.

International Monetary Fund (IMF) (2021a), *World Economic Outlook Database*. April, 2021, available at: https://www.imf.org/en/Publications/WEO/weo-database/2021/April, accessed May 15, 2021.

International Monetary Fund. (IMF) (2021b), *Data*, available at: https://data.imf.org/?sk=4c514d48-b6ba-49ed-8ab9-52b0c1a0179b, accessed May 15, 2021.

Krolzig, H. M. (2003), 'Constructing turning point chronologies with Markov switching vector autoregressive models: The euro-zone business cycle'. *University of Oxford, Discussion Paper in Economics*.

Niedźwiedzińska, J. (2018), 'Inflation targeting: Institutional features of the strategy in practice'. *NBP Working Paper n. 299*. Poland: Narodowy Bank Polski Warsaw.

Palley, T. I. (1996), *Post Keynesian Economics*. Nova York: St. Martin's Press.

Palma, J. G. (2010), 'Why has productivity growth stagnated in most Latin American countries since the neo-liberal reforms?' *Cambridge Working Papers, n. 1.030*.

Rodrik, D. (2008), 'The real exchange and economic growth: Theory and evidence'. *Brookings Papers on Economic Activity*, 365–412.

Rogoff, K. (1985), 'The optimal degree of commitment to an intermediate'. *Quarterly Journal of Economics*, 100, 1169–1189.

Sims, C. (1990), *Macroeconomics and reality: Modelling Economic Series*. Oxford: Clarendon.

Sims, C. (1992), 'Interpreting the macroeconomic time series facts: The effects of monetary policy'. *European economic Review*, 36(5), 975–1000.

Sims, C. and Zha, T. (1998), 'Does monetary policy generate recessions?' *Working Paper 98-12*, Federal Reserve Bank of Atlanta, Atlanta GA.

Walsh, C. E. (1995), 'Optimal contracts for central bankers'. *American Economic Review*, 85(1), 150–167.

Williamson, J. (2003), *Exchange Rate Policy and Development*. New York: Columbia University.

World Bank (2021), *World Development Indicators* (WB/WDI), available at: https://databank.worldbank.org/source/world-development-indicators, accessed May 18, 2021.

APPENDIX

Table 2A.1   Description of variables used for each country analyzed

Country	Variables	Description	Source
Brazil	IRBR	Interest Rate – Selic accumulated in the month in annual terms (basis 252)	Central Bank of Brazil (CBB)
	IPCABR	Broad National Consumer Price Index (IPCA)	Brazilian Institute of Geography and Statistics (IBGE)
	EAIBR	Economic Activity Index – Industrial output (2012 = 100), seasonally adjusted	Brazilian Institute of Geography and Statistics (IBGE)
	ERBR	Exchange Rate – Free – United States dollar (purchase) – end of period – 3695	Central Bank of Brazil (CBB – Sisbacen PTAX800)
Chile	IRCH	Interest rate accumulated in the month in annual terms	Central Bank of Chile (CBC – Statistics Database)
	CPICH	Consumer Price Index (CPI)	Central Bank of Chile (CBC – Statistics Database)
	EAICH	Economic Activity Index – Industrial output INE (2014 = 100), seasonally adjusted	Central Bank of Chile (CBC – Statistics Database)
	ERCH	Exchange Rate United States dollar (purchase) – end of period	Central Bank of Chile (CBC – Statistics Database)
Colombia	IRCOL	Interest rate accumulated in the month in annual terms	Central Bank of Colombia (BANREP – Statistics Database)
	CPICOL	Consumer Price Index (CPI)	Central Bank of Colombia (BANREP – Statistics Database)
	EAICOL	Economic Activity Index – Industrial output INE (2016 = 100), seasonally adjusted	Central Bank of Colombia (BANREP – Statistics Database)
	ERCOL	Exchange Rate United States dollar (purchase) – end of period	Central Bank of Colombia (BANREP – Statistics Database)

Country	Variables	Description	Source
Guatemala	IRGUA	Interest rate accumulated in the month in annual terms	Central Bank of Guatemala (BANGUAT – Statistics Database)
	CPIGUA	Consumer Price Index (CPI)	Central Bank of Guatemala (BANGUAT – Statistics Database)
	EAIGUA	Economic Activity Index – Industrial output INE (2010 = 100), seasonally adjusted	Central Bank of Guatemala (BANGUAT – Statistics Database)
	ERGUA	Exchange Rate United States dollar (purchase) – end of period	Central Bank of Guatemala (BANGUAT – Statistics Database)
Mexico	IRMEX	Interest rate accumulated in the month in annual terms	Central Bank of Mexico (BANXICO – Economic Information System)
	CPIMEX	Consumer Price Index (CPI)	Central Bank of Mexico (BANXICO – Economic Information System)
	EAIMEX	Economic Activity Index – Industrial output INE (2013 = 100), seasonally adjusted	Central Bank of Mexico (BANXICO – Economic Information System)
	ERMEX	Exchange Rate United States dollar (purchase) – end of period	Central Bank of Mexico (BANXICO – Economic Information System)
Peru	IRPE	Interest rate accumulated in the month in annual terms	Central Reserve Bank of Peru BCRP – (Gerencia Central de Estudios Económicos)
	CPIPE	Consumer Price Index (CPI)	Central Reserve Bank of Peru (BCRP – Gerencia Central de Estudios Económicos)
	EAIPE	Economic Activity Index – Industrial output (2007 = 100), seasonally adjusted	Central Reserve Bank of Peru (BCRP – Gerencia Central de Estudios Económicos)
	ERPE	Exchange Rate United States dollar (purchase) – end of period	Central Reserve Bank of Peru (BCRP – Gerencia Central de Estudios Económicos)

Source: BANGUAT (2021), BANREP (2021), BANXICO (2021), BCRP (2021), CBB (2021), CBC (2021) and IBGE (2021).

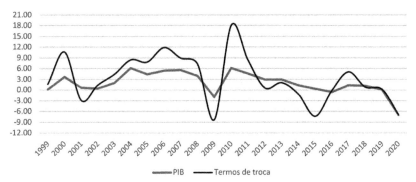

Source: IMF/WEO (2021).

Figure 2.A1   *Model adjustment for Brazil, Chile, Colombia, Guatemala,*
Mexico and Peru

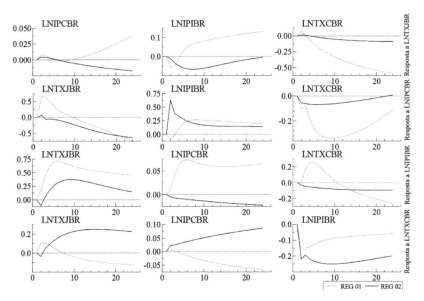

Figure 2.A2a   *Convergence of the models: Brazil, MS2VAR2 model –*
strongly convergent

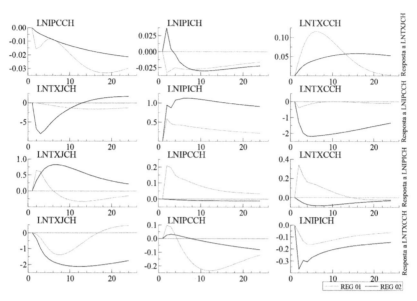

Figure 2.A2b   Convergence of the models: Chile, MS2VAR2 model –
strongly convergent

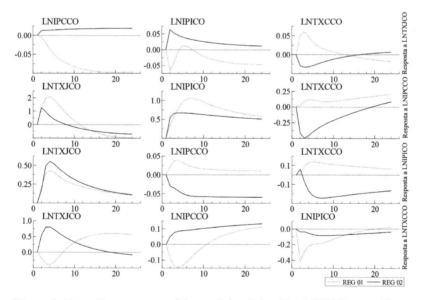

Figure 2.A2c   Convergence of the models: Colombia, MS2VAR2 model –
strongly convergent

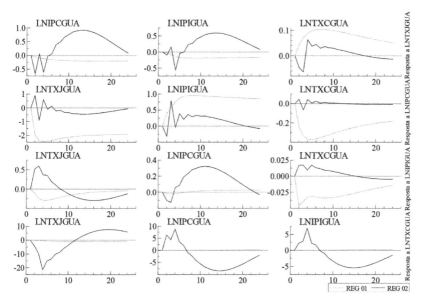

*Figure 2.A2d   Convergence of the models: Guatemala, MS2VAR2 model –
strongly convergent*

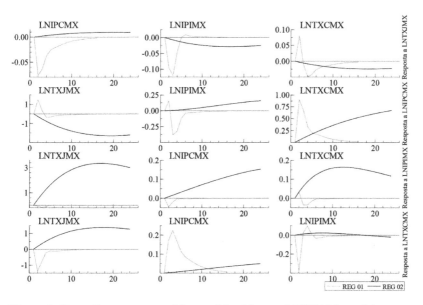

*Figure 2.A2e   Convergence of the models: Mexico, MS2VAR2 model –
strongly convergent*

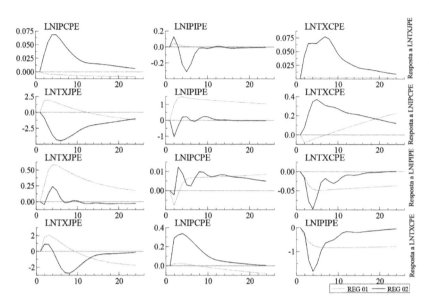

Figure 2.A2f   Convergence of the models: Peru, MS2VAR2 model –
strongly convergent

3. Monetary policy in Brazil under the inflation targeting regime from a Contested Terrain Approach

Assilio Araujo and Fernando Ferrari-Filho

INTRODUCTION

As is well known, monetarist and new-classical economists, such as Friedman (1968, 1970), Kydland and Prescott (1977) and Lucas Jr (1972), argue that monetary policy decisions made by independent central banks are 'neutral'. Thus, the monetary policies operated by central banks reflect society's preference as a whole, with no significant bias in favor of a particular group. In contrast, for the Contested Terrain Approach (CTA), developed by Epstein and Schor (1988), monetary policy mirrors the correlation of forces in society and the central bank's structure. In the current phase of capitalism, marked by the financialization of economies, rentiers are stronger than other groups in society, so that monetary policy tends to favor this class fraction.

Nowadays, in most economies in which the central bank has become independent, and the Inflation Targeting Regime (ITR) was adopted to keep inflation under control, monetary policy has been largely beneficial to rentiers. Thus, economic growth is no longer relevant for most central banks worldwide, especially for emerging economies. In Brazil, for instance, since the implementation of the ITR in June 1999, the no-neutrality of the Central Bank of Brazil (CBB) in terms of operating the monetary policy, that is, the nominal base interest rate (Special System for Custody and Settlement of Government Bonds – SELIC), has favored rentier interest more than other economic interest.

Considering that the CBB became conservative and, as a consequence, its monetary policy favored rentiers, the Brazilian case certainly stands out. Since the mid-1990s, Brazil has had one of the highest basic interest rates. Not even price stability and consistent primary surpluses throughout the 2000s could get the country out of this uncomfortable place, although the real interest rate showed a downward trajectory during this decade and the beginning of the following decade. The context of economic prosperity partially hid the harm associated with this very high interest rate. However, when this phase passed, the obstacle represented by high interest rates was still there. It took a major recession, starting in 2015, for this rate to approach the average level of developing economies, including those in Latin America. At the same, the Brazilian economy became increasingly financialized in this period. In light of this briefly described framework, we consider that the rentier segment of society captured the CBB. This is the main objective of the chapter.

To address this objective, besides this brief introduction, the chapter is divided into three sections: section two presents the theoretical analysis of the CTA; section three describes and analyzes the performances of ITR and monetary policy from 1999 to 2020; and section four concludes.

A THEORETICAL ANALYSIS OF THE CONTESTED TERRAIN APPROACH

The CTA was developed to analyze some advanced developing countries' macroeconomic policies, particularly monetary policy, in the post-World War II period (Epstein and Schor, 1988). For CTA, the central bank is a terrain of class struggle, and therefore the monetary policies will mirror the net outcome of that struggle. Epstein (2001) sought to adapt this model to the reality of developed countries undergoing the financialization of their economies. Apparently, according to him, the influence of rentiers over the central bank in these countries has expanded significantly in recent years, so that the struggle between capitalist class's fractions over monetary policy has lost strength in this period, giving way to a control of the central monetary institution by this segment. Epstein (2019) explains this idea when the term 'contested terrain' was abandoned and, as a result, 'contested control' was used to refer to the new relationship between the dominant class fractions and the monetary authority.

The real interest rate is considered in CTA to be a variable under the control of the central bank and, at the same time, a crucial distributive parameter in the economy (assumptions in line with the Post-Keynesian school, but also with the Marxian approach). In this way, the different classes and fractions, divided simplistically into financial capitalists, industrial capitalists and workers, will seek to influence the central bank's behavior to bring the interest rate closer to the level that maximizes their income share. Financial and industrial capitalists are assumed to want to increase their profits, while workers are concerned with real wages. Monetary policy will be a weighted average of these objectives, with the weight of each determined by the relative power of these groups in society and the state.

Besides the conflict between these classes and fractions, monetary policy is also constrained and influenced by some structural/institutional features of the economy and the central bank itself. Based on econometric studies, documentary analysis, interviews with policymakers, and Marxists theories of State – such as Esping-Andersen et al. (1976) – Epstein and Schor (1988) listed four characteristics as being the main ones, besides the contradictions and the dynamics of capital accumulation:

(i)   The structure of the labor market;
(ii)   The relationship between the industrial sector and the financial sector;
(iii)   The degree of independence of the central bank;
(iv)   The insertion of the domestic economy in the world economy.

The structure of the labor market (or capital–labor relations) is addressed, in the most stylized versions of this model (Epstein, 1992), by referring to only one specific outcome arising from this structure, namely, the relationship (positive or negative) between utilized productive capacity and the share of profits in income. Moreover, Boddy and Crotty (1975) observed that the profit–wage ratio suffers a compression (profit squeeze) in the second phase of cyclical expansion, due to a significant increase in real wages in this phase, because of the fall of the industrial reserve army and greater bargaining power of the working class. At the same time, there is a drop in productivity growth vis-à-vis the first cyclical expansion phase, explained either by technical issues or by the increase in the number of strikes and the lower effort of workers on the factory floor in this period (stimulated by the moment of economic prosperity). This profit squeeze would add to the political-ideological aspects that Kalecki (1943)[1] raised to explain the capitalist class's resistance to situations of full employment of productive factors. A labor market with these characteristics, that is, one that presents the mentioned phenomenon of profit squeeze, has received in CTA the label of neo-Marxist. In this case, industrial capitalists will be opposed to monetary policies that cause full employment.

As extracted from Kaleckian economic theory, if the increase in capacity utilization were accompanied by a decrease in competition and an increase in the market power of firms, firms could increase their mark-up, so that the share of profits in income would also increase or, in the worst case, would remain constant. In this case, industrialists would 'unite' with workers in defense of full employment monetary policies. It should be noted that this direct or inverse relationship between utilized capacity and the share of profits in income is influenced by the organization of the working class in the respective country and by its political capacity to participate in the productivity gains that occur in moments of cyclical expansion. The more robust and less internally divided the workers' movement is, the more the labor market approximates to the neo-Marxist case.

In Epstein and Schor (1988), besides this aspect, labor legislation is also mentioned as a factor that can influence the behavior of the capitalist class concerning monetary policy. Supposing that a given country has employment protection laws that make it expensive to lay off workers, capitalists will tend to adopt a more neutral stance on this issue because, on the one hand, a contractionary monetary policy will possibly not bring the reduction of unit labor cost in the expected proportion, and, on the other hand, it is not advantageous for capitalists to hire workers who will be expensive to lay off later.

It is essential to point out that by treating the distribution of income between capitalists and workers separately from the monetary factors, one excludes the possibility that a reduction in the interest rate (and a drop in the share of rentiers in surplus) would serve as a counter to the crushing of total profits in income. That is, if the model addressed the conflict between workers and capitalists and between industrial capitalists and finance capitalists simultaneously, even if the labor market were neo-Marxist, industrial capitalists' profits could to some extent remain constant or even increase as a result of an expansionary monetary policy leading to a situation of full employment.

According to Epstein (1992), Marx considered that there were grounds for conflicting relations between finance capital and industrial capital, because of the distribution of surplus-value into industrial profits and interest, but also for cooperation between the two vis-à-vis the working class, because they share the exact total after subtracting wages. However, it is generally assumed that industrial capitalists and rentiers are on opposite sides in the struggle to determine the interest rate. This Marx assumption was also endorsed by Keynes. In his *A Treatise on Money: The Pure Theory of Money*, Keynes ([1930] 1976), after defining the industrial circulation and the finance circulation of the capital, argued that monetary policy is not able to reduce quickly the interest rate because the speculators (or rentiers) attempt to stop this drop. As a consequence, 'a state of unemployment may be expected to ensure' (Keynes, [1930] 1976, p. 206). Later, in his *The General Theory of Employment, Interest and Money*, Keynes ([1936] 2007, p. 376) stated that it was necessary to promote the 'euthanasia of the rentiers'; that is, an abrupt reduction of the interest rate to stimulate consumption and, mainly, investment, thus resulting in an economic situation of full employment. In this way, it can be said that workers and capitalists formed the political alliance envisioned by Keynes against rentiers, which paralyzed the creative impulses of society.

The market rate of interest does not drop quickly enough, because speculators of the stock exchange will attempt to stop it above equilibrium level.

Based on Zysman's (1983) classical book, *Governments, Markets, and Growth: Financial Systems and Politics of Industrial Change*, Epstein (1992) argues that the relationship between industrial sector and financial system around the world cannot be framed within the idea that there is a conflict between them. In the so-called credit-based systems, whose emblematic cases are Germany and Japan, the banks, the main financiers of investment in this type of system, have a high share in the assets of the industrial sector, such that they have an interest in a monetary policy that also expands the profits of this sector. In Japan, these sectors are sometimes part of the same industrial group, so a change in the interest rate has the same impact on these companies as a change in the relative prices of the goods produced by different arms of this group. In these cases, the impact on the distribution of income between the industrial and financial sectors caused by a change in the monetary policy stance will be reduced, which encourages cooperative behavior between the two (read: both will defend an interest rate that maximizes their profits jointly). Epstein (1992) called financial systems with these characteristics enterprise finance, in contrast to cases of speculative finance, in which conflicting relations between the two sectors prevail. The generally mentioned examples of the latter are the United States and the United Kingdom, although the large-scale deregulation of financial systems that has been promoted in the last decades has brought a significant part of the economies closer to these cases.

In contrast to credit-based systems, the primary source of investments in these countries are the stock and bond markets (which is why they are called capital-market-based systems). In this context, since banks have a smaller share in the industrial sector, a change in the interest rate causes a redistribution of income across sectors. Consequently, the financial sector will advocate a behavior by the monetary authority that maximizes its profits despite the profits of the industrial sector.

One of the characteristics of developing economies is not having a developed private financial system that provides long-term capital for capital accumulation. In other words, in these economies, the industry still depends largely on self-financing, on the external financial system, and, in some cases, on public institutions and development banks. Thus, the linkages between banks and industry are weak in economies such as Japan and Germany, and the capital market is not as developed as in the United States and the United Kingdom. Given this, we think that the distinction between speculative finance and enterprise finance should be slightly modified to address these economies. Instead of focusing on the source of funds (capital markets or banks) for the financing of industry, one should consider the orientation of banking activity, that is, the extent to which banks are geared towards lending to the real side of the economy or investing in the financial sphere.

Financial capitalists' resistance to an expansionary monetary policy is also linked, in our view, to the general conditions of the economy. If inflation is high, finance capitalists will strongly oppose any measure that expands the money supply in the economy. With inflation under control and at a low level, the central bank should encounter more resistance from the financial system to a fall in the real interest rate when the economy is stagnant than growing at high rates. In this case, they will maintain their profitability even with the fall in return provided by financial assets.

For CTA, the state's internal structure (in this case, the relationship between central bank and government) also matters in determining the policies to be adopted. According to Epstein (1992, p. 11),

> [w]hile classes and class fractions have desired policies, their policies will not be implemented unless they have political power vis-à-vis the state. Thus policy will be determined by a combination of political structure of the economy and the political structure of the state.

Given that, CTA assumes that the more independent the central bank is from the government, the more restrictive monetary policy tends to be, as the support of the financial system will be more important to guarantee this independent position. In the cases seen above in which the industrial and financial sectors share the same interests concerning monetary policy, an independent central bank will adopt monetary policies that also maximize the profits of the industrial sector. Nevertheless, in situations where these interests diverge, the central bank will serve the interests of its natural allies, the rentiers. Thus, it is assumed that workers' interests tend to be ignored by the monetary authority, and they become even more irrelevant in determining monetary policy when the central bank gains independence from the government since the only channel of influence they had over the behavior of this institution (via pressure on democratically elected representatives) is thereby closed.

Besides the econometric evidence, the reasoning above is supported by documentary analysis of the formulation and execution of monetary policy in the United States. Epstein and Schor (2011) examine the battle waged by these divergent interests in the period leading up to the Federal Reserve-Treasury Agreement in 1951, which re-established the independence of the Federal Reserve Bank (FED) after a few years in which monetary policy was subordinated to the need to finance World War II at the lowest possible cost. The history of the agreement shows that not even the financial community was, from the start, unanimous about the independence of the FED. The almost complete support of this community was won by the substitution of the main instrument for the execution of monetary policy – which became the interest rate, instead of banks' mandatory reserves – as well as by decisions taken (first to reduce and then to increase the interest rate) perfectly aligned with the interests of the large banks. Industry's support, in turn, came only belatedly and was motivated by the desire to prevent quantitative credit controls from being implemented and monetary policy from being placed under the command of the Executive Branch, as planned by groups within the government that supported President Harry Truman. In contrast, throughout the clashes, workers showed relative indifference to these issues, being indirectly represented by the most radical elements present in the public administration. The signing of the Accord, according to the Epstein and Schor (2011), represented an attempt to prevent these radical forces from interfering in the execution of monetary policy henceforth, isolating it permanently from (in the words of one of the FED directors) the 'negative' influence of workers.

Beyond domestic conditions, the country's insertion into the world economy is considered by CTA because it affects the interests and constraints faced by central banks. Small and open economies do not constitute the field of analysis of this approach since the monetary authority does not execute policies autonomously. Central banks in larger economies, but with broad insertion in international capital flows, are also often held hostage by the balance of payments imbalances. The more integrated an economy, the greater the chance that a crisis of this nature will strike it, disrupting the scenario for the execution of monetary policy. In turn, having key currencies in the international scenario sharpens the central monetary institutions' concern with domestic stability conditions, stimulating more restrictive behavior on its part. This concern is corroborated by the speculative and outward-looking financial systems found in these economies, for which stability is fundamental to guarantee a continuous flow of investments. Finally, in open economies, a substantive rise in the unit cost of labor is responded to by multinational firms with a shift of production to locations with the cheapest labor (Epstein, 1992; Epstein and Schor, 1988).

As Epstein (2001, p. 1) states, '[...] the increasing importance of financial markets, financial motives, financial institutions, and financial elites in the operations of the economy and its governing institutions, both at the national and international levels', that is, financialization has led to a change in the political economy of central banks, especially in the United States. The interests of capitalists and financiers have become coincident about the optimal level of the interest rate. Whereas before financialization, the greater aversion to inflation of rentiers typically made them want higher interest rates than industrialists, this distance has narrowed significantly in recent decades for many reasons. On the one hand, industrialists have become much more like rentiers, as financial gains have become more critical in their income. However, this has paradoxically not led to a change in their position concerning the interest rate, since inflation is no longer as much of a concern as it used to be, due to changes in the labor market (weakening of unions and competition with cheap labor from developing economies) and the importation of comparatively low-priced goods from these economies. On the other hand, rentiers and industrialists prefer capital gains obtained by speculative bubbles inflated by meager interest rates. In short, both maximize their rate of profit with interest rates at a depressed level.

Epstein (2001) also argues that the success of the ITR among economists and policymakers, and its adoption by several countries over the past decades, cannot be explained from the standpoint of purely technical analysis. One of the main arguments raised by advocates of the ITR is that its adoption would reduce the cost in terms of output and employment associated with the disinflation process, the so-called 'sacrifice ratio'. However, according to Epstein's (2001) literature review, there does not seem to be evidence that this has happened. Furthermore, the great concern with inflation, which motivated the adoption of the ITR, is not justified from the empirical point of view. The results of previous works and of econometric exercises carried out by Epstein (2001) show that moderate inflation (below 20.0 percent) does not generate high costs in terms of reduction of product, investment, the inflow of direct investment, and other real variables. Against this background, he suggests the ITR fever needs to be understood within the context of the financialization of economies and the increasing power of rent-seekers.

As is well known, financialization manifests itself differently in developing economies. Instead of capital gains and low interest rates, one sees gains from financial instruments (government bonds, for example) that pay high interest rates. Moreover, financialization has an 'extroverted' character, that is, it is associated with the inflow of capital and, therefore, with their financial openness. For capital to continue flowing to developing countries, the countries are forced to maintain high interest rates, resulting in an appreciated exchange rate and a negative impact on the productive structure and economic growth and generating more outstanding state indebtedness (Becker et al., 2010). In Brazil, although financialization has its roots in creating the so-called 'indexed currency' in the 1970s, this process gained strength from the 1990s, with the opening (trade and financial accounts balance of payments) of the economy and the macroeconomic paradigm change (Bruno et al., 2011). In this context of financialization and rentier domination of the CBB, Brazil adopted the ITR, whose performance will be analyzed in the next section.

THE PERFORMANCES OF ITR AND MONETARY POLICY IN THE PERIOD 1999–2020

Since the introduction of the ITR, Brazil has had very high nominal and real interest rates, when compared with other countries with similar levels of income: the average nominal and real SELIC, from 1999 to 2020, were 12.4 percent and 5.7 percent per year, respectively.[2]

This raises two questions: how CBB has managed the monetary policy monetary since then to keep such relatively high interest rates? And what have been the main influences on the policymakers in operating the ITR? Looking at the performance of the monetary policy since the 1990s, specifically after the Real Plan, July 1994, there are, at least, two explanations: first, in general and mainly between 1994 and 1998, when the exchange rate was the anchor of the stabilization prices, CBB decided to maintain high nominal interest rates in order to attract capital flows to finance the current account deficits (Ferrari Filho and Paula, 2003); and, second, after the introduction of the ITR, the monetary policy has been operated according to the most important issue highlighted by the New Macroeconomic Consensus (NMC) theoretical framework, in which, in Brazil, the interest rate seems to have only one economic objective, that is, to bring the inflation rate to its target or to its tolerance intervals without worrying about economic growth and employment.[3] Thus, as a result of high interest rates, the monetary policy managed by CBB favors rentier interests (domestic and foreign rentiers) mainly because high interest, in a context of financialization of the economy, insures the rentiers' earnings against possible losses determined by this policy.

Given that, it is possible to argue that monetary policy in Brazil, on the one hand, has been quite ineffective in fulfilling its main objectives, that is, keeping inflation under control and stimulating economic growth, and, on the other hand, it has contributed to income and wealth concentration, considering that high interest rates are an important source for the rentiers gains.

This section presents the macroeconomic model utilized by the CBB to adopt the ITR, analyzes the Brazilian experience with ITR and shows how high interest rates in Brazil ensure the rentiers' earnings.

The NMC Basic Model and the Brazilian Experience with ITR[4]

The NMC model emerged in the beginning of the 1990s and, since then, has become highly influential in terms of both macroeconomic thinking and macroeconomic, mainly monetary, policy (Arestis and Sawyer, 2008).

This model is characterized by three equations: the IS equation representing the demand side; the Phillips curve (PC) equation representing the supply side; and the monetary policy rule (MPR) equation (Carlin and Soskice, 2006).

The MPR is the underpinning of the ITR.[5] The rule fixes the central bank behavior under conditions of mostly demand shocks that deviate inflation from the target under rational expectations by key private players. In this approach, the instrument of monetary policy is the short-run nominal interest rate. When actual inflation rates converge to the inflation target established by the central bank, the interest rate is assumed to be on its natural level.

As mentioned before, CBB introduced the ITR in 1999, along with a target for primary fiscal budget surpluses as a share of GDP, and a floating exchange rate regime. The main theoretical features of the ITR model in Brazil are the following (Arestis et al., 2011):

(i)   Price stability is monetary policy's primary long-term objective. In addition, at least theoretically, the price stability goal may be accompanied by output stabilization;

(ii)   Fiscal policy is no longer viewed as a powerful macroeconomic instrument for stabilizing the economy. Thus, the economic authorities introduced, in 2000, the Fiscal Responsibility Law to improve fiscal discipline in all government entities (Union, states and municipalities). In other words, it was created as a fiscal target in terms of a primary budget surplus to aim at stabilizing the debt-to-GDP ratio;

(iii)   The level of economic activity has to fluctuate around a supply-side long-run equilibrium. This means that the level of effective demand does not play an independent role on the long-run level of economic activity;

(iv)   Finally, considering that the Brazilian economy is open, with a history of external imbalances and payment crises, to avoid the fact that the exchange rate can transmit shocks to interest and inflation rates, the CBB signals a clear commitment to price stability under a floating exchange rate system.

Focusing on the monetary policy, the interest rate target is set by the Monetary Policy Committee (COPOM). The basic interest rate that the COPOM seeks to influence is SELIC, an interest rate for overnight interbank loans, collateralized by those government bonds. The interest rate target is fixed for the period between the COPOM regular meetings (every 45 days). The President of the CBB, though, has the power to change the SELIC interest rate target any time between regular COPOM meetings. Immediately after the COPOM meetings, the CBB publishes an Inflation Report, which provides specific information on economic conditions, as well as the COPOM's inflation forecasts upon which changes in the SELIC are determined.

Table 3.1 shows the point targets, the tolerance intervals, inflation rates, measured by the effective headline Consumer Price Index (IPCA in Brazil), annual interest rates (nominal and real) and annual growth rates from 1999 to 2020.

Based on Table 3.1, we have the following considerations during the 1999–2020 period: (i) the tolerance intervals were missed for four years (2001, 2002, 2003 and 2015); (ii) the inflation rate was over the target for 15 of 22 years; (iii) the inflation rate was high for countries that adopt a ITR – the average inflation rate was 6.3 percent per year; (iv) the nominal and real interest rates (SELIC) were high; (v) as shown in Note 2, the average economic growth rate was only 2.0 percent per year; and (vi) for the entire period ana-

Table 3.1   *Targets, tolerance intervals, inflation (IPCA) rate, nominal and real SELIC and GDP growth rate, %, from 1999 to 2020*

Year	Targets	Tolerance intervals	Inflation (IPCA)	Nominal SELIC*	Real SELIC	GDP growth rate
1999	8	6 to 8	8.94	19	9.2	0.5
2000	6	4 to 8	5.97	15.75	9.2	4.4
2001	4	2 to 6	7.67	19	10.5	1.4
2002	3.5	1.5 to 5.5	12.53	25	11.1	3.1
2003	4	1.5 to 6.5	9.3	16.5	6.6	1.1
2004	5.5	3 to 8	7.6	17.75	9.4	5.8
2005	4.5	2 to 7	5.69	18	11.6	3.2
2006	4.5	2.5 to 6.5	3.14	13.25	9.8	4
2007	4.5	2.5 to 6.5	4.46	11.25	6.5	6.1
2008	4.5	2.5 to 6.5	5.9	13.75	7.4	5.1
2009	4.5	2.5 to 6.5	4.31	8.75	4.3	- 0.1
2010	4.5	2.5 to 6.5	5.91	10.75	4.6	7.6
2011	4.5	2.5 to 6.5	6.5	11	4.2	4
2012	4.5	2.5 to 6.5	5.84	7.25	1.3	1.9
2013	4.5	2.5 to 6.5	5.91	10	3.9	3
2014	4.5	2.5 to 6.5	6.41	11.75	5	0.5
2015	4.5	2.5 to 6.5	10.67	14.25	3.2	- 3.5
2016	4.5	2.5 to 6.5	6.29	13.75	7	- 3.3
2017	4.5	3 to 6	2.95	7	3.9	1.3
2018	4.5	3 to 6	3.75	6.5	2.7	1.3
2019	4.25	2.75 to 5.75	4.31	4.5	0.2	1.1
2020	4	2.5 to 5.5	4.52	2		- 4.1

Note: *End of period.
Source: Author's elaboration based on Ipeadata (2021) and CBB (2021).

lyzed, there is not an inverse relationship between nominal interest rates and inflation rates.

Given that, it is possible to argue that monetary policy under the ITR in Brazil is ineffective in ensuring lower and stable inflation rates, as well as negatively affecting the economic growth. Going in this direction, Modenesi and Araújo (2013) and Araujo et al. (2018), based on an econometric analysis of the monetary policy transmission mechanism in Brazil, endorse our claim that inflation is not directly sensitive to the interest rate,[6] while Libanio (2010) argues that the way that monetary policy has been conducted in Brazil under the ITR, with a floating exchange regime and a liberalized financial account, brings about an upward bias in interest rates that reduces aggregate demand and, as a consequence, the economic growth.

Summarizing this subsection, in Brazil, tight monetary policy and, as a consequence, high interest rates (i) have not been effective at reducing and stabilizing inflation,[7] (ii) have contributed to the poor performance of the GDP growth rate, and (iii) have transferred income to rentiers.

The Rentiers' Interest in the Monetary Policy[8]

The previous subsection raises the following question: why does an economy require high nominal interest rates to achieve lower and more stable inflation rates? According to Dutt (1990–91), from a theoretical perspective, high nominal interest rates, mainly in emerging economies, are able to reduce inflation when capacity utilization is full. Going in the same direction, in 'How to pay for the war', Keynes (1972) argues that when the economy has reached full employment, tight monetary policy is important to reduce and stabilize the inflation rate.

Focusing on the Brazilian economy, considering that Brazil has a large amount of idle capacity, as well as that average GDP growth rates have been modest in the last 22 years, high interest rates, theoretically, are not a plausible explanation to mitigate and stabilize the inflation rate.

Further to this, some new-developmentalist and post-Keynesian economists have an interesting view about the high nominal interest in Brazil.

For Bresser-Pereira and Gomes (2009), the interest rate is very high in Brazil due to an interest/exchange rate trap. Arestis et al. (2011) argue that the SELIC is high because the CBB is 'captured' by rentiers – by the way, this argument is similar to the CTA's idea that rentiers dominate central banks. Ferrari Filho and Milan (2018a) argue that high interest rates managed by CBB means the Brazilian version of the liquidity trap. Thus, according to them, monetary policy and high interest rates are operated by CBB to sustain the rentier's inflationary expectations, and, as a result, their income earnings.[9] Vernengo (2008) argues that the distributive conflict is important for the inflationary dynamics, and that indeed the monetary policy regime favors the financial sector interests within the rentier segment.

But how are rentiers able to shape monetary policy in Brazil? In other words, why do rentiers have power in setting successful interest–income transfer programs?

Bruno et al. (2011) show that the public debt and the corresponding interest payments are a major source of financialized capital accumulation in Brazil. Thus, it is possible to argue, based on this reasoning, that non-financial firms are also earning interest payments and are not opposed to high interest rates, being part of the rentier segment.

In our view, the influence of rentiers over monetary policy in Brazil, a very likely explanation for the stubbornly high interest rates, has more to do with an institutional setting in which central banks are structurally constrained to keep nominal and real interest rates high, but in Brazil this framework has favored the rentier class on an unseen scale, with the result that monetary policy is ineffective in reducing and stabilizing inflation rates to the international average levels, but very effective in transferring income to rentiers.

The CBB sets the short-term interest rate based on a survey of expected inflation mostly by financial institutions. Many issues seem to affect those expectations. For instance, despite the fact that the central government has never defaulted on its domestic debt, financial institutions seem to assume that the risk of default is permanently high, and therefore the interest rates must be kept at high levels in order to finance government deficits. This is an example of the expectational trap.

The rentiers also seem to assume that monetary policy has not been credible, and expected inflation is rigid on the upper levels, even when actual inflation slightly falls. The solution is therefore to increase interest rates even more. Inflation does not fall fast enough? Then, raise the interest rate one more time. If interest rates do not drop, it is because inflationary expectations are rigid due to the lack of true commitment with lower inflation rates. That is, a possible interpretation of rentiers power over monetary policy is that inflation rates do not fall in Brazil because expected inflation by financial firms, whose services have a small participation in the IPCA, are rigid, and they are rigid because interest rates are kept unduly low, even though they are among the highest in the world. Interest rates, according to rentiers in general and financial firms in particular, only reflect the lack of credibility of monetary policy, and they are the only ones capable of defining what is credible and what is not. Credibility is defined as what financial firms think it is or, in our interpretation, whatever policies favor financial interests. If financial firms do not accept a policy, it is not credible by definition (Grabel, 2003).

Therefore, a consequence of their likely view is that expected inflation fully determines actual inflation rates, and the former do not fall because real interest rates are not high enough. But since interest rates also measure the rate at which capitalized monetary and financial wealth grows, it is our argument that rigid expected inflation rates have a major consequence in the form of transfer of funds from the government to the rentiers whose expectations anchor the policy decisions by the CBB. So, it is highly convenient to have expectations disconnected from actual rates of inflation. It would certainly be outrageous for orthodox economists, mainly the ones working for the rentiers, if a rule of wage-setting was established such that nominal wages were automatically adjusted based on the workers' and trade unions' own inflationary expectations, surveyed by the CBB. But that is exactly what rentiers have accomplished themselves in Brazil. Thus, the expectations of rentiers seem to have transformed the ITR into an expectational trap, a powerful mechanism to sustain high interest rates (and earnings) in Brazil even though it has not had significant impacts on actual inflation rates, since they are not sensitive to credit-financed demand.

Ferrari Filho and Milan (2018b) proposes a theoretical classification for the different combinations of nominal interest and actual inflation rates as a way to interpret the structure of monetary policy. The abnormal power of rentiers in Brazil in setting the monetary policy makes it hard to classify the country using this scheme, however, since interest rates in Brazil are very high, but the inflation rates are not low by international standards (although they are not higher than the ones prevailing in many countries in our sample). The recent episode in Brazil, when public banks were enticed to boost competition and reduce market interest rates, along with policy rates reductions by the CBB, is telling in this respect. It led to all types of financial 'revolts' in the Brazilian press, including the financialized industrialists. This episode deserves a deeper treatment that is beyond the scope of this chapter, since it raises the question of why and how the attempt at monetary policy change failed, and the potential role that rentiers' interests played in it besides the public opinion channel.

Yet, the Brazilian anomaly of an expectational trap seems closer to the case of a rentiers' party, with excessive real interest rates based not on low inflation, but instead on exorbitant nominal interest rates, whereas other countries seem to have managed to subdue rentiers' interests, for some reasons that must be addressed by additional research, with nominal interest rates closer to the inflation rates and therefore closer to Smithin's rule of zero real interest rate (Smithin, 1996).

To conclude, it is hard to defend ITR in Brazil as effective in achieving its stated goals. Considering the international standpoint, real interest rates have been excessive on several grounds, despite a fall during the center-left government (which has not led to uncontrolled inflation, as predicted by the NCM defenders), but not enough to bring it down to the international average. Thus, in Brazil, the CBB should be labeled as irresponsible for maintaining very high nominal and real interest rates, with no trivial burdens on the nominal budget deficits (Weisbrot et al., 2017). In this case, the fiscal 'irresponsibility' is more likely a side effect of an 'irresponsible' monetary policy. This policy is wasteful regarding GDP growth and decent employment policies when compared with other countries, although it is still profligate regarding the rentiers' interests being well served by this very monetary framework of unnecessary transfers from taxpayers.

CONCLUSION

As it was shown in this chapter, ITR in Brazil – despite Brazil having one of the highest average nominal and real interest rates – does not seem to be effective in fulfilling its official objectives of keeping low and stable inflation and contributing to sustainable economic growth and low unemployment rate, as expected by the original NMC approach. Moreover, as Note 3 shows, the CBB reaction to inflation has been asymmetric: (i) the increase in the inflation rate generates a more than proportional reaction of the SELIC; and (ii) CBB reacts very gradually (this means it reduces the SELIC very slowly) when there is a fall in the inflation rate and/or a sharp reduction in the output growth.

Thus, it may be concluded that ITR in Brazil was not completely successful over the period 1999–2020.[10]

Given that, it is possible to argue that monetary policy in Brazil has been very abnormal. That is, on the one hand, SELIC does not reduce inflation because there is no excess of demand – as was argued, Brazilian inflation seems to have different determinants, including external transmissions, distributive conflicts, supply shocks and inertia mechanism – and, on the other hand, the high interest rate has stimulated transfer payments in the form of nominal budget deficits to the rentiers, once they earn what they expect to earn in the current monetary framework – more specifically, the expectations trap that frames the monetary policy, in which the CBB overemphasizes the inflationary expectations of rentiers for defining interest rates, contributes to the power of rentiers over monetary policy.

Finally, if Brazil aims at achieving price stability, low unemployment, and sustainable and robust economic growth, the ITR does not seem to have been the answer. To achieve this objective, according to Rochon and Setterfield (2008), it is necessary to have an alternative rule of setting the interest rates to aim at reducing inflation, boosting GDP and employment growth, and minimizing income and wealth concentration. This idea is consistent with Keynes' idea of 'the euthanasia of rentier', as it was mentioned before. However, of course, this is likely to be met with strong resistance from the Brazilian rentiers' interests.

NOTES

1.   For Kalecki (1943), the resistance of capitalists to full employment policies observed throughout the 1930s cannot be explained by a fall in the rate of profit, since the increase in real wages provided by this situation would tend to be reflected more in prices than in profits. Thus, the cause of this opposition was the result of political and social transformations caused by the maintenance of a situation of full employment, as well as the capitalists' natural aversion to any government intervention, particularly those that interfere with the capitalists'

power to determine the level of employment in society. The so-called 'economic experts' and rentiers, who are against the boom because of its effects on the price level and the value of financial assets, support such opposition from the 'captains of industry', whose concern about 'factory discipline and political stability' is more significant than about profits.

2.   Author's calculations based on statistical information from Ipeadata (2021).

3.   From 1999 to 2020 the average annual GDP rate was 2.0 percent, while the average unemployment rate was 8.9 percent per year. Author's calculations based on statistical information from Ipeadata (2021).

4.   This subsection is based on Araujo et al. (2018).

5.   Some theoretical arguments and empirical evidence on ITR can be found in Bernanke et al. (1999).

6.   Exploring closely the idea that the inflation rate is not sensitive to SELIC, Table 3.1 shows that from 1999 to 2005, despite high interest rates, the inflation rates were above the targets, as well as in three years the inflation rates were greater than tolerance intervals. In 2006, 2007 and 2008 it seemed that there is a negative relationship between interest rates and inflation rates, but, again, from 2009 to 2016 a tight monetary policy was not able to bring the inflation rates to their targets. Finally, from 2017 to 2020, the lowest interest rates of the whole period did not affect the inflation rates.

7.   Concerning this point, Arestis et al. (2011) show that the main causes of the Brazilian inflation rate are related to cost-push factors – such as movements in the exchange rate and changes in the international prices of commodities – and distributive conflicts and by partial inertia due to the indexation of the administered prices.

8.   The main arguments of this subsection are based on Ferrari Filho and Milan (2018a).

9.   Going in this direction, Erber (2008, pp. 623–624) points out that the tight Brazilian monetary policy is the result of a coalition of interests that was formed, structured by the public debt and the high interests earned on such debt. This coalition operates under a tacit agreement that the Brazilian State has to pay high interests and so must other debtors. Thus, there is a convention firmly grounded on powerful interests, historically consolidated, about the payment of interest rates. More specifically, this means that the interest rate depends on the expectations of the financial markets, despite the fact that the monetary authorities control the monetary policy.

10.   This argument is supported by Araujo and Arestis (2019).

REFERENCES

Araujo, E. and P. Arestis (2019), 'Lessons from the 20 Years of the Brazilian inflation targeting regime'. *Panoeconomicus*, **66**(1), 1–24.

Araujo, E., E. Araujo and F. Ferrari Filho (2018), 'Macroeconomic performance in Brazil under the inflation targeting regime'. *Investigacion Economica*, **LXXVII**(304), 72–101.

Arestis, P. and M. Sawyer (2008), 'New consensus macroeconomics and inflation targeting: Keynesian critique'. *Economia e Sociedade*, **17**(número especial), 631–655.

Arestis, P., F. Ferrari Filho and L.F. Paula (2011), 'Inflation targeting in Brazil'. *International Review of Applied Economics*, **25**(2), 127–148.

Becker, J., J. Jager, B. J. Leubolt and R. Weissenbacher (2010), 'Peripheral financialization and vulnerability to crisis: A Regulationist perspective'. *Competition and Change*, **14**(3–4), 225–247.

Bernanke, B. S., T. Laubach, F. S. Mishkin and A. S. Posen (eds) (1999), *Inflation Targeting: Lessons from the International Experience*. Princeton: Princeton University Press.

Boddy, R. and J. Crotty (1975), 'Class conflict and macro-policy: The political business cycle'. *Review of Radical Political Economics*, **7**(1), 1–19.

Bresser-Pereira, L. C. and C. Gomes (2009), 'Inflation targeting in Brazil: A Keynesian approach'. In L.R. Wray and M. Forstater (eds), *Keynes and Macroeconomics After 70 Years: Critical Assessments of the General Theory*. Cheltenham, UK and Northampton, MA, USA: Edward Elgar Publishing, 176–195.

Bruno, M., H. Diawara, E. Araujo, A. C. Reis and M. Rubens (2011), 'Finance-led growth regime no Brasil: Estatuto teórico, evidências empíricas e consequências macroeconômicas'. *Revista de Economia Política*, **31**(5), 730–750.

Carlin, W. and D. Soskice (2006), *Macroeconomics: Imperfections, Institutions and Policies*. Oxford: Oxford University Press.

Central Bank of Brazil (CBB) (2021), *Séries Temporais*, available at: http://www.bcb .gov.br, accessed October 25, 2021.

Dutt, A.K. (1990-91), 'Interest rate policy in LDCs: A Post Keynesian view'. *Journal of Post Keynesian Economics*, **13**(2), 210–232.

Epstein, G. (1992), 'Political economy and comparative central banking'. *Review of Radical Political Economics*, **24**(1), 1–30.

Epstein, G. (2001), 'Financialization, rentier interests, and central bank policy'. Paper presented at *PERI Conference on Financialization of the World Economy*, December 7–8, 2001, Amherst: University of Massachusetts.

Epstein, G. (2019), 'Financialization, rentier interests, and central bank policy'. In G. Epstein (ed.), *The Political Economy of Central Banking: Contested Control and Power of Finance, Selected Essays of Gerald Epstein*. Cheltenham, UK and Northampton, MA, USA: Edward Elgar Publishing, 380–406.

Epstein, G. and J. Schor (1988), 'Macropolicy in the rise and fall of the Golden Age'. *World Institute for Development Economics Research of the United Nations University, Working Paper 38*, Helsinki: UNU-WIDER.

Epstein, G. and J. Schor (2011), 'The Federal Reserve–Treasury accord and the construction of the Post-War monetary regime in the United States'. University of Massachusetts Amherst Political Economy Research Institute. Working Paper No. 273, November 8.

Erber, F. S. (2008), 'Development projects and growth under finance domination'. *Revue Tiers Monde*, **195**(3), 597–629.

Esping-Andersen, G., R. Friedland and E. Wright (1976), 'Modes of class struggle and the capitalist state'. *Kapitalistate*, **4-5**, 186–220.

Ferrari Filho, F. and M. Milan (2018a), 'Liquidity trap: The Brazilian version'. *Brazilian Keynesian Review*, **4**(2), 278–299, second semester.

Ferrari Filho, F. and M. Milan (2018b), 'Excess real interest rates and the inflation targeting regime in Brazil: Monetary policy ineffectiveness and rentiers' interests'. *Applied Economics and Finance*, **5**(6), 84–110.

Ferrari Filho, F. and L. F. Paula (2003), 'The legacy of the *real* plan and an alternative agenda for the Brazilian economy'. *Investigación Económica*, **LXII**(244), 57–92.

Friedman, M. (1968), 'The role of monetary theory'. *American Economic Review*, **58**(1), 1–17.

Friedman, M. (1970), 'A theoretical framework for monetary analysis'. *Journal of Political Economy*, **78**(2), 193–238.

Grabel, I. (2003), 'Ideology, power and the rise of independent monetary institutions in emerging economies'. In J. Kirshner (ed.), *Monetary Orders: Ambiguous Economics, Ubiquitous Politics*. Ithaca: Cornell University Press, 25–52.

Ipeadata (2021), *Séries Históricas*, available at: http://www.ipeadata.gov.br, accessed October 25, 2021.

Kalecki, M. (1943), 'The political aspects of full employment'. *Political Quarterly*, **14**(4), 322–330.

Keynes, J. M. ([1930] 1976), *A Treatise on Money: The Pure Theory of Money, Volume I*. New York: AMS Press.

Keynes, J. M. ([1936] 2007), *The General Theory of Employment, Interest and Money*. London: Palgrave Macmillan.

Keynes, J. M. (1972), 'How to pay for the war'. *Essays in Persuasion (The Collected Writings of John Maynard Keynes, Volume IX)*. London: Macmillan, 367–439.

Kydland, F. and Prescott, E. (1977), 'Rules rather than discretion: The inconsistency of optimal plans'. *Journal of Political Economy*, **85**(3), 473–491.

Libanio, G. (2010), 'A note on inflation targeting and economic growth in Brazil'. *Revista de Economia Política*, **30**(1), 73–88.

Lucas Jr, R. (1972), 'Expectations and the neutrality of money'. *Journal of Economic Theory*, **4**(2), 1003–1124.

Modenesi, A. and E. Araújo (2013), 'Price stability under inflation targeting in Brazil: An empirical analysis of the monetary policy transmission mechanism based on a VAR model (2000–2008)'. *Investigación Económica*, **LXXII**(283), 99–133.

Rochon, L. P. and M. Setterfield (2008), 'The political economy of interest rate setting, inflation, and income distribution'. *International Journal of Political Economy*, **37**(2), 5–25.

Smithin, J. (1996), *Macroeconomic Policy and the Future of Capitalism. The Revenge of the Rentiers and the Threat to Prosperity*. Cheltenham, UK and Northampton, MA, USA: Edward Elgar Publishing.

Vernengo, M. (2008), 'The political economy of monetary institutions in Brazil: The limits of the inflation-targeting strategy, 1999–2005'. *Review of Political Economy*, **20**(1), 95–110.

Weisbrot, M., J. Johnston, J.V. Carrillo and V. Mello (2017), 'Brazil's enormous interest rate tax: Can Brazilians afford it?' *Center for Economic and Policy Research*, Washington, DC, April.

Zysman, J. (1983), *Governments, Markets, and Growth: Financial Systems and Politics of Industrial Change*. Ithaca: Cornell University Press.

4. The unfinished stabilization of the *Real Plan*: an analysis of the indexation of the Brazilian economy

José Luís Oreiro and Julio Fernando Costa Santos

INTRODUCTION

The literature on contemporary Brazilian economy is converging in pointing out that the success in fighting Brazilian high inflation in the 1980s and 1990s was due to a change in the diagnosis of its cause. Although the inflationary process is multi-causal and, in this sense, Brazil does not differ from other countries, its specificity lies in that the introduction of price indexation instruments and contracts were able to increase the feedback effect of inertial inflation, making disinflation costly in terms of the increase in unemployment and loss of real output.

The *Real Plan*, adopted between 1993 and 1994, during the Itamar Franco administration,[1] was successful in removing the short-term indexation mechanisms and disarming the inflation memory effect through the introduction of an indexed currency in two different phases. The *Real Plan* was successful in bringing down annual inflation rates in Brazil from 2,477 percent in 1993 to 22.4 percent in 1995 and lower than 10 percent p.y. in the following years (Ipeadata, 2021). However, the plan did not remove all existing indexation mechanisms in the economy since price indexation for periods longer than one year were still allowed. The continuing existence of mechanisms of price indexation avoided restoring the *unit of account* function of Brazilian currency, being mainly responsible for the inflation in Brazil *not* falling below 5 percent p.y. in the long-term.[2]

This chapter aims to review the discussion about price indexation in the Brazilian economy and its effect over the persistence of average long-term inflation at a moderate but still high level over the last two decades. Thus, we begin in the next section by briefly reviewing the history of inflation in Brazil, as well as the origin of indexation and the role of the *Real Plan*. In the third section, we point to the existence of remaining indexation mechanisms on prices, contracts and wages. In the fourth section, we carry out two econometric tests to evaluate an explanatory model for inflation in Brazil and to evaluate the evolution of inflationary inertia over time. Finally, in the fifth section, we present the conclusion of the chapter.

THEORETICAL DISCUSSION ABOUT THE MAIN CAUSES OF BRAZILIAN INFLATION

A Brief Discussion

The debate around the causes of Brazilian inflation throughout the 1980s and 1990s is complex and difficult to summarize. However, in the book entitled *Inflation and Recession* (*Inflação e Recessão*), Bresser-Pereira and Nakano (1984) organized the theoretical pillars of the discussion on the causes of inflation in Brazil in the 1980s and some particularities of the relationship between inflation and growth, which will be useful for what will be listed below regarding the unfinished process of de-indexation of the Brazilian economy.

In general terms, the authors present a very peculiar characteristic of the phenomenon of inflation in the Brazilian economy, which is the coexistence of relatively high inflation, compared with developed countries, with a situation of semi-stagnation.

According to the authors, there are three theoretical basis that could explain this characteristic of inflation, namely:

(a)   The Keynesian theory based on the imbalance between demand and aggregate supply at the height of the economic cycle;
(b)   Structural inflation caused by sectoral imbalances between supply and demand;
(c)   Managed inflation, caused by the monopoly power of firms, unions, and the state.

Thus, the inflation policy in Brazil must have at its core the corresponding diagnosis of the causes of the ongoing inflationary process. For sure, it needs to be clear and precise in order to avoid errors in the conduct of economic policy, generating side effects such as: reduced investments, deindustrialization and fall of real output.

Owing to the intrinsic causal channels of Brazilian inflation, an inflation control policy with a target inflation at a lower level must know how to identify its remedies:

> if inflation comes from demand, the monetary and/or fiscal control of aggregate demand will be the most suitable policy; if inflation is structural, it will be necessary

to live with it while taking long-term measures to reduce structural imbalances; if inflation comes from cost or it is managed, the market will be imperfect and, therefore, price controls and income policy will be the natural path. As these causes are not mutually exclusive, a combination of these policies will likely be necessary. Emphasis, however, must always be given to the main cause of ongoing inflation. (Bresser-Pereira and Nakano, 1984, p. 76; translated from Portuguese by the authors)

The first and second theories are like the monetarist theory, demand theories that only partially explain the dynamics of Brazilian inflation. Therefore, the only theory that brings new elements that help to explain the persistence of inflation (relatively high compared with developed countries) with the semi-stagnation of the economy is the theory of managed inflation. In this sense, economic policies must pay attention to the events that generate managed inflation, which are mainly associated with the remnants of indexation that still exist in the country.

According to the authors, the inflationary process is the result of three mechanisms or factors that act on prices:

(i)   *Maintaining or inflationary inertia factors* are those that cause a certain inflation level to be maintained over time. These factors arise from the ability of economic agents to defend their relative share of income through the automatic transfer of costs caused by the increase in inflation to prices, wages, interest and exchange rates, for example, through indexation mechanisms;

(ii) *Inflation accelerating factors* are those that generate wage increases above productivity, profit margin increases, and, in an open economy, real currency devaluation and rising prices for imported inputs;

(iii) *Factors that sanction the rise in inflation* are those that put upward pressure on the accelerating factors of inflation, such as the increase in the public deficit and in the nominal quantity of money, which occur in an economy close to full employment.

Thus, a policy to fight against inflation in Brazil needs to be aware of the factors that maintain or cause inflationary inertia, which are those that cause the maintenance of the level of inflation, without losing sight of the accelerating and sanctioning factors of inflation.

The Origin of Indexing in the Brazilian Economy

The inflationary spiral is not a particular problem from Brazil, although the country has many peculiarities. Its main consequence is that as it accelerates, it raises the social stress regarding the distribution of national income (Bacha,

1987), which, in other words, is equivalent to intensifying the so-called distributive conflict. When we say that Brazil has particularities compared with other countries, the reason is that due to the maintenance of high levels of inflation for a long period of time, between the 1960s and 1990s, the economy created formal and institutional mechanisms to deal with this social conflict, through the so-called indexation of contracts, wages and prices.

Its origin dates back to 1964, when the so-called Government Economic Action Plan (*Plano de Ação Econômica do Governo* – PAEG) was implemented. In it, the legal institution of inflation indexation of public debt was created, through the Adjustable Treasury Bonds (*Obrigações Reajustáveis do Tesouro* – ORTN). These were government bonds that were issued during a period of high inflation, as a way of maintaining their attractiveness to buyers, since it corrected the amount applied by the past inflation.

At that moment, we marked the beginning of an embryo that, seen as a remedy for public financing in an environment of high inflation, would become a poison for engendering a mechanism that would be spread over other instruments, such as contracts, wages and prices.

The *Real Plan*

The literature about the Brazilian economy points out that Brazil became a great laboratory in the 1980s and 1990s for the design of public policies to reduce high inflation. There was a sequence of plans that were not successful in taming high inflation (Cruzeiro, Verão, Bresser, Color I and Color II). After years of trying to stabilize inflation at lower levels, we can highlight that there were three achievements that marked the turning point on this trajectory.

The first is in the correct diagnosis that the factor that positively fed back current inflation was the degree of indexation of the Brazilian economy. Thus, one of the first designs of the *Real Plan* was to prohibit the indexation of contracts with maturity of less than one year.

The second is in the design of working with a multiphase stabilization plan, with monetary reform being just a phase, and not necessarily the most important. The objective that stands out here was to organize the expectations of economic agents, who had become accustomed to associating stabilization programs with sudden loss of rights.

The third is in the experiment of creating a single price index (*Unidade Real de Valor* – URV), making agents set prices in this unit and avoiding the repricing process (since this unit of account would be indexed[3]). When most economic agents adopted this unit of account, this was the time to also make it the means of payment of the economy, thus removing the memory of past inflation. The intellectual origin of this idea was in a working paper of the

Department of Economics at PUC/RJ (*Pontifícia Universidade Católica do Rio de Janeiro*) and was known as the Larida proposal.[4]

According to Cunha (2006),

> The mechanism would work with the indexation of all contracts by the same price index and for the same time unit, this being the smallest possible. The guarantee of neutrality is given by the conversion of contracts at the average value of the previous period.

Thus, the foundation of the *Real Plan* was in the Larida proposal. The plan would then consist of eliminating the inflationary memory by linking the total assets and prices of the Brazilian economy to a single index, which was called URV (*Unidade Real de Valor*). As a result, there was a complete de-indexation with the conversion of all contracts to the new currency, prohibiting the use of any indexation mechanism for contracts with a maturity of less than one year. Thus, a lower limit was created for the contract readjustment period, in an attempt to neutralize the inertial component of inflation.

Despite the success achieved in bringing Brazilian inflation to single digits over the last 25 years, there are remaining forces through contract, wage and price indexation mechanisms that at some specific moments show their ability to generate an inertial and possibly hysteresis effect on the current inflation in the Brazilian economy. Our idea and arguments aim to expose some examples of these mechanisms and point out some econometric evidences of their latent existence.

THE REMAINING INDEXATION MECHANISM IN THE BRAZILIAN ECONOMY

Indexation Mechanism in the Public Debt

Although in developed countries there are so-called inflation-linked bonds, these bonds have a modest share in public financing compared with other bonds, especially fixed bonds. In this sense, the majority of public debt is usually financed by fixed-rate bonds with short or medium/long maturity (Bills and Bonds).

The Brazilian case reverses this logic. Owing to the long period of high inflation and the creation of mechanisms that would make government financing by public bonds viable under these conditions, we have the most common financing of short-term debt (up to 10 years) being a floating rate (linked to the basic interest rate – SELIC OVER), called Treasury Financing Bills (*Letras Financeiras do Tesouro* – LFT) with part being Fixed, called National Treasury Bills (*Letras do Tesouro Nacional* – LTN). They are zero coupon Bonds. For intermediate maturity (up to 10 years), with payment of a semi-annual coupon, there are the so-called National Treasury Notes – Class F (*Notas do Tesouro Nacional Classe F – NTN-F*). For long maturity (from 5 to 35 years), inflation linked bonds are used, here called National Treasury Notes – Class B (*Notas do Tesouro Nacional Classe B – NTN-B*).[5]

Regarding the maturity of the Brazilian public debt, according to Central Bank of Brazil (CBB) (2021), over the last 20 years, we can say that most of the public debt is short-term (about 75 percent maturing in up to 5 years), with the second tranche a very modest share (about 15 percent maturing in up to 10 years). The remainder (up to 10 percent) matures in a period longer than that. Thus, we have the combination of the following characteristics in Brazilian public financing: it is essentially short-term and non-fixed, as can be seen in Figure 4.1.

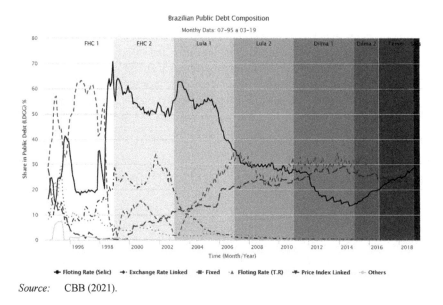

Source: CBB (2021).

Figure 4.1   Composition of Brazilian public debt

Figure 4.1 shows the evolution of the composition of Brazilian public debt between 1995 and 2019. Some points need to be mentioned here: (a) over the years 2000 to 2007, public bonds linked to the exchange rate were no longer issued; (b) although, between 2000 and 2006, most of the debt was financed by floating-rate bonds, owing to the high level of the real basic interest rate, in later years, this space was occupied by the increase in fixed bonds (paying higher interest rate levels); (c) in moments of greater uncertainty, agents migrate from pre-fixed to floating-rate bonds; (d) long-term debt in Brazil is fully financed through bonds that protect against inflation.

Thus, when Brazil raises its short-term interest rate, it has a direct and instantaneous positive impact over 1/3 of its public debt. The other 2/3 may be positively or negatively impacted by new bonds, depending on the current behavior of the term structure of the interest rate to the change in the short-term interest rate. A positive inflationary shock raises one-third of the debt by indexation, another third is raised owing to the short rate adjustment rule by the inflation targeting regime and the final third is adjusted by rising through changes in the term structure of the interest rate.

In relation to previous decades, specifically the 1990s and 2000s, there were two other characteristics in the dynamics of public debt that are no longer present. The first is that most of the treasury financing was external, that is, bonds issued abroad in US dollars. This, of course, caused the debt dynamics to have a repricing according to the exchange rate variation. The second feature is that in the share of the domestic debt (issued in local currency) there were the Class C National Treasury Notes (*Notas do Tesouro Nacional – Classe C – NTN-C*), which were bonds linked to the IGP-M. As this index is heavily impacted by the exchange rate (a wholesale price index), even the domestic debt suffered from exchange rate fluctuations and exchange rate volatility.

Thus, Brazilian composition of public debt after the *Real Plan* was initially characterized by indexation to the exchange rate, making those periods of exchange rate crisis to also be periods of debt crisis. This phase was gradually replaced (between 2000 and 2006) as the composition of public debt profile changed. It stopped being mostly foreign (issued in foreign currency) and became mostly domestic (issued in local currency). At the end of this phase, although the link of public debt to the exchange rate issue was partially addressed,[6] there was still the issue of most of the debt being indexed to inflation rates.

Therefore, the second moment is the one that marks the transition from external debt to internal debt, but with a high share of short-term price-indexed bonds (75 percent of it maturing in up to 5 years). It is temporally marked, starting in 2006 and continuing to the present day (year 2021). In this current phase, Brazil distinguishes itself from other countries because a major share of its public debt is indexed, while other countries have a minor share of public debt indexed (developed and developing countries).

Finally, we argue here that in order for Brazil to regain similar public financing characteristics that exist in a non-inflationary environment, it must gradually replace inflation-linked bonds with fixed bonds at its long part of the interest curve. In parallel, it should allow the CBB to operate at the long part of the interest curve (buying and selling bonds), so that the long interest rate should not be determined only by market clearing conditions, or financial agents' requests.

Indexation Mechanism in the Contracts

We previously presented that after the creation of Brazilian public debt indexation mechanisms, an avenue was opened for other indexation mechanisms to emerge, creating readjustment triggers that feed on past inflation provided by some price index.

In this section, we present some examples of these mechanisms in Table 4.1, as the remaining forms of indexation in the Brazilian economy. The specific indexation for the minimum wage will be shown in the next section, due to its importance, along with the discussion about how those rules changed over time.

Table 4.1   Contracts adjusted by past inflation indexes

Contract	Indexed by	Price group
Consumer's energy prices	IGP-M or IPCA	Managed prices
Telecommunication services prices	IGP-M or IPCA	Managed prices
Water services	IPCA	Managed prices
Individual healthcare	80% IVDA, 20% IPCA	Managed prices
Property rental contracts	IGP-M or IPCA	Housing prices
Ceiling price of medicines	IPCA	Managed prices
Retirements	INPC	Non price
Real estate financing	TR, IPCA	Financial price

Source: Authors' elaboration.

Table 4.1 shows how some contracts are indexed in the Brazilian economy. In the case of consumer energy prices as well as telecommunications services, there is an annual tariff adjustment that can be indexed either by the IGP-M or the IPCA. In the case of water supply services, the readjustment is also annual, and the price is readjusted based on the IPCA. An interesting curiosity is that in 2020, real estate financing contracts became possible to be indexed by the IPCA. Prior to 2020, the only possible index was the TR (*Taxa Referencial*) plus the pre-established interest rate.

The main problem with these indexation rules is that in moments when there is no pressure on the sectorial cost, but there is an increase in any other sector's costs, there is a contamination of prices, increasing the sectorial profit margin, if the revenues remain constant. At times when the sectorial cost grows above the level of the indexed price index, it will have pressure to reduce the sectorial margin and this reflects on the sectorial activity's rate of return, if the revenues remain constant.

The second point that creates a problem is that if we are dealing with an economy in a 'strato-inflation' regime,[7] even in the absence of shocks, due to the indexation mechanism, a shock continues to feed back inflation more than a period ahead, creating the effect inertia. Finally, in the presence of temporary shocks, these dissipate slowly or even do not dissipate, leading them to be added into the time series trend, and this creates difficulties to be solved through the usual instruments of monetary and fiscal policy.

Indexation Mechanism in the Minimum Wages

The minimum wage in Brazil was established by president Getúlio Vargas on 1 May 1940. The value of this minimum wage should be sufficient to ensure a basic quality of life for a person, that is, enough for the worker to pay housing expenses, and for food, health, transport, education, clothing, hygiene and leisure.

The evolution of the minimum wage values in Brazil can be divided into eight phases. with the first phase corresponding to the period 1940–1945, which instituted the provision that aimed to set a minimum value for the worker's survival. This period showed that periodic adjustments to this minimum would be necessary to maintain its purchasing power. Next, there is the period 1946–1951, characterized by the lowering of wages, which practically reached the lowest real value in the country's history.

In the following decades, the minimum wage policy gained importance, mainly because the majority of workers received a lower or equal value. From 1952 to 1959, it is noted that this was the period in which real gains were the most significant in the series, given that values increased fourfold. The period 1960–1964 can be considered a complex moment due to the inflation that started to rise, reducing the real earnings of workers.

After the military coup in 1964, a policy was adopted to maintain the purchasing power of the minimum wage, but in the initial period there was a strong reduction in its real value due to the loss of bargaining power of unions. Subsequently, from 1976–1982, real wages were maintained with the rules for semi-annual readjustments. The minimum wage remained relatively stable, at levels that hovered around R$800, in actual value. Real increases in the minimum wage happened, but only when productivity gains were observed in the economy.

The period of high-inflation,[8] which covers the years 1983–1994, was a complicated phase for the Brazilian economy due to the acceleration of inflation and the failure of economic plans that caused a great erosion of the real minimum wage. Wage triggers were introduced to mitigate the effects of inflation on the value of the minimum wage in real terms, but this mechanism was not successful. Increases were calculated based on expected inflation, which were often underestimated. Thus, in this period, there was a significant drop in the real minimum wage.

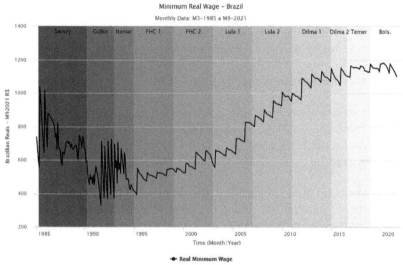

Source: Ipeadata (2021).

Figure 4.2   Brazilian real minimum wage

Although the readjustment rules improved over the following decades and the population's purchasing power increased at those times, it was only after 1994, with the *Real Plan* and the end of hyperinflation, that the minimum wage started to appreciate again, due to several factors, but it is mainly due to the policy of valuing the minimum wage and the favorable economic growth cycle observed in the 2000s.

With the consolidation of democracy in Brazil and the rise of the workers' party (*Partido dos Trabalhadores, PT*) to power, union representations gained strength and began to pressure the government to improve the rules for long-term adjustments of the minimum wage.

In this context, a rule was implemented that started to drive the readjustment of the minimum wage in Brazil in the following way:

$$ " w_t / w_{t-1} = \pi_{t-1} + \max[g_{t-2}, 0] \tag{4.1} $$

where the calculation of the minimum wage adjustment, $\Delta w_t / w_{t-1}$, takes into account the inflation of the previous year π_{t-1} plus the result of the growth rate of GDP with two lags, g_{t-2}. Note that if the GDP growth rate is negative, the value considered for this indicator in the formula is zero.

This calculation was adopted in 2008 and became law in 2011 (law 12,382, of 25 February 2011), but the current model for adjustment of the minimum wage has been applied since 2006. The rules were confirmed in 2011 and 2015, but the actual legislation (Law 13,152, of 2015) only provides for the maintenance of these criteria until 2019. Thus, Senate Bill No. 416, of 2018, is under discussion. The justification for the proposal is to ensure a minimum real gain of 1 percent for the minimum wage every year, in order to ensure that the worker does not lose a real raise in times of crisis. Formally:

$$\Delta w_t / w_{t-1} = \pi_{t-1} + \max[g_{t-2}, 1\%] \tag{4.2}$$

According to the logic of the proposal, it is precisely in times of economic recession that it becomes necessary to increase workers' wages so that there is an increase in aggregate demand through consumption and the economy grows again.

The problem with this proposal is its side-effect, namely, the inflation caused by the distributive conflict between firms and unions for a greater share of national income and the effort that the central bank had to make in terms of increasing the short-term interest rate in order to contain the problem.

Regarding the minimum wage adjustment policy in Brazil, Oreiro (2018, p. 267) defends the use of the *golden rule of wage policy*,[9] which states that wages should grow at a rate equal to the sum of productivity growth in the medium term and the target inflation rate as defined by monetary authorities, as it reduces the distributive conflict and prevents monetary policy from being used to keep this type of inflation (via distributive conflict) under control.

To mathematically demonstrate the consistency of this proposal, the author assumes that firms set their prices based on a fixed mark-up on the short unit of production, so that:

$$\hat{p}_t = \hat{w}_t - \hat{y}_t \tag{4.3}$$

where: $\hat{p}_t$ is the inflation rate; $\hat{w}_t$ is the wage growth rate; and $\hat{y}_t$ is the medium-term productivity growth rate.

Unions need to be convinced that wages will follow the golden rule:

$$\hat{w}_t = \hat{p}_t^T + \hat{y}_t \tag{4.4}$$

where: $\hat{w}_t$ is the wage growth rate; $\hat{p}_t^T$ is the inflation target; and $\hat{y}_t$ is the medium-term productivity growth rate.

Substituting equation (4.4) into equation (4.3), we have:

$$\hat{p}_t = \hat{p}_t^T \tag{4.5}$$

In short, the adoption of the golden rule of wage policy and the removal of the current strict indexing rule makes the inflation rate equal to the inflation target set by the government, so that the control of inflation caused by distributive conflict no longer requires the use of monetary policy as a disciplining variable of the tension between the parties.

EMPIRICAL EVIDENCE OF INDEXATION THROUGH INFLATION INERTIA

Data

In this section, we present the data used to generate an econometric model for explaining the current behavior of Brazilian inflation. For the analysis, we used four price indexes that are widespread and used in the economy, namely the IPCA Free Prices, IPCA Full Prices, IGP-M and IPA. The first two represent consumer price indices while the IGP-M is a mixed index that captures the general behavior of prices, being weighted partly by consumer inflation (30 percent of the CPI), partly by inflation in civil construction (10 percent of INCC) and mostly wholesale price inflation (60 percent of the IPA).

Next, we define the following explanatory variables for the model: the real effective exchange rate of monthly imports; the output gap calculated by using Hodrick–Prescott (HP) and Butterworth (BW) filters in the monthly economic activity index, IBC-BR (calculated by CBB); the real short-term interest rate (ex post) calculated as nominal Selic-over interest rate deflated by the consumer prices index (IPCA); the average expectation of inflation of agents obtained by the FOCUS bulletin of the CBB. All variables are monthly frequency, treated for seasonality through the X-13 ARIMA SEATS.

Finally, the direct measurement of the degree of indexation of the economy and its effect on inflationary inertia is not easy to measure. Thus, we will use the autoregressive component of inflation as a measure of the inertial effect and we will use this as a proxy for the discussion about the presence of indexation. The limitation of this methodology is well defined by De Carvalho (2014): The presence of inflationary persistence can be the result of a numerous range of elements. Among them, it is worth highlighting the presence of price rigidity, informational failures, the possibility of indexing contracts, the adoption of a permanently expansionist fiscal policy and, finally, the occurrence of adverse shocks – from the external sector, for example – which make the exchange rate volatile, causing transitory effects on prices.

An Econometric Model for Inflation in the Brazilian Economy

The empirical analysis of Brazilian inflation has been investigated in different ways and methods over time. Discussions more focused on policymaking have used models with distributed lags (such as VAR, BVAR, SVAR) to capture the temporal effect of a shock on other variables, as well as the sensitivity of a variable to the contemporary effects of another variable and on its lags. Our idea here is simpler than that. We just want to visualize the contemporary effects of the main macroeconomic variables on the following price indices: IPCA free prices, IPCA full prices, IGP-M and IPA. Figure 4.3 shows the behavior of inflation accumulated in 12 months of these indices mentioned.

As can be seen in Figure 4.3, the four inflation indices exhibit different patterns of behavior over time. The most volatile are the IPA and IGP-M, the first being a part of the composition of the second index. This volatility is mainly due to two factors: the fluctuation of tradable goods prices and the effect of exchange rate variation, considering that the IPA is a wholesale price index. In the case of IPCA Free, we are talking about a share of goods in the IPCA basket that does not have price control by the government (whether through regulation or another instrument). Both IPCA Free and IPCA Full show similar behavior in terms of variability. These are consumer price indices with less variance than that observed in the wholesale price index.

The proposed models are estimated using the GMM method and, for each model, the choice of the set of instruments that generates the possibility of accepting the null hypothesis of the J-test of instrument overidentification (in general, the first, second and third lag of model variables as instruments in the GMM). The choice to use the GMM estimation is due to the possible endogenous relationship between the contemporary variables of the model (such as Inflation Indices and REER, Real Basic Interest Rate, Output GAP and so on).[10] We used the parsimony principle to choose the models and numerous attempts at specification were made trying to find the best fit, considering the economic sense.

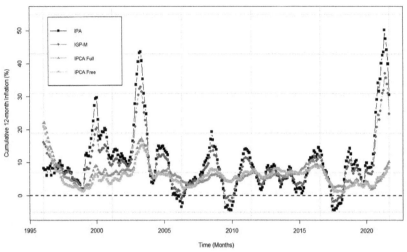

Source: Ipeadata (2021).

Figure 4.3   *Cumulative 12-month inflation (IPCA free, IPCA full, IGP-M, IPA)*

Table 4.2   *Unit root tests*

	Level	
Variable	ADF	PP
IPCA (Free prices)	−3.88***	−7.31***
IPCA (Full prices)	−3.48***	−7.53***
IGP-M	−4.58***	−3.77***
IPA	−4.58***	−4.35***
Real basic interest rate (Selic)	−2.085**	−3.20**
Output gap (Filter BW)	−2.036**	−2.24*
REER (Growth rate)	−4.77***	−11.14***
Inflation expectation (CB focus)	−5.93***	−13.82***

Note: (*) (**) and (***) significant at 1, 5 and 10 percent levels, respectively.

Thus, the series were previously treated for seasonality and deflated. Next, stationarity tests were performed via augmented Dickey–Fuller test (ADF), Phillips- Perron test (PP). All series in level showed stationary behavior with p-value below 0.05 (Table 4.2). In this way, we can use the GMM to estimate without the need to deal with the first difference of the series.

Table 4.3   *Regression results for Brazilian inflation models*

	Econometric estimations for monthly Brazilian inflation indexes							
	IPCA (Free Prices)		IPCA (Full)		IGP-M		IPA	
	(1)	(2)	(3)	(4)	(5)	(6)	(7)	(8)
IPCA free prices (−1)	0.304***	0.305***						
	(0.082)	(0.083)						
IPCA full (−1)			0.288***	0.357*				
			(0.060)	(0.200)				
IGP-M(−1)					0.848***	0.852***		
					(0.055)	(0.059)		
IPA(−1)							0.806***	0.809***
							(0.053)	(0.055)
Real basic interest rate (Selic)	−0.253***	−0.253***	−0.296***	−0.188*	−0.127	−0.097	−0.253*	−0.196
	(0.049)	(0.049)	(0.048)	(0.113)	(0.084)	(0.077)	(0.150)	(0.139)
Output gap (Filter BW)	0.003	0.003	0.005	0.007	−0.006	−0.005	−0.013	−0.011
	(0.003)	(0.003)	(0.006)	(0.009)	(0.006)	(0.006)	(0.010)	(0.010)
REER growth rate	−0.013***	−0.013***	−0.009***	−0.020	0.014***	0.009***	0.028***	0.018***
	(0.004)	(0.004)	(0.003)	(0.013)	(0.004)	(0.003)	(0.007)	(0.007)
REER growth rate (−1)		−0.0001		0.053		0.017***		0.036***
		(0.003)		(0.056)		(0.004)		(0.010)
Inflation expectation (Mean – CB Focus)	0.084***	0.084***	0.098***	0.074***	0.027**	0.024**	0.045**	0.039**
	(0.011)	(0.011)	(0.009)	(0.027)	(0.011)	(0.011)	(0.020)	(0.018)
J-test	0.805	0.823	3.306	1.106	0.879	0.948	0.581	0.678
J-test (*p*-value)	0.37	0.364	0.191	0.293	0.348	0.33	0.446	0.41
N	217	217	217	217	217	217	217	217

Note: (*) (**) and (***) significant at 1, 5 and 10 percent levels, respectively.

Accordingly, the common specification for the four indexes was how current inflation is a function of lag inflation, the short-term real interest rate, the output gap (via BW filter), the real effective exchange rate, the growth rate of real output, the first rate lag exchange rate growth and agents' average expectations for inflation in the next 12 months, via the Focus bulletin.

The results obtained show that all inflation indexes have a significant inertial effect, which highlights the presence of indexation as a memory factor for current inflation.

This evidence found in our chapter is in line with results obtained by other methodologies for the Brazilian case, such as: Figueiredo and Marques (2011); Reisen, Cribari-Neto and Jensen (2003). The former used MS-ARFIMA to capture the long-memory component of inflation in Brazil. They found values between 0.72 and 0.82 for the parameters related to the long run inflation memory. The second paper used an ARFIMA model to analyze Brazilian inflation. The result is like the former one. For other countries, there is the paper of Loungani and Swagel (2001) who used the VAR methodology for different levels of data aggregation. The author found that for South American countries, through the variance decomposition, only 9 percent of the past inflation variance (inertial) can explain the variability of current prices. Therefore, it is suggestive to conclude that the results reported here for the inflation indices in Brazil have an inertial effect greater than that observed in other countries.

The effect of the interest rate on current inflation was negative and with strong statistical significance for the IPCA Free Prices and IPCA Full Price indexes. The effect of the Output Gap on current inflation proved to be weak and without significance (it was tested until the third lag and this remained independent of the specification).

Nevertheless, we ran tests using the exchange rate level. However, the exchange rate level is the variable that does not pass all stationarity tests and when specified in the model, it shows low statistical significance. Thus, we use the growth rate of the real exchange rate and its first lag. The idea is that there may be a lag effect in price readjustments given a shock to the REER due to price rigidity via contracts. Another point to mention is: in order not to incur in a relevant variable omission bias, we use a variable that captures the market consensus on the average expectation of future inflation.

Finally, we see that in all models we accept the H_0 of the J test, showing that the instruments are suitable for the proposed model. Next, we will present the result of the Rolling Regression (ROL) estimation, to obtain the evolution of the estimation of the inertial parameter for the models in a 5-year moving window.

The Autoregressive Effect in the Brazilian Price's Indexes

One of the natural questions that arise regarding the impacts of indexation on the inertial effect of inflation in Brazil is how this autoregressive component has evolved over time. It is already well established in the Brazilian economics literature that the *Real Plan* had the main effect of unlocking the degree of indexation of the Brazilian economy and, in consequence, disarming the inertial component of inflation. That said, a second econometric test is carried out here with a view to evaluating the trajectory of this inertial component over time (mainly in the last three decades).

In this sense, the subject of inflationary persistence over time is not unique to Brazil. There are also papers in the literature about inflation dynamics showing that the persistence effect still occurs today in the CPI indices in other countries. The paper of Devpura et al. (2021) makes it clear that, using a unit root test with endogenous structural break, Asian countries have the inertial effect of inflation (inflation persistence) still present today.

Thus, we perform tests here comparing the first-order autoregressive effect of inflation indices in Brazil with the first-order autoregressive effect of the US economy CPI. More specifically, we used the Rooling Regression (ROL) technique to estimate the first-order autoregressive component in a 60-month rolling window. It should be noted that their interpretation is that the current estimate represents the average effect of the last 5 years. We plot the upper limit of this component on Figure 4.4 as being equal to one. This mark is important because it represents the threshold level above which it creates an explosive dynamic (also recognized as a trajectory of explosive inflation).

The results for the inflation indices are that despite the period before the *Real Plan* we had an autoregressive component oscillating around 0.8 and 1.0, after the reform we had a drop and, in some moments, a new acceleration. Two obvious points in time are: in the period of the 1999 crisis in emerging countries (which even culminated in the abandonment of the exchange rate band regime and adoption of the inflation targeting regime) and in this period there was a sudden drop in expectations due to the risk of exchange rate crisis, which implied a strong acceleration of inflation. The second point was the American subprime crisis (around 2007/2008), which also generated a drop in expectations, a sudden exchange rate depreciation due to the outflow of capital flows and, consequently, an acceleration of inflation.

Still in relation to the Figure 4.4, we used a dark grey line to show the similar estimation for the same period using the American Consumer Price Index (CPI) data, as a benchmark. We can see that although time series like that, by construction, may have autoregressive components, the four Brazilian inflation indices always have a higher level than the one shown by the US economy.

Thus, as mentioned above, the increase in the inertial effect does not exactly mean an increase in the degree of indexation of the economy, but the still high degree of indexation of the economy implies a rigidity in the reduction of the inertial effect. The year 2021 is a good example of the case. Due to the Brazilian economic scenario and deteriorating expectations about economic

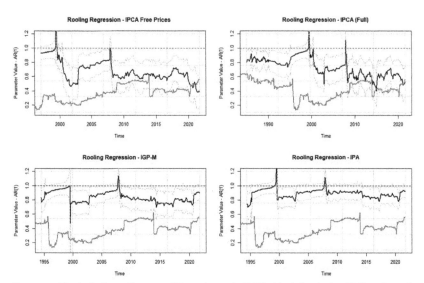

Note: The dashed grey line = confidence intervals (95%); black line is the AR(1) estimated for the Brazilian price index and the solid grey line is the AR(1) estimated for the US consumers price, as a benchmark.

Figure 4.4   Time varying autoregressive – AR (1) – parameter estimation by rooling regressions

growth, we had a strong currency devaluation. This currency devaluation and the boom in commodity prices accelerated inflation in the wholesale price index (IPA). This rise in wholesale inflation had a major impact over the general price index, IGP-M. It so happens that the value of residential rents in Brazil is readjusted based on the IGP-M. Thus, a shock that impacted the IPA spread to the general price index, IGP-M, and ultimately impacted the consumer price index, IPCA.

However, in times of economic recession, it is common among agents of the Brazilian economy to enter into a compromise between the sides so that the complete transfer of the price adjustment does not occur.

FINAL REMARKS

Throughout this chapter we analyzed the effects of persistence of price indexation mechanisms over the dynamics of Brazilian inflation after the implementation of the *Real Plan*. Although the plan was successful in bringing down inflation rates in Brazil to moderate levels in the first years after its implementation, long-term average inflation showed a remarkable resistance to fall below 5 percent p.y. due to the continuing existence of price indexation for periods higher than one year.

As were shown by our econometric exercises, although the auto-regressive component of Brazilian inflation had fallen after the implementation of the *Real Plan*, it remained at high levels compared with the Benchmark case, which is the US consumer price index. This result clearly highlights the role of price indexation in the long-term rigidity of inflation in Brazil, which makes inflation control by means of monetary policy much more difficult, since it requires very high short-term interest rates to keep inflation at moderate levels in the face of the continuous external shocks faced by the Brazilian economy in the period 1995–2020.[11] Since Brazil had a very open capital account, high interest rates result in overvaluation of the real exchange rate, having as a side effect the *premature deindustrialization* of the Brazilian economy (Oreiro, Martins da Silva and Dávila-Fernandez, 2020; Oreiro, D'Agostini and Gala, 2020).

Since the *Real Plan* did not eliminate all price indexation mechanisms in the Brazilian economy and thus restore the unit of account function of Brazilian currency, it can be said the inflation stabilization in Brazil is still an unfinished process.

NOTES

1. Itamar Franco was the vice-president elected in the Presidential elections of 1989. After the impeachment of the President Fernando Collor de Mello on October 2, 1992, Itamar Franco took office as the President of Brazil until the end of the mandate of Fernando Collor de Mello.
2. The average inflation in Brazil measured by annual change of IPCA (Índice de Preços ao Consumidor Amplo) was 6.82 percent p.y. in the period 1995–2020.
3. In the working paper, Arida and Lara Resende (1984) argues that under these conditions, inflation goes to zero for the simple reason that, measured in terms of the indexed currency, the prices of goods and services are constant.
4. Nickname attributed by Rudiger Dornbusch to the proposal of the working paper co-authored by Pérsio Arida with André Lara Resende in 1984 at an international conference organized by John Williamson. (Arida and Lara Resende, 1984).
5. For more details on Brazilian public financing in its historical context and public bond classes, see Silva, Carvalho and Medeiros (2010).
6. We use the partial term because despite the reduction in the participation of the external debt in the total debt, the internal debt was still indexed to the IGP-M, a wholesale price index that is strongly influenced by the exchange rate.
7. See note 6 for definition of *strato-inflation regime*.
8. It could also be called 'strato-inflation', in the terms of Carvalho (1993) or Jackson, Turner and Wilkinson (1972) who define that as inflation far from the expected equilibrium of a capitalist regime. Although the term 'hyperinflation' was widely used for high inflation in the Brazilian economy in the 1980s and 1990s, we do not use this nomenclature because the concept of hyperinflation is

related to the moment when the currency loses its role as a means of payment, and this has never occurred in the Brazilian case.

9. See Flassback (2017) about the importance of a *golden rule of wage policy* for macroeconomic stabilization.

10. Of course, other econometric forms of estimation would also be possible: (a) ARDL, for example, could be used with the advantage of accepting the use of a simultaneous set of variables I(1) and I(0), but at the cost of not being consistent for endogeneity; (b) VAR, for example, could be used to model distributed lags but we would lose information about the effect of a single lag.

11. About the high levels of interest rates in Brazil see Oreiro and De Paula (2021, chapter 2).

REFERENCES

Arida, P. and Lara Resende, A. (1984), 'Inertial inflation and monetary reform in Brazil'. Paper prepared for the Conference *'Inflation and Indexation'*. Institute of International Economics, Washington, DC, pp. 6–8.

Bacha, E. (1987), 'Moeda, Inércia e Conflito: Reflexões sobre políticas de estabilização no Brasil'. *Textos para discussão n.181*, PUC-RJ.

Bresser Pereira, L. C. and Nakano, Y. (1984), *Inflação e Recessão*. São Paulo: Editora Brasiliense.

Carvalho, F. J. C. (1993), 'Strato-inflation and high inflation: the Brazilian experience'. *Cambridge Journal of Economics*, 17(1), 63–78.

Central Bank of Brazil (CBB) (2021), *Séries Temporais*, available at: http://www.bcb .gov.br, accessed October 25, 2021.

Cunha, P. H. F. (2006), 'A Estabilização em Dois Registros'. *Estudos Econômicos*, 36(2), 383–402.

De Carvalho, A. R. (2014), 'A persistência da indexação no Brasil pós-Real'. *Revista de Economia Política*, 34(2), 135, 266–283.

Devpura, N., Sharma, S. S., Harischandra, P. K. G. and Pathberiya, L. R. C. (2021), 'Is inflation persistent? Evidence from a time-varying unit root model'. *Pacific-Basin Finance Journal*, 68, 1015–1077.

Figueiredo, E. A. and Marques, A. M. (2011), 'Inflação Inercial sob Mudanças de Regime: Análise a partir de um Modelo MS-ARFIMA, 1944–2009'. *Economia Aplicada*, 15(3), 443–457.

Flassback, H. (2017), 'Germany´s trade surplus: Causes and effects'. *American Affairs*, 1(3).

Ipeadata (2021), *Séries Históricas*, available at: http://www.ipeadata.gov.br, accessed October 25, 2021.

Jackson, D., Turner, H. and Wilkinson, F. (1972), *Do Trade Unions Cause Inflation? Two Studies: With a Theoretical Introduction and Policy Conclusion*. Cambridge: Cambridge University Press.

Loungani, P. and Swagel, P. (2001), 'Sources of inflation in developing countries'. *IMF Working Paper n. 01/198*, available at: https://ssrn.com/abstract=880326, accessed October 25, 2021.

Oreiro, J. L. (2018), *Macrodinâmica pós-keynesiana: crescimento e distribuição de renda*. Alta Books: Rio de Janeiro.

Oreiro, J. L, and De Paula, L. F. (2021), *Macroeconomia da Estagnação Brasileira*. Rio de Janeiro: Alta Books.

Oreiro, J. L, Martins Da Silva, K. and Dávila-Fernandez, M. (2020), 'A new developmentalist model of structural change, economic growth and middle-income traps'. *Structural Change and Economic Dynamics*, 55, 26–38.

Oreiro, J. L., Manarin D'Agostini, L. L. and Gala, P. (2020), 'Deindustrialization, economic complexity and exchange rate overvaluation: The case of Brazil (1998–2017)'. PSL Quarterly Review, 73(295), 313–341.

Reisen, V., Cribari-Neto, F. and Jensen, M. (2003), 'Long memory inflationary dynamics: The case of Brazil'. *Studies in Nonlinear Dynamics and Econometrics*, 7, 1157–1173.

Silva, A. C., Carvalho, L. O. and Medeiros, O. L. (2010), *Public Debt: The Brazilian experience*. Brasília: Estação Gráfica.

5. The role of capital flow management measures when the bubble bursts: the Brazilian experience in the global financial crisis and in the COVID-19 pandemic

Luiza Peruffo, Pedro Perfeito da Silva and André Moreira Cunha

INTRODUCTION

The 2007–2009 Global Financial Crisis (GFC) has brought to the fore the debate on capital controls. Since the end of the Bretton Woods System in the early 1970s, mainstream economics had pressed for unrestricted cross-border financial deregulation in developing and emerging economies (DEEs). The understanding was that capital-account liberalization was not only "an inevitable step on the path of development, which cannot be avoided and should be embraced," but also because "the potential benefits outweigh the costs [...] increasing economic growth and welfare", as Stanley Fischer (1998, pp. 2–3) summarized. This view had been contested at least since the 1997–1998 Asian crisis, but it was not until after the GFC – when loose monetary policy in advanced economies triggered a surge in capital inflows to several DEEs – that the macroeconomic and financial stability risks engendered by unmanaged capital flows were acknowledged as a key feature of the International Monetary and Financial System (IMFS). As the GFC unfolded, the International Monetary Fund (IMF) revised its institutional view to accept the use of capital controls, although only as a last resort measure (Ostry et al., 2011; IMF, 2012, 2016). To smoothen the legitimation of what until then was a forbidden policy instrument (Grabel, 2017, p. 198), a technocratic label of "capital flows management measures" (CFMs) was created to refer to "measures that are specifically designed to limit capital flows" (IMF, 2012, p. 8).

Over a decade later, the COVID-19 pandemic once again prompted a large wave of capital reallocation, mostly drifting away from DEEs towards safer markets and asset classes. While volatile international capital movements have penalized DEEs as they usually do in moments of global shocks, the issue of CFMs is no longer at the core of policy discussions. This time around, there has been much less coordination in terms of global macroeconomic policies, not least due to the abdication by the United States of its traditional leading role in global financial governance (and beyond). In fact, there has been no parallel in the COVID-19 pandemic for the collective discussions that took place in the G20, the IMF, the Financial Stability Board (FSB), among other forums in the context of the GFC, and which contributed to the formulation of the IMF's new institutional view on CFMs. A possible explanation for the lack of a coordinated macroeconomic policy debate now is that one of the consequences of the GFC was what Grabel (2021, p. 2) calls "incoherence": an increasing "dissensus in the domain of ideas, and inconsistency in the domain of policy". In a way, this "incoherence" is a hangover from the unfinished discussions that started at the GFC. Another complementary reason is that, during the COVID-19 crisis, DEEs were hardly seen by advanced economies as part of the solution as they were during the GFC, so there has been much less incentive to invite them to the decision table.

Among the different experiences with CFMs, Brazil has been a flagship case-study for analyzing the issue of CFMs. Brazil was one of the DEEs which had historically resorted to capital controls, defying mainstream recommendations, and which emerged as a "winner" from the GFC. Brazil's advocacy in global economic forums, backed up by its accomplishments at the time, particularly with the CFMs implemented between 2009 and 2013, contributed to endorsing the review in theory and practice that admitted the use of capital controls (Gallagher, 2014). But while Brazil was internationally praised as one of the last countries to enter the GFC and one of the first to come out of it (*The Economist*, 2009), the same has not happened with the economic crisis triggered by the COVID-19 pandemic. Moreover, Brazil has also changed its approach in relation to the adoption of CFMs, undergoing another liberalization cycle since the post-GFC controls started to be relaxed from 2012 onwards.

In light of the striking contrast between the performance of the Brazilian economy during the GFC and during the COVID-19 pandemic, this chapter discusses the role of CFMs (i) to manage the global financial cycle in developing and emerging economies (DEEs) and (ii) to create policy space for them to fight crises. In particular, it investigates the relation between the degree of financial integration and macroeconomic performance by looking at CFMs put forward by Brazil before, during and after the two global crises of the 21st century.

This chapter argues that the contrasting performance of Brazil in these two crises can be attributed both to a structural component of the IMFS, in which Brazil and other DEEs occupy an unprivileged position, and to Brazil's domestic policy decisions which have shaped the profile of its integration into global markets. Building on the Brazilian experience, this chapter reasons that CFMs are important not just when the bubble bursts, but rather as a perennial macroeconomic tool to reduce the negative effects of the global financial cycle to DEEs in a hierarchical IMFS.

Following this introduction, the next section presents a theoretical review of the role of CFMs for DEEs in the context of a hierarchical IMFS. The third section presents an overview of Brazil's financial liberalization and financial integration. The fourth section analyses the empirical data, comparing the Brazilian economic performance in the GFC and in the COVID-19 crisis, and discusses the relation between Brazil's degree of international financial integration and its macroeconomic performance. The fifth section concludes the chapter.

THE ROLE OF CFMS IN A HIERARCHICAL INTERNATIONAL MONETARY AND FINANCIAL SYSTEM

The "macroeconomic policy trilemma" (Obstfeld and Taylor, 1997), or "impossible trinity", rests on the assumption that there exists a fundamental tension between exchange rate stability, international financial capital mobility, and monetary policy autonomy. According to this theoretical framework, an economy that wants to keep its monetary policy autonomy needs to give up either its exchange rate stability or restrain its capital mobility, employing CFMs. CFMs serve to loosen the linkages between the policies designed to meet domestic objectives, such as income and employment, and the consequences these policies might have in terms of an economy's external balance, reflected in its balance of payments and in its international investment position. Yet, the issue of capital mobility and the use of CFMs is much more complex than the trilemma formulation suggests.

A first issue concerns the goal of international financial capital mobility itself. While it is quite clear why countries would want to have exchange rate stability and monetary policy autonomy, the international capital mobility objective rests on the theoretical benefits that cross-border flows would bring. Some of the theoretical benefits of international capital markets pointed out by the literature are: (i) the diversification of risks and increase of returns beyond domestic assets; (ii) access to foreign savings, which would allow countries to accelerate economic growth and stabilize consumption over the economic cycle; (iii) more efficient allocation of global savings; (iv) transfer of technology and development of the financial sector; and (v) discipline of policymakers, inducing "better" policies and acting as a brake against "bad" macroeconomic management (see for example Prasad et al., 2003, pp. 23–26).

However, empirical data has failed to provide robust evidence to support these theoretical benefits. Even strong supporters of free trade such as Jagdish Bhagwati (1998) have long noticed that ideology and interests (i.e., lobbies from the financial sector) explain free capital mobility policies much more than actual welfare and income benefits, benefits which proponents of free capital mobility have been unable to measure. With the increased frequency and intensity of financial crises since the mid-1980s, the IMF itself conducted a series of studies in the early 2000s to evaluate the empirical evidence on the effects of financial globalization for DEEs (see for example Prasad et al., 2003). In one of these efforts, its staff concluded that "a systematic examination of the evidence suggests that it is difficult to establish a robust causal relationship between the degree of financial integration and output growth performance" (Prasad et al., 2003, p. 6). After the GFC, this literature expanded even wider among mainstream economists. Rey (2015, p. 19), for example, reasons that the benefits of international financial integration are "elusive" and that the costs may be very large, since great gross capital flows disrupt asset markets and financial intermediation. Therefore, a first element in the discussion of capital mobility and the use of CFMs is the distorted view of mainstream models that international capital mobility should be a goal of policymakers as much as exchange rate stability and monetary policy autonomy.[1]

A second issue is that capital mobility can be regarded as a structural feature of the IMFS (Eichengreen, 2019; Ruggie, 1982), meaning that the notion that each country can choose to restrain, or not, capital mobility is misleading. Some rules of the international system are set by global powers, and their preferences spill over to the rest of the world. This is the case of CFMs, whose acceptance as a legitimate policy tool has fluctuated throughout history – from being widely accepted during the Bretton Woods System to being highly discouraged following its collapse and, in the aftermath of the GFC, to be reintroduced in the macroeconomic policy toolkit as a last resort measure. During the Gold Standard, choosing to impose capital controls would most likely result in a country being excluded from Britain's trade and financial relations (Eichengreen, 2019, Chapter 2). Later, the access to America's trade and financial networks was conditional on being part of the Bretton Woods System (BWS), whereby states could limit capital movement in order to pursue domestic objectives (Eichengreen, 2019, Chapter 4). The fact that there is an asymmetry between advanced economies and DEEs in the IMFS, in which DEEs face a greater credit constraint in relation to their developed peers, makes it even harder for them to deflect from the "right policies" at each time.

The recognition of international capital mobility and, more precisely, of the existence of a global financial cycle, as a structural feature of the international system, is why Rey (2015) argues the "trilemma" is actually a "dilemma". The notion of a global financial cycle refers to the fact that there are global factors which work as major determinants of international capital flows, and which are not necessarily aligned with countries' individual macroeconomic fundamentals (an argument that further challenges the idea that free capital flows would help to "discipline policymakers"). The global financial cycle is revealed in the co-movements of gross flows, asset prices, leverage of global institutions and credit creation, generating procyclical and volatile boom and bust cycles in DEEs and advanced economies alike. Accordingly, Rey challenges the theoretical framework of the "trilemma" and reasons that "independent monetary policies are possible if and only if the capital account is managed, directly or indirectly via macroprudential policies," i.e., regardless of the exchange rate regime (Rey, 2015, p. 3).

The identification of the global financial cycle as a structural component of the IMFS has also been accompanied by a clearer acknowledgement of the underlying asymmetries that characterize it. Specifically, mainstream economics has increasingly recognized the role played by US monetary policy as a major driver of the global financial cycle (Rey, 2015; Ilzetzki et al., 2017; Gourinchas et al., 2019; Gopinath and Stein, 2021). This is because of the dominance of the US dollar in international transactions. While there are almost as many currencies as countries, the greenback accounts for more than two thirds of foreign exchange reserves, denominates over 62 percent of international debt and 56 percent of loans, represents nearly half of global foreign exchange turnover and works as a payments currency for some 40 percent of global transactions (ECB, 2018). The reasons for the existence of a currency hierarchy have been long debated, but the fact is that the interplay of features that characterize the current IMFS – the fiduciary dollar standard, floating exchange rates and almost free capital mobility – has served to increase the dollar dominance (Ilzetzki et al., 2017; Paula et al., 2017; Fritz et al., 2018; Ocampo, 2018) and to exacerbate the negative consequences of international capital mobility, since capital flows can more easily punish or reward governments for policy decisions (Kirshner, 2003).

These critical reflections on the actual benefits of international capital mobility and on the existence of a global financial cycle that is detached from countries' macroeconomics conditions has underpinned the debate on the role of CFMs in the aftermath of the GFC. Another element that contributed to endorsing a review on the use of CFMs (even if only as a last resort measure) was the fact that a number of DEEs which employed CFMs before the GFC – thus defying the mainstream rule at the time – emerged as "winners" in the immediate aftermath of the GFC (Grabel, 2017, p. 199; Gallagher, 2014). DEEs successful experiences with CFMs revealed CFMs' importance (i) to manage the global financial cycle and (ii) to create policy space for them to fight crises (as this chapter will later discuss for the specific case of Brazil).

While the global financial cycle also creates boom and bust cycles in advanced economies, it is increasingly accepted that DEEs are more vulnerable to the global financial cycle, and that this vulnerability is not necessarily due to DEEs' policy failures or weaker institutions, as mainstream economics traditionally argued (see Reinhart et al., 2003, for example). In short, the practical implication of the dollar dominance is that it is considered the safest and most liquid currency, especially in times of uncertainty (crises) (Andrade and Prates, 2013; Paula et al., 2017; Gourinchas et al., 2019). Other currencies which are also used beyond its borders for international purposes – such as the euro, the yen, the pound, etc. – also enjoy some of the benefits of being safe and liquid, although to a lesser extent than the dollar. In contrast, currencies issued by DEEs hardly have any demand across borders. More than that, it is possible to argue that the demand for DEEs' currencies is more for their role as financial assets than as currencies (something that can be used as a unit of account, medium of exchange or store of value). Among mainstream economics, Eichengreen et al. (2007) had already suggested that currencies play different roles in the IMFS with the "original sin" concept (although their view was far from unanimous). The "original sin" is defined as "the inability of a country to borrow abroad in its own currency" (Eichengreen et al., 2007, p. 122), which would be due both from countries' domestic policies and institutions, and from "factors largely beyond the control of the individual country" (p. 124), especially the structure of global financial markets. Outside mainstream economics, these asymmetries had long been outlined under different perspectives.

In this light, discussions and proposals to reform the IMFS which assumed a "level playing field" among nations in the past (for a critical review see Akyüz, 2017; Ocampo, 2018) were replaced by perceptions that DEEs cannot isolate themselves from global financial shocks, even those with good macroeconomic fundamentals. This has been particularly corroborated by studies that relate the Volatility Index (VIX)[2] and capital flows (Nier et al., 2014; Rey, 2015), where low VIX levels are associated with an expansion of the global financial cycle and high VIX levels indicate the reverse. This is consistent with the "flight for safety" movements that usually characterize moments of crises, and which exacerbate DEEs' vulnerability to externally determined financial cycles.[3]

While international structural factors render to DEEs an unprivileged position in the IMFS, DEEs' domestic policy decisions also play a role in explaining their external vulnerability by shaping the profile of their integration into global markets. This includes their CFMs policies. The next section reviews the specific case of Brazil and looks at CFMs put forward by Brazil before, during and after the two global crises of the 21st century.

FINANCIAL LIBERALIZATION AND FINANCIAL INTEGRATION IN BRAZIL: AN OVERVIEW[4]

The profile of Brazil's international financial integration has been conditioned both to Brazil's unprivileged position in the hierarchical structures of the IMFS and to Brazil's domestic policy decisions over time. The result of these external and domestic forces should also be placed within the historical process of the development of the IMFS itself, particularly of the development of international capital markets. The expansion of international capital markets since the 1960s has culminated in the rise of globalization, neoliberalism and financialization in the 1990s, resulting in greater financial elites' power worldwide. As Polanyi would have predicted, the (financial) market expansion prompted increasing contradictions among social groups, contradictions that materialized in the 1990s' crises. However, it was only when these crises affected the core of the system during the GFC that the Polanyian double movement more clearly played out, unfolding in a legitimacy crisis for the neoliberal globalized financial regime (Helleiner, 2010; Dale, 2012; Grabel, 2021). This process has gained new contours as Western states, in general, and the United States, in particular, have left much to be desired in terms of responding to the COVID-19 global pandemic (Silver and Payne, 2020). These broader transformations in the IMFS are key to understand the rebranding and legitimation of capital controls in the post-GFC period. To be sure, the legitimacy crisis of neoliberalism eroded the consensus in the realm of ideas and opened space for experimentation and autonomy in the domain of policy (Grabel, 2017, 2021), including among unprivileged players such as Brazil.

Historically, Brazil's access to international capital markets has been externally determined. For example, in the 1960s, US expansionary policies increased the international credit supply and allowed countries such as Brazil, which had no regular access to financial markets hitherto, to become large-scale borrowers (Batista, 1987, p. 11; Goldfajn and Minella, 2007, pp. 361–362). Of course, this access was also made possible by the domestic financial and monetary reforms put forward by the military government that took office in 1964, which loosened the wide apparatus of CFMs that had been established for the Import Substitution Industrialization (ISI) strategy in the immediate post-war years (Van der Laan et al., 2012). These reforms also guaranteed that the foreign exchange market remained subject to oversight and regulation by the Central Bank of Brazil (CBB) (Law 4,131/1962 and Federal Law 4,595/1964). To that extent, laws and regulations have been usually elaborated considering the central government's concern with foreign exchange controls. Accordingly, the inflow and outflow of funds in Brazil can only be made through financial institutions authorized to operate in the foreign exchange market (Van der Laan et al., 2012).

During the 1960s and 1970s, Brazil's capital account convertibility enabled the authorization of profit remittances to Foreign Direct Investment (FDI), loans and other forms of finance. However, all this came to a halt with the reversal of international market conditions at the end of the 1970s and early 1980s (Goldfajn and Minella, 2007, pp. 353–357). With the Mexican moratorium in 1982, international capital markets closed for most DEEs, including Brazil, which entered a long process of external debt negotiation with the IMF, the Paris Club and a consortium of private banks. This lasted until 1994, with the issuance of the Brady bonds and the resumption of voluntary capital flows to Brazil.

The problem of the external constraint has also guided Brazil's financial liberalization policies over the years. On the one hand, this can be traced back to the issue of the currency hierarchy, credit needs and the incapacity to borrow abroad in its own currency, as discussed in the previous section. On the other hand, Brazil's financial openness policies were also an option of domestic elites. Countries that equally faced external constraint problems found alternatives other than Brazil's option for a broad financial liberalization. The case of China, for example, is illustrative of how DEEs can develop different profiles of international financial integration, which can be at least in part traced back to their CFMs policies. Brazil's engagement with international capital markets has been mostly characterized by a "play by the rules" approach, deploying CFMs usually for financial stability purposes. China, in turn, has traditionally used CFMs as part of a broader development strategy to maintain a competitive exchange rate and attract certain types of flows, resisting more the external pressures for financial liberalization policies. Over the years, the profile of Brazilian foreign liabilities has resulted mostly in portfolio and debt flows, whereas Chinese foreign liabilities constitute mostly direct investments (see Figure 5.1).

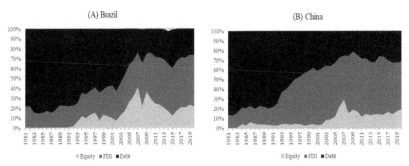

Note: Averages: (A) Brazil – 1981–2000: Equity + Debt (79%), FDI (21%); 2001–2020 Equity + Debt (57%), FDI (43%); (B) China – 1981–2000: Equity + Debt (71%), FDI (29%); 2001–2020 Equity + Debt (45%), FDI (55%).
Source: Lane and Milesi-Ferretti (2021), adapted by the authors.

Figure 5.1   Composition of foreign liabilities (1981–2020)

It is possible to argue that this means Brazil is more exposed to short-term changes in the global financial cycle than China, which enjoys a longer commitment by foreign capital. This is illustrated, for example, by the greater volatility of the Brazilian exchange rate to the global financial cycle (proxied by the VIX) in comparison with China (see Figure 5.2). The reasons for Brazil and China's different policy approaches aside (for a discussion see Peruffo et al., 2021; Cunha et al., 2020), the point to highlight is that DEEs hold some degree of agency in deciding how to engage with the financial globalization process despite their unprivileged position in the power structures of the IMFS.

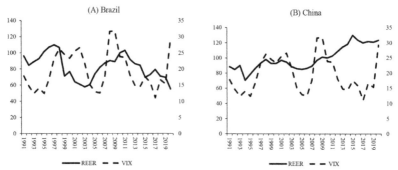

Note: REER: +/– = appreciation/depreciation.
Source: Word Bank (2021) and Chicago Board Options Exchange (2021), adapted by the
authors.

Figure 5.2   *Real effective exchange rate (REER) and global financial*
                 cycle (VIX CBOE) (1991–2020)

In the context of rising globalization, Brazil began a process of financial liberalization (Goldfajn and Minella, 2007, p. 370). Brazil started to liberalize capital inflows in the late-1980s, and in the 1990s the government committed more explicitly with capital account openness, liberalizing capital outflows, removing restrictions over FDI, and granting foreign institutional investors the right to acquire derivatives and domestic firms' equities (Goldfajn and Minella, 2007, p. 372). Following the currency stabilization program which started in 1994, the *Real Plan*, Brazil's financial system also went through a deep restructuring process, which resulted in a larger presence of foreign banks and a reduced share of public banks. Overall, by the late 1990s Brazil was much more open financially. This financial opening process partially explains why the CBB was incapable of containing the speculative attack against the Brazilian currency in January 1999, which forced the abandonment of the fixed exchange rate regime and marked the inauguration of a new macroeconomic regime, known as the "macroeconomic tripod" – a combination of a floating exchange rate regime, inflation targeting, and a fiscal policy aimed at maintaining a primary surplus.

The years that followed, until the GFC, witnessed an intensification of Brazil's financial liberalization policies. Non-resident investors were granted access to all segments of the domestic financial market, including the derivatives market (Resolution 2689/2000), and the exchange rate market was further liberalized. This encompassed, for example, the unification of the exchange rate market (Resolution 3265/2005), the end of the Central Bank's monopoly on the exchange rate, and the end of the need for foreign exchange coverage for exports (Resolution 3389/2006). These lower controls for foreign participants to operate in the Brazilian market meant that they accounted for an increasing share of domestic assets, rendering Brazil's external vulnerability increasingly denominated in domestic currency. Over time, these liberalization policies would amass to create new external vulnerabilities for Brazil (Kaltenbrunner and Painceira, 2015, 2018).

The greater share of foreign players in the domestic market would be translated, for example, into a higher vulnerability of the Brazilian real to the global financial cycle, reducing the ability of Brazilian policymakers to pursue domestic objectives without subordinating them to the external balance. Soon enough, the double bonanza of rising commodity prices and loosening monetary policy in advanced economies in the early 2000s triggered an appreciation cycle of the Brazilian real (see Figure 5.3). From May 2004 until August 2008, the real–dollar exchange rate appreciated from R$3.20 to R$1.56 per dollar. This appreciation cycle prompted a debate on the future consequences of what several economists in Brazil and abroad considered to be an overvalued exchange rate level, particularly regarding the risk of regressive specialization and primarization of exports (Palma, 2005; Bresser-Pereira, 2010; Jenkins, 2012).[5]

Hence, a key concern of the Brazilian government was to contain a new cycle of exchange rate appreciation in the aftermath of the GFC, when the monetary authorities of advanced economies announced large-scale bond-buying programs (known as Quantitative Easing, QE), which flooded the international market with cash. Between October 2009 and December 2012, the Brazilian regulatory authorities deployed 13 controls to manage the capital boom prompted by the QE policies of advanced economies, particularly those of the United States. There were three types of controls: (i) capital controls, such as the IOF[6] (eight out of the 13); (ii) prudential regulation measures, such as reserve requirements (two out of the 13); and (iii) foreign exchange derivatives[7] regulation (three out of the 13) (Prates and Fritz, 2016, pp. 195–196). Foreign exchange derivatives simulate the impact of capital flows on the exchange rate without actually generating any capital flows (because they are

Source: Elaborated by the authors with data from the CBB (2021).

Figure 5.3   Brazil's nominal exchange rate (Jan 1999–Aug 2021) (R$/US$)

non-deliverable) and thus are not affected by capital controls nor prudential regulation. Yet these operations have an enormous impact on the future exchange rate, and by arbitration in the spot rate alike, justifying its regulation in Brazil, which was an innovation inaugurated in the context of the crisis. Starting from R$2.50 per dollar in December 2008, the most depreciated level after the bankruptcy of Lehman Brothers, the Brazilian real appreciated until the lowest level of R$1.53 per dollar in July 2011, coinciding with when the government tightened prudential regulation and foreign exchange derivatives regulation (Prates and Fritz, 2016, p. 197).

Since these post-GFC CFMs started to be relaxed from 2012 onwards, Brazil has experienced another liberalization cycle. This has been marked, for example, by Brazil's official request to become a member of the OECD in May 2017, followed by efforts to meet with the organization's standards, including its Code of Liberalization of Capital Movements, whose ultimate goal is to liberalize capital movements. Towards this goal, in May 2019 the CBB submitted a bill of law to the House of Representatives (PL 5387/2019) proposing fundamental changes to the legal framework of Brazil's exchange rate market regulation, which is currently under appreciation. This bill of law aims at replacing various previous laws with one piece of legislation. In short, it sets forth an equal legal treatment for foreign and domestic capital, opening room for a full convertibility of reais into foreign currency. If approved, the new law will allow, for example, both private individuals and entities to have bank accounts in foreign currency in Brazil, something impossible under the current rules. It will also allow the operation of fintech companies in the exchange rate market and will further remove restrictions to the use of exports' revenues abroad. This ongoing liberalization cycle has been marked by a continued depreciation of the Brazilian currency, which peaked at R$5.93 per dollar amidst the COVID-19 pandemic in May 2020.

All in all, since the late 1980s, Brazil's financial policies in general have shadowed the historical evolution of the IMFS towards financial globalization. The exception was during the immediate aftermath of the GFC, when Brazil challenged the mainstream with its CFMs, but this was a period of policy experimentation in other parts of the world too. Over the years, Brazil's relatively passive engagement to financial globalization, coupled with its unprivileged position in the hierarchical structures of the IMFS, resulted in a greater vulnerability to the global financial cycle in comparison with DEEs which adopted other strategies to deal with the external constraint problem, such as China. Brazil's weaknesses would be particularly exposed in moments of crises, as the next section argues.

THE RISE AND FALL OF BRAZIL: FROM THE GLOBAL FINANCIAL CRISIS TO THE COVID-19 CRISIS

The contrast between the performance of the Brazilian economy during the GFC and during the ongoing COVID-19 pandemic (see Table 5.1) is illustrative of the structural challenges faced by DEEs, particularly the most financially open ones. The case of Brazil is also a strong reminder that external vulnerabilities may be being built over time, even if masked by favorable short-term international conditions. That means the bonanza period that preceded the GFC helps to explain the relative policy space Brazil had to fight that crisis, and the (economic and political) international uneasiness that characterized the post-GFC period also helps to explain why there has been much less policy space for Brazil to respond to the COVID-19 pandemic. At the same time, the policy spaces Brazil had in both crises are interconnected by its own domestic policy decisions – before, during and after the crises. As argued in the previous section, new external vulnerabilities began to be built in Brazil in the early 2000s as the share of foreign players in the domestic market increased. To that extent, the lower policy space Brazil had to fight the COVID-19 crisis can be in part also attributed to Brazil's policy decisions two decades earlier (and before that as well).

Table 5.1   *GDP data, Brazil and selected country groups (2007–2020)*

GDP (percent change)	World	Advanced economies	DEEs	Brazil
2007–2009	2.8	−0.1	5.6	3.7
2010–2014	4.0	1.9	5.8	3.4
2015–2019	3.4	2.1	4.4	−0.5
2020	−3.1	−4.5	−2.1	−4.1

Source: Data from IMF (2021, World Economic Outlook October).

A confluence of international and domestic factors explains Brazil's relatively better performance in the GFC than in the COVID-19 crisis. The years that preceded the GFC were fairly good for DEEs in general, and Brazil in particular. The rise in commodities prices, which started in the early 2000s (see Figure 5.4), contributed to a surge in Brazilian exports that was large enough to compensate both the rise of imports and Brazil's structural deficit in the primary income account. As a result, even with the exchange rate appreciation movement that began in 2003, Brazil accumulated surpluses in the current account between 2003 and 2007, reducing the traditional external constraint. The favorable international scenario, marked by a low VIX (see Figure 5.4), also allowed a policy of international reserve accumulation, yielding Brazil the reputation of a sound economy. This included the pre-payment of Brazil's debt with the IMF in 2005, two years ahead of schedule, and a sequence of achievements in terms of economic growth, rising investment rates, and economic and political stability. Standard & Poor's upgrade of Brazil's long-term foreign currency debt to investment grade in April 2008 epitomized this positive outlook, a movement that was shortly followed by Fitch Rating (May 2008) and Moody's Investors Service (September 2009). Thus, when the GFC erupted, Brazil had considerable economic policy space and political capital[8] to fight the consequences of the crisis.

In contrast, the years that followed the GFC were marked by international and domestic turbulence. As Figure 5.4 shows, commodity prices rebounded shortly after the bankruptcy of Lehman Brothers and rose until mid-2011, a movement that contributed to Brazil's quick rebound to the negative consequences of the GFC. Thereafter, however, commodity prices started a slow downtrend that accelerated from 2014 onwards. This, coupled with a much less favorable global economy environment in the years that followed the GFC, including the Eurozone crisis, the Russian financial crisis in 2014, the Brexit referendum and the US presidential elections in 2016 (see the VIX line in Figure 5.4). For Brazil, these years were also marked by high domestic economic and political instability (including a downgrade from S&P's

investment-grade credit rating in September 2015), an instability that was embodied in the impeachment of President Dilma Rousseff in August 2016 and its long-lasting consequences. To that extent, the Brazilian economy was much more fragile when the COVID-19 pandemic erupted.

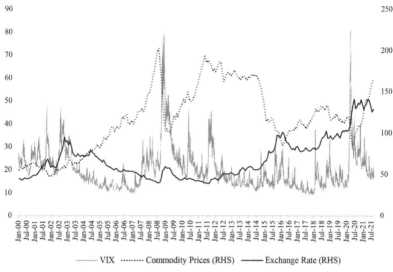

Note: The exchange rate is multiplied by 25 to allow for better representation.
Source: Elaborated by the authors. VIX data from CBOE. Monthly commodity prices data from the IMF. Monthly exchange rate data from the CBB (2021).

Figure 5.4   International risk aversion, commodity prices and exchange rate (Jan 2000–Aug 2021)

As Figure 5.4 shows, both crises prompted a drop in commodity prices and a rise in the VIX index, but the Brazilian exchange rate responded differently at each time. In the GFC, the depreciation happened in the wake of an appreciation process, and the exchange rate began to appreciate again in late 2008, as discussed in the previous section. In fact, the Brazilian government deployed a set of CFMs to prevent the continued appreciation of the exchange rate in the context of the QE policies deployed by advanced economies. These CFMs were relaxed from 2012 onwards and this coincided with a long depreciation trend, which peaked in the context of the COVID-19 pandemic. Unlike the GFC, the Brazilian exchange rate has remained depreciated, meanwhile the Brazilian government has continued to promote financial liberalization policies. The exchange rate behavior can be at least in part linked to Brazil's CFMs policies in the last two decades. As Figure 5.5 shows, the early 2000s up to the

GFC were marked by a financial liberalization process, which was partially reversed by the CFMs deployed in the context of the GFC.

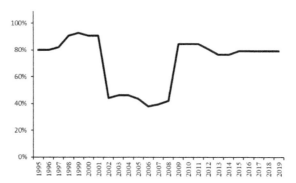

Note: This reformulated version of the CCI took into consideration the average level of capital controls over four types of flows: direct investments, portfolio investments, other investments, and derivatives.
Source: Fernández et al. (2016), reformulated by the authors.

Figure 5.5   *Brazil's capital controls index (1995–2019)*

These liberalization policies allowed for a greater share of foreign participants in the domestic market, a process that has been reflected in Brazil's external liabilities. As Figure 5.6 illustrates, the exchange rate devaluation in both crises was linked to a strong capital outflow, which in its turn can be linked with the "flight for safety" movement that is typical from stress moments. During the GFC and the COVID-19 pandemic alike, the capital outflow movement from Brazil was led by non-residents with positions in assets denominated in domestic currency – typifying the idea of the "new forms of external vulnerability" put forward by Kaltenbrunner and Painceira (2015, 2018), and of an "original sin redux" discussed by Carstens and Shin (2019). These capital outflows contribute both to a deflation in domestic asset prices and to a devaluation of the exchange rate.

Over the years, domestic policy decisions coupled with Brazil's position in the hierarchical structure of the IMFS engendered a cumulative process that increased Brazil's vulnerability to short-term changes in the global financial cycle, with important consequences for Brazil's external position, as illustrated by Figure 5.7. The financial opening process that was heightened in the 2000s coincided with the commodity boom and the favorable international scenario, which concealed the ongoing increase of Brazil's external vulnerability. Under the surface of the current account surpluses between 2003 and 2007, which nonetheless helped Brazil to build the conditions that allowed it to have the

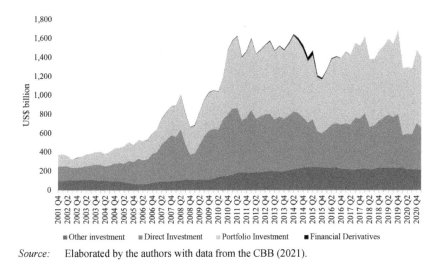

Source: Elaborated by the authors with data from the CBB (2021).

Figure 5.6   Composition of Brazil's external liabilities (Q4 2001–Q1 2021)

policy space to fight the GFC, was both the surge in the share of non-residents in the domestic financial market and the primarization of exports. The latter was in part an outcome of the Brazilian exchange rate appreciation process in the previous period which, as discussed, can be linked to the greater susceptibility of the exchange rate to the global financial cycle. To that extent, it is not surprising that the period following the GFC was much more challenging to Brazilian policymakers. With the end of the commodity boom, current account deficits became once again the rule, reflecting Brazil's structural deficit in the primary income account, aggravated by the fact that the trade balance result became more dependent on commodity prices due to the primarization of exports. Not even the sharp depreciation of the Brazilian currency has been enough to reverse the current account deficits. In this process, the demand for capital inflows increases and heightens even more Brazil's financial integration profile led by liabilities which, in turn, further accentuates the current account deficit due to rising income payments to non-residents.

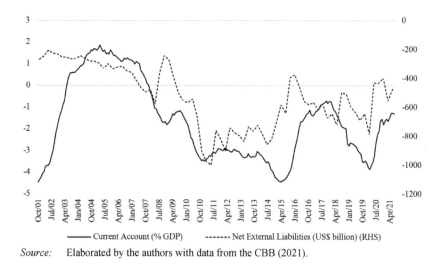

Source: Elaborated by the authors with data from the CBB (2021).

Figure 5.7   Brazil's current account (% GDP) and net external liabilities (US$ billion) (Q4 2001–Q1 2021)

FINAL REMARKS

This chapter contrasted the performance of the Brazilian economy during the 2007–2009 GFC and during the ongoing COVID-19 pandemic to discuss the role of CFMs (i) to manage the global financial cycle in developing and emerging economies (DEEs) and (ii) to create policy space for them to fight crises. It explained the contrasting performance of Brazil in these two crises episodes by taking into account both a structural component of the IMFS, in which Brazil and other DEEs occupy an unprivileged position, and Brazil's domestic policy decisions, which have shaped the profile of its integration into global markets. It argued that the decisions of Brazilian policymakers to increase Brazil's financial liberalization before the GFC contributed to building the vulnerabilities that made responding to the COVID-19 crisis more challenging.

NOTES

1.   As noted by Kirshner (2003, p. 5), "the competing argument is not that capital flows are bad but rather that completely deregulated capital would lead to a sub-optimally high level of flows".
2.   The VIX is the Chicago Board Options Exchange (CBOE) Market Volatility Index, an indicator of the implied volatility of the S&P 500 index options. It is widely used as a proxy to global factors.

3.   The "flight for safety" is not linked with countries macroeconomic fundamentals but rather with the position their currencies have on the international currency hierarchy. A distinctive example in this regard was the appreciation of the dollar against most currencies following the collapse of Lehman Brothers in September 2008. To be sure, not even the fact that the GFC originated in the American financial system could change international investors' perception about the dollar as a safe haven (Akyüz, 2017). During the COVID-19 crisis, the dollar has once again appreciated against most currencies worldwide.

4.   The terms "financial integration", "financial liberalization", and "financial globalization" often appear as synonyms in the literature. This is because most models assume that economies will automatically achieve a perfect level of financial integration under full capital mobility. In practice, however, "financial liberalization" refers to the removal of legal restrictions that will allow for greater "financial integration," i.e., financial liberalization is a necessary but not sufficient condition for financial integration. In its turn, "financial globalization" refers to greater global linkages through international financial markets, while "financial integration" refers to an individual country's linkages (Prasad et al., 2007; Akyüz, 2017; Ocampo, 2018).

5.   A concern which has proved to be accurate, as shown by Nassif and Castilho (2020).

6.   IOF is the Portuguese acronym for the Tax on Financial Operations, a tax levied on various types of financial transactions in Brazil – foreign exchange, investments, credit – that can be set by Presidential Decree, independently from Congress approval

7.   Foreign exchange derivatives refer to financial derivatives whose payoff depends on the foreign exchange rates of two or more currencies.

8.   "Political capital" is a concept that describes the accumulation of resources and power built through trust, relationships and influence, which can be used to accomplish policy reforms and other political goals.

REFERENCES

Akyüz, Y. (2017), *Playing with Fire: Deepened Financial Integration and Changing Vulnerabilities of the Global South.* Oxford and New York: Oxford University Press.

Andrade, R. and D. M. Prates (2013), 'Exchange rate dynamics in a peripheral monetary economy'. *Journal of Post Keynesian Economics*, **35**(3), 399–416.

Batista Jr., P. N. (1987), 'International financial flows to Brazil since the late 1960s: An analysis of debt expansion and payments problems'. *World Bank Discussion Papers*, 7. Washington, DC: The World Bank.

Bhagwati, J. (1988), 'The difference between trade in widgets and dollars'. *Foreign Affairs*, **77**(3), 7–12.

Bresser-Pereira, L. C. (ed.) (2010), *Doença holandesa e indústria*. Rio de Janeiro: Editora FGV.

Carstens, A. and H. S. Shin (2019), 'Emerging markets aren't out of the woods yet: How can they manage the risks'. *Foreign Affairs*, 15 March.

Central Bank of Brazil (CBB) (2021), *Estatísticas*, available at: https://www.bcb.gov.br/, accessed October 21, 2021.

Chicago Board Options Exchange (2021), *VIX Index*, available at: https://www.cboe.com/tradable_products/vix/, accessed October 21, 2021.

Cunha, A. M., D. M. Prates and P. P. Silva (2020), 'External financial liberalization and macroeconomic performance in emerging countries: An empirical evaluation of the Brazilian case'. *Development and Change*, **51**(5), 1225–1245.

Dale, G. (2012), 'Double movements and pendular forces: Polanyian perspectives on the neoliberal age'. *Current Sociology*, **60**(1), 3–27.

Eichengreen, B. (2019), *Globalizing Capital. A History of the International Monetary System*, 3rd ed. Princeton: Princeton University Press.

Eichengreen, B., R. Hausmann and U. Panizza (2007), 'Currency mismatches, debt intolerance and original sin: Why they are not the same and why it matters'. In S. Edwards (ed.), *Capital Controls and Capital Flows in Emerging Economies: Policies, Practices and Consequences*. University of Chicago Press, 121–169.

European Central Bank (2018), *The international role of the euro*. Interim report, June, Frankfurt am Main.

Fernández, A., M. W. Klein, A. Rebucci, M. Schindler and M. Uribe (2016), 'Capital control measures: A new dataset'. *IMF Economic Review*, **64**, 548–574 (updated August 2021, available at: http://www.columbia.edu/~mu2166/fkrsu/, accessed October 21, 2021.

Fischer, S. (1998), 'Capital account liberalization and the role of IMF'. In S. Fisher et al. (eds), 'Should the IMF pursue capital-account convertibility?' *Essays in International Finance*, 207, 1–10, Department of Economics, Princeton University.

Fritz, B., L. F. R. Paula and D. M. Prates (2018), 'Global currency hierarchy and national policy space: A framework for peripheral economies'. *European Journal of Economics and Economic Policies: Intervention*, **15**(2), 208–218.

Gallagher, K. P. (2014). *Ruling Capital: Emerging Markets and the Re-regulation of Cross Border Finance*. Ithaca: Cornell University Press.

Goldfajn, I. and A. Minella (2007), 'Capital flows and controls in Brazil: What have we learned?' In S. Edwards (ed.), *Capital Controls and Capital Flows in Emerging Economies: Policies, Practices and Consequences*. Chicago: University of Chicago Press, 349–419.

Gopinath, G., and J. Stein (2021), 'Banking, trade, and the making of a dominant currency'. *The Quarterly Journal of Economics*, **136**(2), 783–830.

Gourinchas, P., H. Rey and M. Sauzet (2019), 'The international monetary and financial system'. *NBER Working Paper* no. 25782.

Grabel, I. (2017), *When Things Don't Fall Apart: Global Financial Governance and Developmental Finance in an Age of Productive Incoherence*. Cambridge, MA: MIT Press.

Grabel, I. (2021), 'Post-American moments in contemporary global financial governance'. *Political Economy Research Institute Working Paper Series*, n. 511. University of Massachusetts Amherst.

Helleiner, E. (2010), 'A Bretton Woods moment? The 2007–2008 crisis and the future of global finance'. *International Affairs*, **86**(3), 619–636.

Ilzetzki, E., C. M. Reinhart and K. S. Rogoff (2017), 'Exchange rate arrangements entering the 21st century: Which anchor will hold?' *NBER Working Paper Series*, no. 23134, NBER, Cambridge, MA.

International Monetary Fund (2012), *The Liberalization and Management of Capital Flows: An Institutional View*. Washington, DC: IMF.

International Monetary Fund (2016), *Capital Flows – Review of Experience with the Institutional View*. Washington, DC: IMF.

International Monetary Fund (2021), *World Economic Outlook October*, available at: http://ww.imf.org, accessed October 21, 2021.

Jenkins, R. (2012), 'China and Brazil: Economic impacts of a growing relationship'. *Journal of Current Chinese Affairs*, **41**(1), 21–47.

Kaltenbrunner, A. and J. Painceira (2015), 'Developing countries' changing nature of financial integration and new forms of external vulnerability: The Brazilian experience'. *Cambridge Journal of Economics*, **39**(5), 1281–306.

Kaltenbrunner, A. and J. Painceira (2018), 'Subordinated financial integration and financialisation in emerging capitalist economies: The Brazilian experience'. *New Political Economy*, **23**(3), 290–313.

Kirshner, J. (2003), 'The inescapable politics of money'. In J. Kirshner (ed.), *Monetary Orders: Ambiguous Economics, Ubiquitous Politics*, Chapter 1. Ithaca and London: Cornell University Press, 3–24.

Lane, P. R. and G. M. Milesi-Ferretti (2021). *The External Wealth of Nations*, available at: https://www.brookings.edu/research/the-external-wealth-of-nations-database/, accessed October 19, 2021.

Nassif, A. and M. R. Castilho (2020), 'Trade patterns in a globalised world: Brazil as a case of regressive specialisation'. *Cambridge Journal of Economics*, **44**(3), 671–701.

Nier, E., T. S. Sedik, and T. Mondino (2014), 'Gross private capital flows to emerging markets: Can the global financial cycle be tamed?' *IMF Working Paper* no. 14/196, October. Washington, DC: IMF.

Obstfeld, M. and A. M. Taylor (1997), 'The Great Depression as a watershed: International capital mobility over the long run'. *NBER Working Paper*, n. 5960, Cambridge, MA: NBER.

Ocampo, J. A. (2018), *Resetting the International Monetary (Non)System*. Oxford: Oxford University Press.

Ostry, J. D., A. R. Ghosh, M. Chamon and M. S. Qureshi (2011), 'Capital controls: When and why?' *IMF Economic Review*, **59**(3), 562–580.

Palma, G. (2005), 'Four sources of de-industrialisation and a new concept of the "Dutch Disease"'. In J. A. Ocampo (ed.), *Beyond Reforms: Structural Dynamics and Macroeconomic Vulnerability*. Stanford, CA: Stanford University Press.

Paula, L. F., B. Fritz and D. M. Prates (2017), 'Keynes at the periphery: Currency hierarchy and challenges for economic policy in emerging countries'. *Journal of Post Keynesian Economics*, **40**(2), 183–202.

Peruffo, L., P. P. Silva and A. M. Cunha (2021), 'Capital account regulation and national autonomy: The political economy of the new welfare economics'. *Contexto Internacional*, **43**(1), 173–197.

Prasad, E., K. Rogoff, S. Wei and M. A. Kose (2003), *Effects of Financial Globalization on Developing Countries: Some Empirical Evidence*. Washington, DC: IMF.

Prasad, E., K. Rogoff, S. Wei, and M. A. Kose (2007), 'Financial globalization, growth and volatility in developing countries'. In A. Harrison (ed.), *Globalization and Poverty*. Chicago: University of Chicago Press.

Prates, D. M. and B. Fritz (2016), 'Beyond capital controls: regulation of foreign currency derivatives markets in the Republic of Korea and Brazil and the global financial crisis'. *Revista de la CEPAL*, **118**, 184–201.

Reinhart, C. M., K. Rogoff, K. and M. Savastano (2003), 'Debt intolerance'. *Brookings Papers on Economic Activity*, **1**, 1–74.

Rey, H. (2015), 'Dilemma not trilemma: The global financial cycle and monetary policy independence'. *NBER Working Paper*, no. 21162.

Ruggie, J. G. (1982), 'International regimes, transactions, and change: Embedded liberalism in the postwar economic order'. *International Organization*, **36**(2), 379–415.

Silver, B. J. and C. R. Payne (2020), 'Crises of world hegemony and the speeding up of social history'. In P. Dutkiewicz, T. Casier and J. A. Scholte (eds), *Hegemony and World Order: Reimagining Power in Global Politics*. New York: Routledge, 17–31.

The Economist (2009), 'Brazil takes off'. November 12.

Van der Laan, C., A. M. Cunha and P. C. D. Fonseca (2012), 'Os pilares institucionais da política cambial e a industrialização nos anos 1930. *Revista de Economia Política*, **32**(4), 597–614.

World Bank (2021), *Databank, The World Bank*, available at: https://data.worldbank .org/, accessed October 21, 2021.

6. Back to a high-inflation regime? The Argentine economy from the 2000s to the COVID-19 crisis [1]

Hernán E. Neyra and Andrés Ferrari Haines

INTRODUCTION

High inflation was typical of some Latin American economies in the late 1970s and 1980s. Those inflation rates would be considered hyperinflation by classic authors such as Cagan (1956), and modern ones such as Fischer, Sahay and Végh (2002). However, in these countries, three-digit annual inflation rates could be commonly observed. People, thus, had to learn how to live in such a complex environment. Normally, some kind of inertial component was added into prices by agents who, in this way, simultaneously, adapted themselves to the high inflation environment, but also continued it. Thus, high-inflation became self-perpetuating, making it more difficult to end it.

At the time in Argentina, several other mechanisms surged to cope with high inflation. Although not uniquely defined, together they became known as the High Inflation Regime (HIR). In Argentina, HIR was most thoroughly analyzed by Frenkel (1989). Following his analysis of the Argentine high-inflation context in the 1970s, we will study current inflation in Argentina to see if the features that characterized it are once again present.

If, in fact, HIR can be identified today in the Argentine economy, it would surely represent a tremendous setback for a country that thought it had, finally, defeated inflation. Argentina has suffered the presence of inflation almost continuously since, at least, the 1940s up to 1990. In 1991, in the context of the market-friendly Washington Consensus era, a drastic Currency-Board Convertibility scheme was implemented where the domestic currency, *peso Argentino*, emission needed an equivalent quantity in US dollars held as reserves by the Central Bank of the Argentine Republic (CBAR). In practice this meant a tight monetary policy that at the same time brought confidence to the public that the government would respect it. Thus, inflation dropped dramatically and quickly.

But the other side of convertibility was a growing recession as it led to over-valued domestic prices internationally. At the end of 2001, a social rebellion brought that plan down. Amid the political and economic chaos that followed, inflation returned but in a milder manner compared with the high-inflation period. The commodity boom also helped, prompting elevated growth rates. Inflation never went away, but, although cumbersome, it did not return to be a grave feature as before. In the last few years, though, it regained strength under governments of different political outlook, and it gained momentum with the pandemic.

In the 1980s, fear of runaway inflation was probably the main concern in Argentina, confirmed by the hyperinflation at the turn of that decade. Here, we wish to explore if previous experience with HIR has helped people at present to adapt themselves similarly, as suggested by Frenkel (1989) during the earlier epoch.

To this end, this chapter continues with five sections starting with a historical overview of inflation in Argentina. Afterwards, Frenkel's HIR will be presented and, in the following section, his explanatory model of inflationary dynamics will be tested. To complement this analysis, ongoing trends in some particularly sensitive markets will be examined next. The final section presents some conclusions.

ARGENTINE INFLATION 1975–2021

Argentina has had a long history of inflation and macroeconomic instability.[2] In comparison with other large Latin American economies – such as Brazil, Mexico and Colombia – Argentine inflation in 32 of the last 50 years has been the highest. In addition, in 26 years, it has had an inflation rate higher than the sum of the other three countries. Today, once again Argentina is the only country in the region experiencing long inflation periods.[3] This new inflationary phase comes after the very low and deflationary records of the 1990s. In 2002, as a consequence of the social unrest, a totally new macroeconomic regime surfaced that completely changed how prices were fixed.

Between the 1970s and 1980s, several Latin American economies were going through HIRs. It was widely understood that the presence of high inflation was impeding output growth. During the 1990s, each country sorted out in different ways their problem with high-inflation.[4] Argentina did it with the 1991 Convertibility Plan that functioned like the traditional Currency Board of the gold-standard era, but with the US dollar now backing domestic fiat money. That experience ended dramatically with a social unrest in 2001–2002. After that, the country managed to recover, riding on the commodities boom, but suffered when this slowed down. However, at all times, inflation was lurking and gradually creeping back. Even before being aggravated by the pandemic years, monthly inflation rates were once again running in high figures.

Like most countries in Latin America, the Argentine economy developed – with very successful results – along the so-called 'Primary Export Model'. In the 1930s, as a consequence of the world economic crisis, it began switching to the 'Import Substitution Model' (ISM)[5] – which lived with a chronically high inflation rate. As a result of political tensions, and hit by world recession, the ISM was, economically and politically, violently interrupted by a military coup in 1976. But before, in June 1975, amid deep political and social tensions, the then Peronist Economic Minister Celestino Rodrigo implemented a huge devaluation and tariff adjustment. This *Rodrigazo*, as it became known, was totally unexpected and produced immediate reactions of all kinds from people and interest groups trying to avoid enormous losses in their purchasing power. All in all, in the end, the episode totally wrecked the existing price system. It also left a deep scar in the population regarding inflation. It made the inflation rate jump to a totally new plateau.[6] Since 1975, Argentina suffered permanently from a minimum 100 percent annual inflation rate every year until 1991 (84 percent), save for 1980 (88 percent) and 1988 (82 percent). Some years, it was quite above that level, leading to the hyperinflationary 1989–1990 years.

Thus, 1975–1991 is the "high inflation" period of the Argentine economy, while the 1991–2001 decade became known as the "Convertibility years". The period since 2002 until now, has had no defining aspect. Different governments have managed their monetary policy according to their ideological views and political understanding of the circumstances. While HIR surged before Argentina developed a critical immense external debt, since the early 1980s servicing it fatally fueled the country's high inflation rates – particularly when it led to hyperinflation in 1989–1990. Twice Argentina thought wrongly it had resolved this issue – in 1992 when it signed the Brady Plan and in 2004 when Economic Minister Roberto Lavagna managed a huge 70 percent cut of private holders' outstanding claims. In both cases, external indebtedness would grow again, followed by an intense capital flight process. Currently, it has become a central concern vis-à-vis the management of the pandemic for the incumbent government as, in 2018, President Macri unexpectedly indebted Argentina by US$50 billion with the IMF.[7]

Characteristically, countries hit by elevated inflation rates implement currency changes to cut off numerical digits from prices in order to make market operations easier to handle. These changes sometimes even modify the name of the currency to help people to distinguish 'old' and 'new' price denomination. Argentina has been no exception. In 1970, a new standard was introduced the "*peso ley*" ($ley) looking to stabilize the economy. But high inflation forced another change in 1983 when the *peso Argentino* ($a) replaced the "*peso ley*" at the rate 1 $a = 10,000 $ley. Soon, runaway inflation again swelled nominal prices. In a bid to end inflation in 1985, a more cohesive approach was introduced with a new nomenclature, The Austral Plan. The *austral Argentino* (₳) replaced the *peso ley*, this time knocking off three zeros.[8] Following the hyperinflation years at the turn of the decade, once more people were dealing with enormous figures. In 1992, on the back of the success of the Convertible Plan that was sharply reducing inflation, the *peso* ($) replaced the austral (1$=10,000₳). Since 1992, the *peso* is still the legal tender, but after 2002 it is no longer convertible.

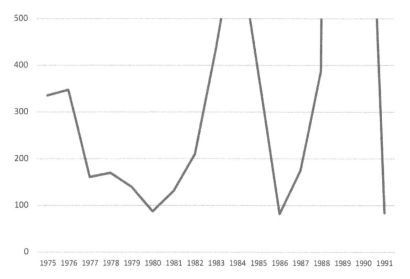

Source: Author's elaboration based on INDEC (2021).

Figure 6.1   *Inflation rate (%), 1975–1991*

In Figure 6.1, the "classic" period of the HIR can be observed. It began after the maxi-devaluation of 1975, which led people to start using indexation clauses. Inflation peaks cannot be represented in the graph because of their magnitude. In 1984, the inflation rate reached 688 percent per year and in 1989, with the first hyperinflationary episode, it went to the astonishing figure of 4,923.6 percent.[9] The next year, a second hyperinflation made annual values go to 1,343.9 percent. After 1991 started with a new inflationary acceleration, in April the Convertibility Plan was launched, which brought down the values to 84 percent for that year.

    Price dynamics changed completely in the decade of the Convertibility Plan. Not only did the annual one-digit inflation rate become normal, but in its last three years deflation was in fact registered. Of course, as, under this regime, pesos could only be minted against an equivalent amount of US dollars held as reserves by the CBAR, this made true the clause that there should be a nominal equivalence between an Argentine peso and a US dollar (Cavallo and Runde, 2020). To intensify the convertibility project, domestic banks were allowed to operate with dollar deposits and loans, leading to a wholly bi-monetary system.

Convertibility was extremely popular in Argentina, not only because it tamed inflation, but also because it allowed output to grow once again after several years of recession. Save for 1995, hit by the Mexican 'Tequila Crisis' of the previous year, between 1991 and 1997 the economy expanded at high rates by Argentine standards. However, after 1998, the fixed exchange rate of the Convertibility law prevented domestic prices from being corrected through a nominal devaluation. Argentina, with its hands tied and unable to adjust its domestic prices, was saved by a deflationary recession. This process then suffered the devaluation of the Brazilian real in 1999, the currency of its main trading partner. All in all, the Argentine economy fell into a spiral of a deflationary process that led to a fall in output that pressed for a further drop in prices and economic activity (OEI, 2004) (Figure 6.2).

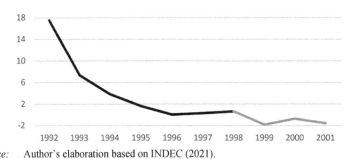

Source: Author's elaboration based on INDEC (2021).

Figure 6.2   *Inflation rate (%), 1992–2001*

After the 1999 elections there was a change of government in December of that year – but little could be adjusted as there were widespread fears of the conse-quences of giving up the convertibility scheme. In fact, the new administration opted to enhance the features of the ongoing economic plan and deepen defla-tionary dynamics with tougher market-friendly policies and financial support from the IMF. But social unrest grew exponentially and, in December 2001, President De la Rúa had to resign after several days of social unrest, including rioting and violence, throughout the country. After an extremely agitated and confused period, the convertibility regime was abandoned. In this way, a new monetary phase began in 2002, but in no clear manner.[10]

Leaving behind the dollar backing of the peso meant that different compensation mechanisms had to be implemented, and sustaining them politically meant defining 'winners and losers'. This was done during some very tense and disrupted months in which political might by different interest groups was a practical feature. Nevertheless, political and monetary authorities during this adjustment period were cautious to avoid falling back to the high-inflation period. Notably, the prohibition of indexation that had been stipulated in the Convertibility Law in 1991 was preserved. To accommodate some prices, a unit was created to update some debts in the process of reordering payments between private parties that had been set in dollars (Cavallo and Runde, 2020). Normalization was helped by political stability after Nestor Kirchner was elected in 2003 – followed by two spells by his wife Cristina Kirchner (2007–2014). Both used heterodox economic tools in a more benign environment of the global commodities boom to enable important output growth.

The evolution of prices in the post-convertibility period (2002–2020) is shown in Figure 6.3. In 2002, amidst the chaotic exit out of the convertibility scheme, inflation reached 40 percent, the highest level since 1991.[11] But afterwards it stayed for a decade below 10 percent. That is *officially* because, after 2007, INDEC, the official agency responsible for inflation data, started to falsify it. Consequently, the rates since then until 2015, when new President Mauricio Macri came to power, became seen with suspicion. Clamor from the political opposition and other social organizations led to investigations into INDEC itself, while the government suffered severe reprimands from the IMF.[12] However, regardless of this issue and the validity or not of official figures, it can still be seen that a long-term trend of price increases was manifesting itself.

Macri, aligned to an orthodox economic vision,[13] at first let the 'real inflation rate' be acknowledged by deregulation policies and a strong devaluation in May 2018, and then proceeded to tackle it through traditional anti-inflationary mechanisms. But several severe fiscal budget cuts and a deep recession could not avoid rising inflation. When he left office in December 2019, the inflation rate had reached the highest level in the century. With the impact of the COVID-19 Pandemic, the economy was hit and recession brought the price level down somewhat, helped by containment of the official exchange rate by the incoming 2020 Administration of President Alberto Fernández, with Cristina Kirchner as Vice President.

Despite this, annualized inflation (from September 2021 to September 2020) reached 51.7 percent, after the last nine months presented yearly increases. Thus, inflation is gradually approaching the highest values of the decade that occurred after the May 2018 devaluation, when it reached 56.8 percent, which

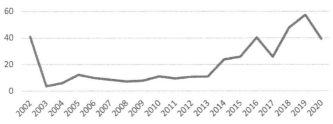

Source: Author's elaboration based on INDEC (2021).

Figure 6.3   Inflation rate (%), 2002–2020

the new Administration made responsible for the rise in inflation (Central Bank of the Argentine Republic, 2020a, 2020b). Thus, the government had to intervene in the last trimester in the sensitive meat market, a traditionally crucial component in Argentine households. At the time of writing (October 2021), the government is trying to implement a three-month price freeze on a basic goods-basket, which is proving both highly contentious with private firms and politically troublesome.

Taking into account all the latest inflationary developments, it is not surprising that people's behavioral patterns regarding price formation and the signing of contracts reveal that, in the last few years, increasingly, they have adapted to live in such an environment.[14] Even though inflation rates have not returned to levels of those of the 1975/1990 years, they are still considerable. Thus, people have started to protect their income with mechanisms similar to those under the HIR.

THE HIGH INFLATION REGIME

Roberto Frenkel called the HIR the way agents adapt to living in a context of inflationary instability,[15] and presented the following features.

(1)   *Temporary structure of nominal contracts.* As most economic activity is organized around explicit and implicit contracts, each contract stipulates a certain period in which nominal prices are valid. The higher the inflation, the shorter this period will be, to allow more flexibility for price revision.

(2)   *Existence of adaptive price mechanisms.* Some of these price mechanisms take to shortening contracts time spells as much as possible, sometimes down to months or even days. Crucial for this is the existence of available information; as inflation is calculated on a monthly basis, monthly calculations tend to prevail. This was particularly seen for sala-

ries, rents and services, as well as in bank deposits and credits. Even so, regular adjustment was not able to preserve the structure of relative real prices, due to fluctuations in different rhythms.

(3)   *Coordination.* The comprehensive use of the mentioned mechanisms leads to an intertwined network of contracts across all economic sectors, a network that ends up being coordinated to enhance contract indexation as an institutional framework. Thus, inertia becomes grounded and extremely difficult to overcome, as history has shown.[16]

(4)   *Pricing expectations and decisions.* In the absence of shocks or increases in administered prices (typically tariffs and exchange rates), future inflation tends to be equivalent to past inflation, as prices are set on the basis that inflation will follow the prior monthly rate.

(5)   *Shocks generate greater volatility.* As different agents have different capacities to face unexpected shocks, those with greater ability react by raising their prices over the ongoing inflation rate, thus accelerating it.

(6)   *Distributive struggle.* Distributive conflicts intensify because volatility leads agents to try to protect themselves with over-the-top increases in nominal prices or by pressuring for fiscal resources or assistance from the Central Bank.

(7)   *Flexible markets act as accelerators/decelerators of inflation.* 'Flexible prices' refers to goods traded in open markets – in the Argentine case, exportable goods that are socially sensitive as they are also domestically consumed foodstuffs, such as meat or vegetables. Thus, as they are additionally affected by external demand, any excess in supply or demand has an accelerating or decelerating effect on inflation, consequently affecting the expected future inflation.

(8)   *Indexation.* For Frenkel, indexation was a crucial feature of HIR. But here it is listed last because it has been forbidden since 1991. In effect, Law 23,928, on Convertibility of the austral, specifically prohibited it in its article 7 and repealed any previous contractual clause in article 10. As these two clauses remain nominally in force, indexing continues to be prohibited. Indexation was a crucial aspect of HIR for Frenkel; thus, strictly speaking, it could not be presented today in Argentina. Notwithstanding, despite its legal prohibition, indexation has, in practice, recently reappeared in some forms.

AN EXPLANATORY MODEL FOR THE 2018–2021 INFLATION

To check whether HIR is present today in Argentina, this section will estimate again the CEDES (Centro de Estudio de Estado y Sociedad) 1988 econometric model of the Argentine inflation during the 1970s and 1980s, as presented by Baldi-Delatte (2004).[17] Fundamentally, the model looks to verify, as point (7) stated above, whether flexible-market prices and administered tariffs act as accelerators/decelerators of the general price level.

The CEDES model is formed with the following variables:

$$IPC = \alpha W + \beta E + \gamma Pub + \delta Pflex \qquad (6.1)$$

where IPC = Inflation rate, W = wages, E = nominal exchange-rate, Pub = public services and Pflex = meat and vegetables prices.

The original results of the estimation for the 1977/1988 period were:

$$IPC = 0,38W + 0,14E + 0,34Pub + 0,14Pflex$$

This meant that the price index rate depended significantly on the variation in wages and public service rates, with statistically relevant values.

To replicate the experiment for the last few years, the same model was estimated with a slight adjustment. Conforming to primary source data made available today by INDEC, "flex prices" will be represented by Meat (M) and Vegetables (Veg) prices. Consequently, the estimate for the years 2018–2021 shows:

$$IPC = -0.16W + 0.37E + 0.11Pub + 0.35M + 0.08Veg \ .$$

Comparisons between the two estimations reveal some interesting results. First, surprisingly, the two explanatory variables estimated in 1988, wages (W) and rates (Pub), are no longer relevant because they no longer have statistically significant values. Second, the variables that became explanatory are the remaining ones, the exchange rate and the flexible prices – meat in fact.[18] Thus, the same model continues to have statistical relevance. However, now variables have exchanged their explanation capacity for the price movements between 2018 and 2021.

The existence of an inverse relationship between wages and inflation seems, at first glance, problematic. However, at the particular 2018/2021 juncture of recent years in which the economy is in recession, private employment is falling and labor-market conditions are similar to those of the late 1990s – that is, affected negatively by a long recession. Hence, following Frenkel and González Rozada (1998, p. 62), we can conclude that this outcome is logical considering that labor markets are relatively segmented, such as those of the different branches of industry. Consequently, contraction in employment levels is observed at different intensities across the labor-market, because, as they point out, "the hypothesis is then that wages fell more (or rose less) in the branches where the greatest contractions in employment were observed."

Noticeably, these updated results confirm the significance of one flexible price; that of meat. Its importance as a cause of the accelerations and decelerations of inflation in recent years can be, likewise, confirmed by the fact that the government has been trying to tamp its price down in the last few months.[19]

Another observation must be made regarding the exchange-rate. The newest model revealed it as explanatory, calculated using the dollar price set by the Central Bank. Nevertheless, to further comprehend the significance now of the exchange rate, some clarification is needed. In Argentina, the long inflationary history – especially during the 1970/1980 HIR years – made people reach for the US dollar for purchasing power protection. Crucially, this led finally to the full convertibility of the national currency in 1991. Until that point, the exchange market did not operate freely and the rate was decided by the government, usually well below what it would have reached otherwise. As a result, a so-called "black" exchange rate market would commonly emerge, where individuals carried out transactions between national monies, but without any legal registration or control by authorities. Convertibility made this double market ineffectual, but the re-entrance of inflation once more split the exchange market.

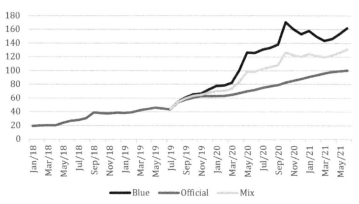

Source: Author's elaboration based on Central Bank of the Argentine Republic (2021) and Ambito Financiero (2021).

Figure 6.4   *Official exchange rate, "blue" and mix (monthly averages, in pesos per dollar)*

Once Macri in December 2017 abandoned inflation-targeting after the rate reached 25 percent, the exchange-market began to split as government confidence waned. Although people went for the dollar, the official price was not modified. Thus, a parallel market grew which was not forbidden, where the dollar rate surpassed the official one. As it was not illegal nor was it tax evasion, but operated outside the formal economy, this lighter characteristic led to be it known as a "blue market", to infer a milder form of black market. After 2018, particularly after the May devaluation, the blue dollar began showing a noticeable gap with the official one, which grew considerable in 2019 before the failure to stabilize the economy after taking a historic US$50 billion IMF loan.

The significance the US dollar again acquired in the functioning of the Argentine economy cannot be overstated; thus, the distance between the "official" and the "blue" dollar-rate, as Figure 6.4 illustrates, can be quite considerable. For this reason, it seemed appropriate to estimate the model to verify which exchange rate influenced the inflationary level. Results revealed that the model had explanatory power if the official exchange rate values are taken, but not when the "blue" exchange rate or, even, a mix of both, is considered. The blue dollar has experienced fluctuations not accompanied by inflation rates. For instance, on October 23, 2020, the dollar reached its highest daily value ($195), dropping to $145 December, 5, without affecting the inflation rate in any meaningful manner.

TRENDS AND BEHAVIOR OF SOME PARTICULAR MARKETS

Before inspecting the remaining assumptions of an HIR reviewed in the second section, it is important to state again that its main characteristic is that the previous inflation rate (represented by the latest published CPI data) coordinates inflation expectation for the following month – unless some relevant new information appears. In this case, "any impact that affects the monthly inflation rate becomes replicated with all its force on expectations" (Fanelli and Frenkel, 1989). When the system as a whole reaches this level of adaptation to inflation, it is because uncertainty is excessively high and, as a result, the economy acquires a very short-term way of functioning, making propagation extremely fast due to the high elasticity against any inflationary surge (Fanelli and Frenkel, 1989).

Synthetically, what must be verified is that: (1) the temporary structure of contracts is shortened; (2) adaptation to high inflation shortens deadlines to the minimum time of available relevant information – i.e., a month since there are no weekly inflation data published; (3) progressively, all contracts end up being coordinated; thus, a system of coordinated contracts evolves; (4) in the absence of shocks, future inflation will be same as past inflation; (5) a shock increases volatility; (6) there is the existence of a distributive struggle; (7)

flexible prices act as accelerators or decelerators of inflation; and (8) indexing is a common practice.

Real-estate Rent Market

Household rentals have had a new regulatory framework from June 2020. It is a decentralized market with free pricing at the beginning of each contract. The original bill began to be discussed in 2018 and sought to balance relations between tenants and owners, since inflation was surpassing wage increases. Hence, being dealt with between the high inflation rates of 2018/2020, the main concern was to regulate the impact of the general price index rise over rents. The formula that was implemented combined in equal share the rise in the CPI (general retail inflation) and the average wage index of registered workers.[20] Additionally, it was established that the minimum contract extension increased from two to three years, with a once per year rent update allowed. This regime came into force for contracts signed from July 2020, that is, already in the midst of a pandemic.

With the annually inflation rate being more than 50 percent but wages increasing lower than that level, a property owner would have to acknowledge that they would charge rent at a lower rate than inflation. This reckoning would be enhanced by the clause of the minimum three-year rent-period. As a result, the market could either adjust through prices (rent increases at the beginning of the contract or prices set in dollars) or through quantities (where some owners opted to withdraw from the rent-market, either choosing to sell their properties or just wait for better times). Additionally, others decided on short-terms rents to tourists.

Real estate market analysts calculated that, in 2021, the number of units offered for rent fell 20 percent in comparison to 2020. Over time, the yearly price adjustments cannot compensate owners for the loss in the original rent in real terms. It was estimated that one out of four apartments, when it ended its rent contract, returned to the market to be offered once again, while the number of apartments put up for sale increased very strongly.

Regarding agricultural and livestock land (fields and ranches), prices were determined as a fraction of output produced in them – a percentage of the harvest or a certain amount of quintals per hectare. As these are commodities or meat, which have an international price in dollars, in that way, and although priced in pesos, these contracts end up dollarized. Consequently, in this case, owners do not have uncertainty around exchange rate fluctuations.

Labor Market

Working conditions in Argentina are settled in collective agreements. The norm (Law No. 14,250) that regulates them leaves it to the discretion of the negotiating parties to determine wage levels.[21] Hence, the terms of each agreement ends up being decided by those involved. In practice, as expected under HIR, workers have tended to reduce the temporal validity of settlements so as to be able to renegotiate their wages sooner.

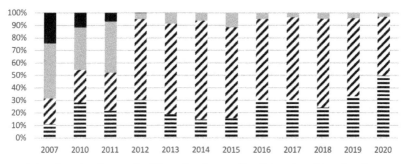

≡ Up to 6 months ⌐ Between 7 and 12 months ▦ Between 13 and 24 months ■ 24 months and more

Source: Author's elaboration based on Ministry of Labor (Ministerio de Trabajo et al., 2021) data.

Figure 6.5   Temporal validity of wage agreements

After 2012, "longer than 24 months" agreements, which represented 25 percent of all settlements in 2007, disappeared, while "Between 13 and 24 months" dramatically lost ground (Figure 6.5). In fact, between 2019 and 2020 just 3 percent of total agreements were made for more than 12 months, whereas "up to 6 months" reached 50 percent of the total in 2020.

A closer inspection, examining the quantity quarterly evolution of wage-contracts (Figure 6.6), reveals a positive trend for "up to 6 months" agreements particularly after the mid-2018 devaluation, in the same way that it did following the December 2015 devaluation.[22] This trend can be observed after there were hardly any settlements established at the beginning of 2018, due to the intense economic uncertainty, while simultaneously there is a very strong drop in "between 7 and 12 months" clauses.

This trend was reinforced by the impact of the COVID-19 pandemic. As a consequence, because of high-inflation uncertainty, the tendency of labor contracts is for an adjustment through quantities (no contracts are signed) when insecurity is deemed very high, and through price (in the form of shorter-term contracts) when uncertainty decreases.

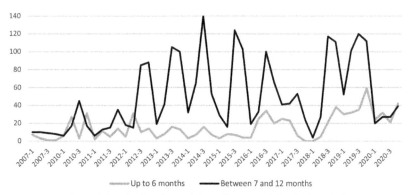

Source: Author's elaboration based on Ministry of Labor (Ministerio de Trabajo et al., 2021) data.

Figure 6.6   Quarterly amount of clauses "up to 6 months" and "between 7 and 12 months"

Distributive Struggle

In an economy functioning under high-inflation rates, a tense distributive struggle cannot but manifest itself in different ways and across almost all markets. This is further enhanced when a recession also creeps in, as it did in Argentina in 2018 and which is still dragging on.

This struggle can even be observed in disputes over how public funds are appropriated by different kinds of social and economic groups, manifested occasionally in some "hidden ways" as direct or indirect subsidies (such as tax exemptions), which at first glance seem not to express this conflict. Nevertheless, these exemptions can be substantial: since 2016, it has been between 2.3 and 2.8 percent of GDP.

In the money market (Figure 6.7) it is evident there is a preference for shortening the terms in bank deposits. This was observed regardless of the type of currency, dollar or peso deposits. Thus, the latter had around 80 percent of its deposits in less than 60 days, while the former around 60 percent. Another critical aspect concerning this area is the catastrophic collapse of the con-vertibility-scheme: dollar operations in the domestic financial system became restricted to credits to financing exports or companies that had confirmed sales contracts with exporters, ensuring the ability to repay in dollars (BCRA, Communication "A" 6428). Nevertheless, a "hidden side" of the distributive struggle in the money market is manifested twofold. First, by the considerable gap between the official and "blue" dollar rate. Second, by political proposals to straightforwardly "dollarize" the Argentine economy – that is, directly wrap-up the national currency and adopt the US dollar. Conspicuously, this view is most openly held by defenders of the convertibility-scheme, arguing that it failed because it did not go far enough.[23]

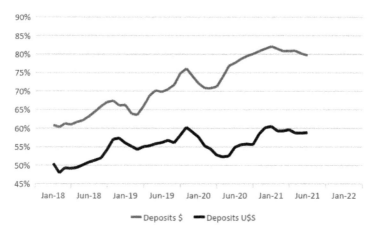

Source: Author's elaboration based on Central Bank of the Argentine Republic (2021).

Figure 6.7   *Ratio of deposits up to 60 days over total deposits in $ and in U$S*

Tensions are also expressed in the great discrepancy in price increases of different goods, as presented in Table 6.1. Additionally, the working of some as accelerators and decelerators can be seen. For instance, balanced animal food prices took-off after devaluations. Goods in the lower rows of the table seemed able only to raise their prices when consumption conditions improved, as in the period 2016–2017 when the economy was growing. Wines or beer prices could rise above the average level on that occasion, while, on the contrary, in the 2020–2021 crisis they could only rise below it. Implicitly, it can be stated that they depend on an improvement in employment conditions and income distribution.

Electrical energy price movements reflect clearly the ideological input of the distribution struggle in its political dimension. The incoming 2016 Macri administration followed policies friendlier to big private corporations and, thus, prompted price raises well over the general level of price increases in the economy – and despite the recession that was affecting it. This was justified as having been done to 'normalize' these prices that it said had been tampered down for political reasons by the more popularly based Kirchner governments (2003–2015). But Macri was followed in 2020 by the government of Fernández-Cristina Kirchner, leading those prices to again be held back. However, with inflation reaching considerable heights, in 2021 they were allowed an important readjustment.

Table 6.1   Wholesale price increases for some selected products

	2016	2017	2018	2019	2020	2021
Balanced animal food (1,250.3%)	62.1	10.0	103.5	64.4	82.8	23.9
Tires (1,231.4%)	37.8	20.9	80.5	88.7	64.7	42.5
Electricity (1,173.6%)	106.8	88.4	54.1	46.0	1.2	43.6
Vegetable oils (1,038.4%)	66.0	5.0	78.4	64.0	83.2	21.9
Cereals and oil seeds (972.8%)	40.9	7.7	106.4	59.1	80.8	19.1
Beers (477.4%)	59.3	27.5	55.6	37.3	15.7	15.1
Wines and cider (465.6%)	79.0	24.5	23.4	35.6	16.2	30.5
Non-alcoholic beverages (418.1%)	32.4	25.5	51.8	53.6	17.6	13.7
Bakery products (395.6%)	45.1	10.2	39.4	59.7	14.8	21.3

Source: Author's elaboration based on INDEC (2021).

CONCLUSION

In recent years Argentineans have once again adapted to living under high inflation rates, after a long stretch believing they had left behind such a scenario for good. During the 1970–1980 period, Frenkel presented an economic analysis that showed how people learned to get by living with high-inflation rates. While at that time some other Latin American countries passed through similar experiences with high inflation, currently it has been rather uncommon. Accordingly, Argentina, alas, stands out on this aspect.

Frenkel presented this adaptability to high inflation standards (levels that internationally would even be considered hyperinflation in many places) as a regime characterized by several facets, as well through an economic model. Despite some different behaviors and denominations, it seems plausible to argue that the Argentine economy is once more functioning under a high inflation context, and, as a result, a HIR has re-emerged.

This statement is sustained due to the ascertainment that, just as in the previous case, in Argentina today agents have adapted to continuous high-inflation rates in much the same manner described by Frenkel (1989) as a structure of explicit and implicit contracts in which the readjustment period for indexed contracts has been reduced to the minimum imposed by the availability of information.

In short, it can be stated that an HIR was present in Argentina at the time of writing, in all but its formal recognition. That is the reason why a truly inertial inflation with perfect adjustment cannot be confirmed, as it was more observable during the 1970–1980 period in which Frenkel wrote. Under such circumstances, inflation expectations for the next period ($t + 1$) would be the same as the previous inflation; save for some unaccounted unforeseeable shock that would readjust the inflation scale.

Consequently, only missing from a complete HIR is total and legal indexation. Although in Argentina, as stated, indexing is legally prohibited, "the prohibition does not make the essence of the institution disappear" (Frenkel, 2008, p. 5). Thus, as an environment of high-inflation progressively returned, so did indexation even if it meant working around its forbiddances. As a result, it looks as if legal indexation is quietly gaining ground – particularly as the ongoing COVID-19 pandemic seems to be enhancing the trends to a proper HIR.

NOTES

1. The authors appreciate the collaboration of Alonso Ahumada in the econometric analysis.
2. For a comprehensive view of Argentine economic history, see Della Paolera and Taylor (2003), while for a very brief view, see Glaeser, Di Tella and Llach (2018) and Rapoport (2007).
3. Not considering Venezuela as it has different institutional political and economic frameworks. For hyperinflation in Venezuela see Kulesza (2017) and Vera (2018).
4. For a modern general view of inflation in Latin American countries see Capistrán and Ramos-Francia (2009). For an analysis during the high-inflation period see Arida (1986), Damill and Frenkel (1990) Frenkel (1986, 1995) and Heymann and Leijonhufvud (1995). For the effect of inflation on growth see De Gregorio (1991) and on exchange rates see Edwards (1993).
5. For a comprehensive view of ISM see the original formulation by Prebisch (1959) and the inflationary effects of its operation see Banco Mundial (1987) and Hirschmann (1996).
6. Marongiu (2006) analyzes the *Rodrigazo* and its effect for high inflation rates, and Rapoport (2007) analyzes the whole spectrum concerning the *Rodrigazo*.
7. The original external debt was formed after the late 1970s orthodox financial liberalization plan that broadly exposed the country to external goods and capital movements. Besides being exposed as a cause of inflationary pressures itself, it has also become a very controversial and complex political issue. For a deeper view on this subject see Gaggero, J. (2004) and Rapoport (2014).
8. For an analysis of the Plan Austral see Canitrot (1992).
9. For a detailed account of the hyperinflation process see Fanelli and Frenkel (1989) and Canavese and Di Tella (1988).
10. See Damill, Frenkel and Juvenal (2003) for the economic process that led to the collapse of the convertibility regime.
11. For the transition period out of the convertibility scheme see Della Paolera and Taylor (2003). Specifically for the financial system see Damill, Salvatore and Simpson (2003).

12. Former Economic Minister Domingo Cavallo, who had implemented the Convertibility Plan, stated in 2007 "INDEC has started to lie on inflation rate" (Cavallo and Runde, 2020, p. 446).
13. Macri explicitly followed inflation-targeting as it was being proposed by several orthodox economists such as Abeles and Borzel (2004), Pagnotta (2002) and, finally his future President of the Central Bank, Sturzenegger (2011).
14. On inflation in the period following the 2002 economic adjustment see Heymann and Ramos (2010).
15. Thus, Frenkel focuses on how agents adapt to a high-inflation environment that persists, and not on the reasons of the inflation process in Argentina. Regarding its causes, see Rapoport (2011) for a general overview of the different main outlooks.
16. For an analysis of inertial inflation, see Arida and Lara-Resende (1986) and Bacha (1988).
17. Frenkel's original estimation was produced as a member of CEDES and was not published, although it did informally circulate in some academic circles as a CEDES paper. However, it appeared in 2004 when Anne-Laure Baldi-Delatte picked it up and used it as the "CEDES model".
18. The econometric report on the estimation is presented in the Appendix.
19. Graziano (2021) analyzes the mechanisms through which the price of meat accelerates the inflation rates in Argentina.
20. It must be taken into account that in Argentina a significant number of workers are not registered and do not have retirement benefits.
21. In the labor market, wages are freely established through collective bargaining between representatives from workers unions and employers' associations. Subsequently, they are presented to the State, becoming binding for both parties.
22. To see cases of devaluation with different pass-through inflation, see Costa and Ruffo (2019).
23. A full dollarization began to be proposed during the Convertibility decade – for example, Hanke and Schuler (1999). As inflation grew in the last years, it has become a project commonly proposed from orthodox economists such as Cachanovsky and Ravier (2014) and O'Grady (2018).

REFERENCES

Abeles, M. and Borzel, M. (2004), 'Metas de inflación: Implicancias para el desarrollo', *Documento de Trabajo*, *1*, Buenos Aires: Centro de Economía y Finanzas para el Desarrollo.

Ambito Financiero (2021), *Dollar*. Available at: https://www.ambito.com/contenidos/dolar.html, accessed October 25, 2021.

Arida, P. (1986), 'Macroeconomic issues for Latin America'. *Journal of Development Economics*, *22*(1), 171–208.

Arida, P. and Lara Resende, A. (1986), 'Inflación inercial y reforma monetaria: Brasil', *Inflación Cero.* Bogotá: Oveja Negra.

Bacha, E. (1988), 'Moeda, inércia e conflito: Reflexão sobre políticas de estabilização no Brasil'. *Pesquisa e Planejamento Econômico*, *18*(1), 43–56.

Baldi-Delatte, A. L. (2004), 'Los factores de la estabilidad de los precios y de la moneda en Argentina desde la crisis'. *Centro Interdisciplinario para el Estudio de Políticas Públicas, Documento de Trabajo 39*.

Banco Mundial (1987), *Informe sobre el desarrollo mundial*. Washington, DC.

Cachanovsky, N. and Ravier, A. (2014), 'A proposal of monetary reform for Argentina: flexible dollarization and free banking'. *Journal of Political Economy, 19*(3), 397–426.

Cagan, P. (1956), 'The monetary dynamics of hyperinflation'. In M. Friedman (Org.) *Studies in the Quantity Theory of Money*. Chicago: University of Chicago Press, 25–117.

Canavese, A. and Di Tella, G. (1988), 'Estabilizar la inflación o evitar la hiperinflación? El caso del Plan Austral: 1985-1987'. *El Trimestre Económico, 62*, 189–229.

Canitrot, A. (1992). La macroeconomía de la inestabilidad: Argentina en los 80. *Boletín Informativo Techint, No. 272*, 37–54.

Capistrán, C. and Ramos-Francia, M. (2009), 'Inflation dynamics in Latin America'. *Contemporary Economic Policy, 27*(3), 349–362.

Cavallo, D. F., and Runde, S. C. (2020), *Historia Económica de la Argentina*. Buenos Aires: El Ateneo.

Central Bank of the Argentine Republic (2020a), *Mercado de cambios, deuda y formación de activos externos, 2015–2019*.

Central Bank of the Argentine Republic (2020b), *Informe de política monetaria. Mayo de 2020*.

Central Bank of the Argentine Republic (2021), *Statistics*. Available at: http://www .bcra.gob.ar, accessed October 25, 2021.

Costa, J. and Ruffo, A. (2019), 'Regímenes de inflación y dinámica de precios minoristas. Un estudio empírico para la Argentina'. *Revista De Economía Política de Buenos Aires, 18*, 9–49. Available at: http://ojs.econ.uba.ar/index.php/REPBA/ article/view/1571, accessed October 15, 2021.

Damill, M. and Frenkel, R. (1990), *Malos Tiempos: La economía argentina en la década de los ochenta*. Buenos Aires: CEDES.

Damill, M., Frenkel, R., and Juvenal, L. (2003), *Las cuentas públicas y la crisis de la convertibilidad en Argentina*. Buenos Aires: CEDES.

Damill, M., Salvatore, N., and Simpson, L. (2003), 'Diagnóstico y perspectiva del sistema financiero argentino'. *CESPA Paper no. 4*.

De Gregorio, J. (1991), 'The effects of inflation on economic growth: Lessons from Latin America'. *IMF Working Paper no. 91/95*. Available at: https://ssrn.com/ abstract=885073, accessed October 15, 2021.

Della Paolera, G., and Taylor, A. M. (eds) (2003), *A New Economic History of Argentina*, vol. 1. Cambridge: Cambridge University Press.

Edwards, S. (1993), 'Exchange rates, inflation and disinflation: Latin American experiences'. *NBER Working Paper no. 4320*.

Fanelli, J. M. and Frenkel, R. (1989), *Desequilibrios, políticas de estabilización e hiperinflación en Argentina*. Buenos Aires: CEDES.

Fischer, S., Sahay, R. and Végh, C. A. (2002), 'Modern hyper-and high inflations'. *Journal of Economic Literature, 40*(3), 837–880.

Frenkel, R. (1986), 'Salarios e inflación en América Latina. Resultados de investigaciones recientes en la Argentina, Brasil, Colombia, Costa Rica y Chile'. *Desarrollo Económico*, 587–622.

Frenkel, R. (1989), *El régimen de alta inflación y el nivel de actividad*. Buenos Aires: CEDES.

Frenkel, R. (1995), *Las políticas antiinflacionarias en América Latina*. Buenos Aires: CEDES.

Frenkel, R. (2008*). La inflación tolerable.* Available at: http://itf.org.ar/pdf/lecturas/lectura32.pdf, accessed October 15, 2021.

Frenkel, R. and González Rozada, M. (1998), *Apertura, productividad y empleo. Argentina en los años 90.* Buenos Aires: CEDES.

Gaggero, J. (2004), 'La cuestión fiscal, huella de la historia política y económica'. In R. Boyer and J. Neffa (eds), *La economía argentina y su crisis (1976-2001).* Buenos Aires: Miño y Dávila Editores.

Glaeser, E. L., Di Tella, R. and Llach, L. (2018). 'Introduction to Argentine exceptionalism'. *Latin American Economic Review, I*(27), 1–22.

Graziano, W. (2021), 'Las dos principales causas de la inflación permanecen ocultas'. May, 21. Available at: https://www.ambito.com/economia/inflacion/las-dos-principales-causas-la-permanecen-ocultas-n5194278, accessed October 15, 2021.

Hanke, S. and Schuler, K. (1999), 'Una propuesta de dolarización para Argentina'. *Cato Institute.* Available at: https://www.elcato.org/una-propuesta-de-dolarizacion-para-argentina, accessed October 15, 2021.

Heymann, D. and Leijonhufvud, A. (1995). *High Inflation: The Arne Ryde Memorial Lectures.* Oxford: Oxford University Press.

Heymann, D. and Ramos, A. (2010), 'Una transición incompleta. Inflación y políticas macroeconómicas en la argentina post-convertibilidad'. *Revista de Economía Política de Buenos Aires, 4*(7, 8), 9–48.

Hirschmann, A. O. (1996), 'La economía política de la industrialización a través de la sustitución de importaciones en América Latina'. *El trimestre económico, 63*(250), 489–524.

INDEC (2021), *Statistics.* Available at: www.indec.gob.ar, accessed October 25, 2021.

Kulesza, M. (2017), 'Inflation and hyperinflation'. *Working Papers no. 93/2017.* Berlin: Institute for International Political Economy.

Marongiu, F. (2006), 'Políticas de shock en la agonía del estado peronista: el Rodrigazo y el Mondelliazo'. *MPRA Paper 6338.* Available at: https://mpra.ub.uni-muenchen.de/6338/1/MPRA_paper_6338.pdf, accessed October 15, 2021.

Ministerio de Trabajo, Empleo y Seguridad Social, Dirección de Estudios y Estadísticas de Relaciones de Trabajo (DEyERT) (2021), *Statistics.* Available at: http://www.trabajo.gob.ar, accessed October 25, 2021.

OEI, Oficina de Evaluación independiente (2004), 'Informe sobre la evaluación del papel del FMI en Argentina, 1991–2001'. Available at: https://www.imf.org/external/np/ieo/2004/arg/esl/063004.pdf, accessed October 25, 2021.

O'Grady, M. A. (2018), 'Argentina needs to dollarize'. Available at: https://www.wsj.com/articles/argentina-needs-to-dollarize-1536524297, accessed October 25, 2021.

Pagnotta, E. (2002), 'Elementos de análisis para la adopción de metas inflacionarias como estrategia monetaria'. *Anales de la Asociación Argentina de Economía Política.*

Prebisch, R. (1959), 'Commercial policy in the underdeveloped countries'. *The American Economic Review, 49*(2), 251–273.

Rapoport, M. (2007), 'Mitos, etapas y crisis en la economía argentina'. *Nación-Región-Provincia en Argentina, Pensamiento político, económico y social,* 9–28.

Rapoport, M. (2011), 'Una revisión histórica de la inflación argentina y de sus causas'. In J. M. Vázquez Blanco and S. Franchina (Comps.), *Aportes de la economía política en el Bicentenario.* Buenos Aires: Prometeo.

Rapoport, M. (2014), 'La deuda externa argentina y la soberanía jurídica: sus razones históricas'. *Ciclos, 22*(42-43), 3–43.

Sturzenegger, A. (2011), 'Inflacionar las metas de inflación'. *Asociación Argentina de Economía Política, XLVI Reunión anual.*
Vera, L. (2018), 'Cómo explicar la catástrofe económica venezolana'. *Nueva Sociedad,* (274), 83–96.

APPENDIX

Table 6A.1

	IPC	W	Pub	E	Meat	Vegetables
feb-18	62.500	0.830	8.711	2.261	4.361	−5.738
mar-18	−3.846	1.871	0.541	0.246	3.154	−3.852
apr-18	4.000	2.719	13.002	1.961	0.344	−3.553
may-18	−26.923	1.502	−7.211	22.115	2.080	14.984
jun-18	105.263	0.846	0.144	15.748	5.460	8.488
jul-18	−28.205	2.655	0.915	−5.102	2.500	14.442
aug-18	46.429	2.859	13.905	34.050	4.007	6.144
sep-18	60.976	2.846	1.105	12.567	10.243	−11.526
oct-18	−22.727	3.668	12.427	−12.589	3.173	12.363
nov-18	−43.137	2.917	3.270	4.891	1.700	0.575
dec-18	−3.448	2.473	−0.016	0.000	1.210	−5.496
jan-19	0.000	3.119	1.308	−1.036	4.929	1.546
feb-19	35.714	2.626	11.887	4.974	10.332	8.926
mar-19	26.316	3.949	6.658	10.474	9.187	8.761
apr-19	−33.333	2.247	5.708	2.032	1.663	−8.366
may-19	−6.250	2.826	1.161	1.327	−0.441	0.260
jun-19	−13.333	1.832	1.666	−5.022	0.484	5.953
jul-19	−19.231	4.898	0.620	3.218	0.100	12.473
aug-19	85.714	2.430	0.807	35.857	3.673	7.052
sep-19	48.718	2.698	1.159	−3.279	6.728	3.569
oct-19	−44.828	3.216	0.355	7.627	1.584	−1.406
nov-19	28.125	2.369	−0.798	−1.969	6.724	7.005
dec-19	−7.317	2.615	0.587	1.205	5.036	−3.702
jan-20	−50.000	6.015	0.000	0.000	5.883	2.922
feb-20	−5.263	3.861	−0.278	1.587	1.844	6.676
mar-20	100.000	3.035	−0.380	2.734	4.328	12.862
apr-20	−61.111	0.147	−0.993	4.563	3.506	11.550
may-20	7.143	−0.074	−0.744	2.545	−0.542	4.556
jun-20	33.333	0.625	−0.118	4.255	0.920	2.757
jul-20	−20.000	1.792	−0.082	3.741	2.479	−3.915
aug-20	75.000	1.976	1.043	2.295	3.368	8.234
sep-20	0.000	2.501	1.252	2.564	1.916	13.693
oct-20	28.571	4.089	0.632	4.375	3.533	15.799

	IPC	W	Pub	E	Meat	Vegetables
nov-20	−16.667	3.301	0.122	3.593	5.440	−6.792
dec-20	23.333	1.758	0.149	3.179	13.912	−16.637
jan-21	−10.811	3.266	0.756	3.361	6.401	0.514
feb-21	9.091	4.349	−0.298	2.439	2.737	9.590
mar-21	44.444	5.013	−0.204	3.175	6.773	6.324
apr-21	−21.154	3.192	1.061	1.026	4.700	−0.898

Note: IPC = retail inflation, W = wages, Pub = electrical tariffs, and E = official exchange rate.

Table 6A.2

Descriptive analysis

	IPC	W	Pub	E	carne	verd
Mean	9.925	2.689	2.047	4.538	3.985	3.491
Standard error	6.618	0.205	0.701	1.460	0.506	1.259
Median	0.000	2.698	0.632	2.564	3.506	4.556
Mode	0.000	#N/A	#N/A	0.000	#N/A	#N/A
Standard deviation	41.330	1.280	4.379	9.115	3.159	7.860
Sample variance	1,708.137	1.640	19.173	83.090	9.982	61.786
Kurtosis	−0.211	0.633	2.247	5.448	1.540	−0.290
Coefficient of skewness	0.603	0.119	1.485	2.043	1.107	−0.466
Range	166.374	6.089	21.116	48.447	14.455	32.435
Minimum	−61.111	−0.074	−7.211	−12.589	−0.542	−16.637
Maximum	105.263	6.015	13.905	35.857	13.912	15.799
Sum	387.086	104.857	79.830	176.991	155.429	136.135
Observations	39	39	39	39	39	39

Correlation analysis

	IPC	W	Pub	E	Meat	Vegetables
IPC	1					
W	−0.161613	1				
Pub	0.1160563	0.0833047	1			
E	0.3770701	−0.124699	0.0232715	1		
Meat	0.3503811	0.1453617	0.0917914	0.0963106	1	
Vegetables	0.0825845	0.1533808	−0.074853	0.0741154	−0.270324	1

Table 6A.3

Regression model	
Resume	
Regression statistics	
Multiple correlation coefficient	0.4916729
Coefficient of determination R^2	0.2417423
R^2 adjusted	0.1996169
Typical error	36.975182
Observations	39

Table 6A.4

	Coefficient	Standard error	Statistic t	Probability	Inferior 95%	Superior 95%	Inferior 95.0%	Superior 95.0%
Interception	−13.73	9.87	−1.39	0.17	−33.75	6.29	−33.75	6.29
E	1.57	0.66	2.38	0.02	0.23	2.91	0.23	2.91
Meat	4.15	1.91	2.17	0.04	0.28	8.02	0.28	8.02

7. The new foreign debt trap and its long run consequences: the persistence of Monetarism as a social doctrine in Argentina

Juan Matías De Lucchi and Matías Vernengo

INTRODUCTION

The currency and debt crisis of 2018 in Argentina was, to some extent, expected. The country had experienced an effective external constraint since at least 2011 and, despite the promises of the electoral campaign in 2015, the government of Mauricio Macri used the devaluation of the currency to accelerate inflation, reduce export taxes, slow down wage negotiations and reduce real wages. Furthermore, in the short term, it was expected that the reduction in wages and the fiscal adjustment would lead to a fall in gross domestic product (GDP). In other words, the devaluation with its contractionary and inflationary effects, although not announced, was expected (Vernengo, 2016a).

But the Macri economists did believe in old fashioned Monetarist views, and did think that well-behaved macroeconomic policies would restore confidence and eventually growth in a virtuous cycle. The role that José Alfredo Martinez de Hoz, and Domingo Cavallo played in other neoliberal cycles, was played by Federico Sturzenegger this time around. This chapter looks at the combination of mismanagement and structural problems that were left by the Macri administration and that were aggravated by the pandemic.

The rest of this chapter is divided into four sections. The next section analyzes the causes of the crisis, suggesting that the problems were essentially financial, and reinforced by a misdiagnosis that led to growing external indebtedness. The subsequent section describes the currency crisis and its long-term consequences. The fourth section analyzes the Argentine economy after the Macri administration and the foreign debt restructuring during the pandemic crisis. A brief conclusion closes the chapter, suggesting that the malpractice associated with the Monetarist diagnosis of Argentine problems endangers the possibility of a resumption of growth, and increases the chances of a *default*.

The persistence and return of Monetarism as a social doctrine, as Bhaduri and Steindl (1983) had identified for advanced countries in the 1970s, is not, however, a mere error, but the ideological defense of a series of policies that benefit certain interests in Argentina.

MISDIAGNOSIS AND EXTERNAL INDEBTEDNESS

Cambiemos' economic policy was designed on the basis of the false perception that an excess supply of foreign currency existed and, consequently, a downward pressure on the nominal exchange rate was at least feasible. The economic team believed that it could quickly lower the inflation rate simply by reducing and demonetizing public spending, while the Central Bank of the Argentine Republic (BCRA) was moving towards an inflation targeting system and with the intention to remove the organic charter reform of 2012, or at least that's what they officially said. As if it were not enough, in turn, the BCRA President at that time publicly argued that based on the general equilibrium agreement he was convinced that the tariff adjustment of the Ministry of Energy – chaired by the former CEO of Shell – would not impact on the inflation rate (Sturzenegger, 2016). In other words, the government expected a reduction in the demand for foreign exchange caused by the rapid deflation, and a strong increase in the supply of foreign currency, resulting from a large increase of capital inflows, generated by the confidence shock of a new market-friendly administration.

However, as shown in Figure 7.1, none of this happened and the nominal exchange rate increased 500 percent and the BCRA sold a net amount of US$17 billion in the foreign exchange market between December 2015 and December 2019, with at least three episodes of exchange rate runs in March 2016, March–September 2018 and August 2019 which again opened the discussion about debt *defaults* and restructuring. This suggests that, in part, the problem of the Macri administration was related to the decisions made by its economists, some of whom were part of the team in the previous debacle and *default* at the end of Convertibility in the early 2000s.

In other words, although it is true that the Argentine economy faced a current account deficit-to-GDP of 5 percent in 2018, the main factor explaining the currency crisis in that year was a lethal combination of theoretical and operational errors. In this context, the beginning of a reckless pattern of indebtedness in foreign currency, the implementation of an inconsistent monetary and exchange rate policy and, finally, the unnecessary and desperate agreement with the International Monetary Fund (IMF) by a government overwhelmed by circumstances are the main errors of practice the Peronist government had to confront in order to stabilize the exchange rate and avoid a debt *default*.

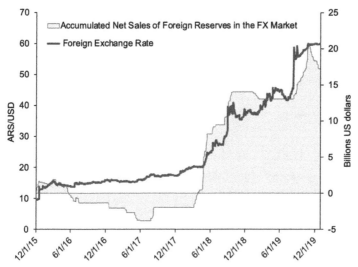

Source: Own elaboration based on data from Central Bank of the Argentine Republic (BCRA) (2021).

Figure 7.1   *Exchange rate and central bank interventions (12/2015–12/2019)*

As in the times of Kirchnerism (2003–2015), the external problem and exchange market pressures continue to be a financial phenomenon rather than a real or current account one, also considering the high speculative component of the agricultural export settlements in the exchange market. In particular, it is important to note that countries with similar, and even more severe external deficits, such as Brazil, which has had a current account deficit for a longer period than Argentina, have not suffered exchange rate crises, in part because they were able to accumulate a significant volume of international reserves attracting capital flows, in a context in which interest rates in the United States have been at historically low levels.

In addition, there was no reason to assume that Argentine inflation was caused by an excess aggregate demand caused by disproportionately large government spending. Since 2011, on average, the economy had been stagnant and the use of installed capacity had declined. On the other hand, the rudimentary Monetarist explanations completely ignored the endogenous mechanisms of monetary reflux, even when there was a monetization of the fiscal deficit. In this sense, it is important to note that Sturzenegger's (2016) discussion retains theoretical elements of an outdated version of Monetarism. Even within the mainstream of the profession the quantitative version that emphasizes the importance of monetary aggregates has been abandoned long ago for an updated version of the Wicksellian model in which central banks control the interest rate and have explicit inflation targets.

In this regard, far from being explained by an alleged excess of aggregate demand, as shown in Figure 7.2, the inflation rate has been determined by the dynamics of the macroeconomic prices – particularly the exchange rate, but also tariffs and wages – which affect production costs, in a marked context due to the relative scarcity of foreign exchange (see Figure 7.2).

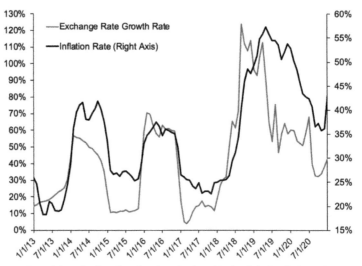

Source: Own elaboration based on data from Instituto Nacional de Estadística y Censos (INDEC) (2021) and BCRA (2021).

Figure 7.2   Currency devaluations and price inflation

Further, the substitution of public debt in *pesos* (Argentine currency) held by public agencies, especially the BCRA, with public debt held by resident and non-resident private investors and international organisms in foreign currency, was an inadequate anti-inflation policy, as should be expected. This policy has seriously compromised, once again, the external and financial stability of the country. Here is another important misdiagnosis of the *Cambiemos*' economists: the inability to distinguish between debt in domestic currency and debt in foreign currency.[1]

In order to gradually reduce transfers from the BCRA to the National Treasury, the government had to choose between two borrowing patterns to cover the fiscal deficit. On the one hand, it could have started issuing debt in *pesos*. Once the exchange market had been unified, and exchange rate controls lifted, the conditions had been created for the development of a sovereign debt market in local currency, as was quickly demonstrated by the boom in the Central Bank's Bills (LEBAC) market and casual placement of Treasury bonds, even at rates below the BCRA policy rate, with an inversion of the yield curve.[2]

However, the government chose to issue securities in foreign currency, and for that it faced an unnecessary negotiation with the so-called Vulture Funds, with which much more was spent than was appropriate or necessary. Based on its unrealistic forecast of exchange rate stability, and observing the interest rate differential in *pesos* and dollars, the government believed that the fiscal cost of the debt would be lower if it was issued in dollars. In formal terms:

$$\delta > \delta_f + \hat{E}_G^e$$

$$\delta_f = \delta^* + \rho$$

where δ is the interest rate in *pesos* set by the BCRA, $\hat{E}_G^e$ is the official expected growth rate in the nominal exchange rate, δ_f is the rate of return on dollar-denominated treasury bonds, δ is the international interest rate and ρ is the country risk premium.

In addition, considering that the BCRA was implementing an inflation targeting system, the interest rate in *pesos* can be formalized for simplicity with a Taylor rule (Taylor, 1999):

$$\delta = r^n + \hat{P} + \alpha \left(\hat{P} - \hat{P}^T \right)$$

where $\hat{P}$ is the inflation rate, $\hat{P}^T$ is the inflation target and the r^n is the Wicksellian natural rate. Thus, the reaction function of the BCRA is derived as follows:

$$\delta - \hat{P} - r^n = \alpha \left(\hat{P} - \hat{P}^T \right)$$

$$\Rightarrow r - r^n = \alpha \left(\hat{P} - \hat{P}^T \right)$$

where r is the real interest rate. However, considering that r^n is an unobservable variable, the following differential equation suggested by Kriesler and Lavoie (2007) better reflects the Taylor rule in practice:

$$\dot{r} = \alpha \left(\hat{P} - \hat{P}^T \right)$$

Therefore, the monetary policy framework and budget financing strategy was the basis of the following official forecast:

$$\left(r^n + \hat{P} + \alpha \left(\hat{P} - \hat{P}^T \right) \right) > \left(\delta^* + \rho + \hat{E}_G^e \right)$$

However, while the government followed this financing strategy and got into debt in dollars, the exchange rate increased 360 percent and Argentina's EMBI increased 290 percent between January 2016 and December 2019. Figure 7.3 shows how Argentina's rate of return on dollar denominated bonds measured in *pesos* has skyrocketed since 2016 and the official strategy has turned into a complete failure.

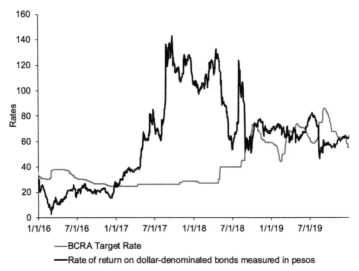

Source: Own elaboration based on data from BCRA (2021).

Figure 7.3   *BCRA policy rate in pesos and rate of return on dollar-denominated bonds measured in pesos*

Here, malpractice manifested itself in at least two aspects. First, beyond the forecasts, the government prioritized the fiscal balance in *pesos* over the external balance in dollars, which reveals a fundamental flaw of the conventional macroeconomic vision. On the other, and perhaps more serious still, their position reveals a certain *hubris*, and they did not have any degree of skepticism about the possibility of stabilizing the economy in the context of a financially open and integrated small economy. Given that the history of Argentina is marked by repeated foreign debt and balance of payments crises, no government can ignore the systemic risk that debt in foreign currency entails.[3]

Central banks cannot act as lenders of last resort when it comes to, for example, treasury or public debt in foreign currency with third parties (PDFC-TP), that is, the resident private sector, foreigners and international organizations. Public debt in the hands of public agencies such as the BCRA, the National Social Security Administration (ANSES) or the Banco de la Nación Argentina (BNA) are obligations within the national State itself that are canceled in the consolidated statement. Even if they were intrastate commitments in foreign currency, their cancellation or renewal are administrative acts that depend on the same political authority and, therefore, escape the logic of the market. In this sense, the debt in domestic currency carries much less risk, and that is why in the Kirchner administrations there was a marked effort to reduce the debt in dollars. That was in part because the 2001 *default* was still fresh in the memory, but also because there existed an understanding about the differences in debt in domestic and foreign currency.

As can be seen in Figure 7.4, Argentina declared the *default* in December 2001 when the PDFC-TP amounted to approximately US$136 billion (42 percent of GDP). Then, with the restructuring of 2005 it dropped to US$66 billion (34 percent of GDP) and, later, Kirchnerism leave it at US$70 billion, approximately (16 percent of GDP). When Macri left the government in December 2019, the PDFC-TP reached almost US$170 billion, an increase of more than 140 percent in only four years (44 percent of GDP).

Compared with the United Kingdom, Canada, the United States or Japan, which have public debt-to-GDP ratios between 90 and 250 percent, the current 44 percent of Argentina would appear to be very moderate. However, once again, far from there being a debt intolerance, as Reinhart and Rogoff (2009) argue, the structural difference lies in the fact that developed countries assume their commitments in their own currencies while Argentina does, to a great extent, in foreign currency.

Although it is clear that the current level of PDFC-TP-to-GDP is an alarming figure when compared with recent history, a debt sustainability analysis requires greater depth: not only does the stock of debt matter, but also its average life, fundamentally, the interest charge and capital maturities in the short term. But not only this, obviously the ability to pay in foreign currency

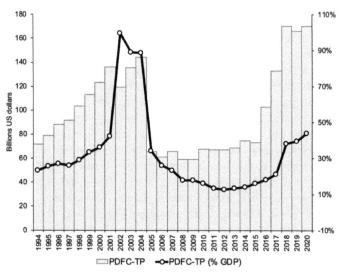

Source: Own elaboration based on data from the Ministry of Finance of Argentina (2021).

Figure 7.4   *Public debt in foreign currency held by third parties as percentage of GDP*

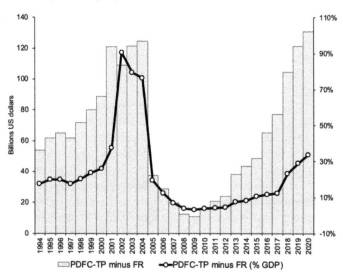

Source: Own elaboration based on data from the Ministry of Finance of Argentina (2021).

Figure 7.5   *Net public debt in foreign currency held by third parties as a percentage of GDP*

also matters, which could be measured in the short term by the stock of international reserves, and in the long term by the evolution of export dynamics. In this way, without pretending to carry out a comprehensive analysis of the sustainability of the external debt, it is worth observing the difference between liabilities and assets; that is, the difference between the PDFC-TP and BCRA's foreign reserves (hereinafter, net PDFC-TP) as a slightly more elaborate indicator. As can be seen in Figure 7.5, currently the net PDFC-TP amounts to US$108 billion (30 percent of GDP) and has not yet exceeded the US$121 billion (38 percent of GDP) in 2001.[4]

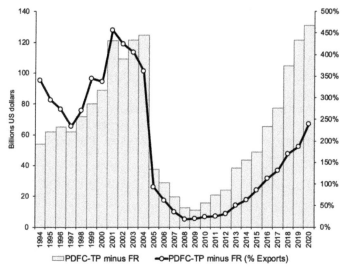

Source: Own elaboration based on data from the Ministry of Finance of Argentina (2021).

Figure 7.6   *Net public debt in foreign currency held by third parties as percentage of exports*

On the other hand, when we analyze Figure 7.6 the net PDFC-TP in terms of exports, the current situation is more favorable when compared with the end of Convertibility. While, in 2001, this ratio reached 457 percent, in 2020 it was 239 percent. However, the net PDFC on exports was 80 percent in December 2015, which marks a growth of 125 percent in less than three years. Observing the conventional ratio between gross debt and GDP, most analysts, including within the government, had interpreted that the indebtedness of Kirchnerism had effectively created the conditions for the restart of a new cycle of indebtedness in foreign currency. For example, according to the *Financial Times* (2017): "luckily, the foreign debt was low when Mr. Macri took office because the previous government was unable to borrow abroad. Most analysts believe that the debt–GDP ratio in Argentina is still very sustainable". However, although the indebtedness was significant compared with the 2001 crisis, the Macri government already began its administration with a high floor of external fragility, especially due to the relative scarcity of international reserves.[5]

Argentina was one of the few developing countries that did not take advantage of the possibility of creating a large domestic market for sovereign debt in local currency during the improvement in terms of trade that occurred in the 2000s, when the commodity boom and the great international liquidity resulting from the unconventional monetary policy of the Federal Reserve and the rest of the developed countries created the ideal conditions. Moreover, in reality, Argentina was one of the few countries that did not take advantage of the relatively positive international situation to increase foreign reserves and, as a result, create insurance against the possibility of a new currency crisis, and this would probably be the only serious criticism of macroeconomic policy, beyond what one can say about other policies, such as the industrial one, during the Kirchner governments. To put things in perspective, it is worth comparing the evolution of the net PDFC of Argentina and Brazil (Figure 7.7), which during the governments of the Workers' Party (PT) accumulated significant reserves in dollars.

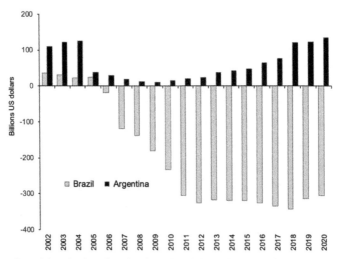

Source: Own elaboration based on data from the Ministry of Finance of Argentina (2021), BCRA (2021) and Central Bank of Brazil (CBB) (2021).

Figure 7.7   *Net PDFC-TP as a percentage of GDP in Argentina and Brazil*

Until 2005, both countries had a positive net PDFC, although in the case of Argentina the level was much higher in absolute terms and in relation to GDP. However, from 2007 onwards, Brazil was able to stabilize the net PDFC at negative levels because it managed to develop an important domestic market for debt in *reais* (Brazilian currency) and, consequently, began an unprecedented process of accumulation of international reserves.[6] On the other hand, in the Argentine case, the combination of low interest rates in *pesos*, deeply negative in real terms, and the chronic tendency to nominal depreciation of the exchange rate, which later led to quantitative restrictions in the exchange market, made unfeasible the development of a local debt market and consolidated the conditions for capital flight. During the period of exchange controls, between 2011 and 2015, the BCRA lost around US$25 billion of reserves and, subsequently, doubled the level of PDFC between 2016 and 2018. The latter led the Bank of International Settlements (BIS) to affirm in its September 2017 Report that the Argentine case was exceptional at the international level:

> [t]he share of domestic bonds denominated or connected to foreign currencies is minimal in almost all countries. Many countries have reduced external indebtedness. Argentina is an exception to this pattern, and has increased domestic and international debt denominated in foreign currency. (Bank of International Settlements, 2017)

It is important to note that the arrangement with the vulture funds, and the return to the international capital markets, generated the possibility of a continuous flight of capital during the Macri administration. In addition, it was well-known that several government officials had close relationships with the local and international capital markets, in particular, with J. P. Morgan, the Wall Street house that issued the international bonds for the Argentine government. Beyond that it seems that there was malpractice, in the sense that the diagnosis of many of the government economists was wrong, and it is important to note that a series of vested interests favored economic groups close to the government.[7] Although the notion that the problem was fiscal – and that inflation would be solved by adjustment, and growth would come from the confidence generated by well-behaved macroeconomic policies that would attract capital flows, and this, in turn, would lead to exchange rate appreciation, in our central vision to understand the crisis – can be seen as a policy mistake, it is also true that the fact that these mistakes were beneficial to certain groups should not be completely dismissed as an explanation for the crisis.

THE CURRENCY CRISIS OF 2018

The exchange rate crisis was specifically gestated as a result of the implementation of the 20/23 plan. With the victory of the internal wing that questioned financial speculation with the LEBACs, the government announced that its informal objective was to reach by December 2018, an interest rate at 20 percent, and a dollar at 23 *pesos*, that is, a 20 percent rise of the nominal exchange rate. The new monetary and exchange policy generated a strong incentive to dollarize portfolios that, later, would be formalized with the IMF program.

The most surprising element of this strategy was that the BCRA began to lower the interest rate in the context in which the yield on US 10-year bonds increased from 2.4 percent to 3 percent between January and February of the same year (Figure 7.8). At the end of January, after the sell-off on Wall Street, the exchange rate pressure intensified and the BCRA froze the cycle of interest cuts, but did not reverse course and increase the interest rate. Then, from the beginning of March until the start of the run at the end of April, the BCRA was forced to abandon its flexible exchange rate policy, and began to systematically intervene, eventually using US$2.4 billion to prevent the wholesale dollar from taking off. At this point, the monetary and exchange policy had already failed.

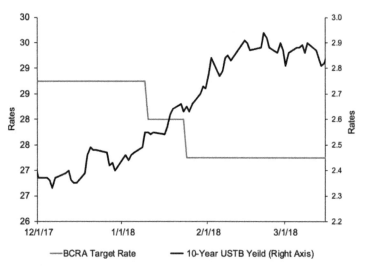

Source: Own elaboration based on data from BCRA (2021) and Federal Reserve Bank (FED) (2021).

Figure 7.8   *The BCRA begins the rate reduction cycle while the international rate increases*

From the beginning, the BCRA showed improvisation in its market operations. However, the operational problems became more evident and damaging with the exchange rate pressure in April and May. The BCRA behavior was erratic, at times validating devaluations, at times suggesting that small increases in the policy rate and the credibility of the administration's policies would contain the avalanche. The BCRA ended up being a destabilizing factor, and the administration was forced to ask for the IMF's assistance, which led to a stand-by loan for the extraordinary amount of US$57 billion. Even after that, the BCRA had to inject another US$1.2 billion to stabilize the markets (De Lucchi, 2018, 2019).

The BCRA was overwhelmed by the circumstances and became a factor of propagation of the exchange rate run. However, the market did not stabilize because it found equilibrium. The BCRA changed its position and decided to go out strongly to fix the price of the dollar: it placed a daily offer of US$5 billion in the exchange market at the rate of 25 Pesos per US dollar to stop the speculative attack and limit devaluation, now backed by the significant amount of dollars provided by the IMF. Monetary policy assumed an explicit old Monetarist bias with a goal of zero growth of the monetary base, flexible exchange rate and fiscal austerity.[8] However, faced with the inflationary acceleration derived from exchange rate volatility, the BCRA modified the exchange rate stance with the aim of having a more interventionist role in the exchange market. These changes, however, were marginal alterations within the same approach, and it was understood that the IMF loans were to pay the external debt obligations and preclude a *default*, and not to sustain the exchange rate.

Within the context of the second agreement with the IMF, the BCRA eventually formally abandoned the purely flexible exchange rate approach and announced a band system, or no-intervention zone as it was called. However, this regime had obvious inconsistencies. First, the exchange rate band had a range that was too wide to serve as a reference (30 percent gap). Second, the BCRA was willing to auction only US$150 million a day in case of exceeding the ceiling of the band and, even, without specifying at what exchange rate. Finally, the daily adjustment of the bands suggested that the BCRA was pursuing a certain objective for the real exchange rate, when the real problem was, and continues to be, the uncertainty about the nominal exchange rate. With the breadth of the band and the very low intervention fees, the BCRA implied that it did not commit to any ceiling for the nominal exchange rate. As expected, the regime failed because the BCRA was prevented from operating freely in the spot and futures markets, a necessary condition to manage devaluation expectations.

For this reason, at the end of April, the BCRA once again modified its exchange rate policy. On the one hand, it increased the daily intervention quota to US$250 million in case the exchange rate exceeded the ceiling of the band. On the other hand, it announced that it would intervene within the band without pre-established quantitative limits. Finally, the band was reduced to zero, making explicit the need for a more interventionist policy. However, the new scheme still showed design inconsistencies, and it was ambiguous about when the BCRA would be willing to intervene. In other words, the mere mention of interventions above the ceiling of the band suggested that the BCRA still did not have a maximum exchange rate that it would defend to the bitter end. A new currency crisis was inevitable, and, in August 2019, in the context of the presidential primary election, it occurred. Overwhelmed by the situation, the Macri administration re-introduced the capital controls, that they had decried as a sign of incompetence, and that his administration had removed in December 2015. Finally, Macri lost the presidential election in October 2019, an event not entirely disconnected from the currency crisis.

AFTER MACRI, *DEFAULT* AND THE PANDEMIC

In December 2019, the newly elected Peronist government had to deal with an extreme macroeconomic situation. The National Treasury was virtually in a situation of sovereign debt *default* because the country could not meet the financial commitments denominated in foreign currency. In addition, as if that was not enough to create financial and exchange rate uncertainty, the Macri administration had declared a compulsive restructuring of short-term treasury bills denominated in local currency, essentially an unnecessary *default* in the debt in domestic currency. In other words, the new administration of Alberto Fernández had to deal not only with the international credit rationing but also with an increasing credit risk on peso-denominated securities, a self-inflicted injury if we consider that the BCRA is the monopoly supplier of bank reserves and, consequently, it can always act as lender of last resort in its own currency.

The new government had two immediate financial and macroeconomic objectives. On the one hand, the restructuring of dollar-denominated bonds, particularly those ones issued under the United States law, and after that, the roll-over of the IMF loan. On the other hand, an urgent recovery of the real wage and economic growth, which was stagnant during the last phase of the Kirchner administration and over the whole of the Macri period. Under these macroeconomic guidelines, the BCRA initiated an interest rate cutting cycle. Following the monetary policy, the interbank rates reduced from the range 50–40 to 30–25 percent, approximately. In addition, the term structure of interest rates in the banking system was affected, although with different degrees of elasticity depending on the types of bank loans and term deposits: the weighted average interest rate for bank loans was reduced from 60 to 50 percent, approximately, during that period.

It was in this context that the World Health Organization (WHO) announced on March 11 2020 that the outbreak of the novel COVID-19 was a global pandemic and one week later the Argentine government was declaring a strict lockdown to buy time and delay the first wave while the national health system adjusted. As occurred around the world, economic policy had to be adjusted to the new situation. After the announcement of the lockdown, the BCRA accelerated the rate-cutting cycle and the interbank rate reduced substantially, below 10 percent, while the inflation rate was almost 50 percent. The primary objective of this aggressive rate reduction was not based on the mainstream interest-elasticity of investment, particularly, if we consider that the private credit-to-GDP ratio in Argentina is below 10 percent. The goal was to support the financial needs of the non-financial private sector under the lockdown and, consequently, to avoid an eventual collapse of the domestic payments system. In addition, the BCRA implemented a credit policy based on credit card debt relief, loans to Small and Medium sized Enterprises (SMEs) for working capital and capital goods at 24 percent interest rate, for pay check protection in the range of 0–15 percent interest rate and loans to independent workers at zero interest rate. It is important to mention that a substantial portion of those loans were also guaranteed by the government through a special treasury fund (Fondo de Garantías Argentino, FoGAr).

The pandemic-related monetary policy intensified upward pressures in the exchange markets. While the Coronavirus shock on exchange markets was transitorily in most developing countries, it reinforced the structural problems of the balance of payments in Argentina. In a context of a crawling-peg system with strict capital controls, already implemented by the previous government to curb the speculative attack, the exchange market pressures provoked a higher upward volatility in the parallel exchange rates and induced more BCRA interventions in the official market.[9]

The monetary easing induced a higher portfolio dollarization of the private sector through different mechanisms. Financial operators increased the local currency short-selling by leveraging dollar purchases in parallel exchange markets under the belief that short-term interest rates were low enough to compensate the expected currency devaluation. Other investors simply withdrew their time deposits in *pesos* from the banking system to purchase dollars in the parallel market. This speculative or precautionary demand for dollars explains why the parallel exchange rate increased 40 percent approximately since the interest rate drop at the end of March until mid-May 2020. Private firms also leveraged early repayments of dollar-denominated external debt under the belief that the crawling-peg system was not sustainable and sooner or later a currency devaluation in the official market would occur. Finally, the trade balance had a speculative dynamic: tradable goods were perceived as dollar-linked real assets. For this reason, there was speculative imports and agricultural firms increased their stock of past harvests, mainly soybeans, and cereal and soybean exporting firms delayed their settlements in the official exchange market.

In order to deal with those undesired collateral effects of the pandemic-related monetary and fiscal policy, the BCRA quickly initiated a gradual monetary policy in the opposite direction. Between April and May, the BCRA increased two times the reverse repo policy rate and simultaneously implemented a minimum time deposit rate policy for the retail banking system to discourage the portfolio dollarization. The minimum time deposit rate was determined by the fraction 0.7 of the LELIQ rate, which was 38 percent in mid-April, which implied an increase in retail time deposit rates from approximately 20 percent to a minimum of 26.6 percent. In addition, since June, the BCRA began to regulate the access of the wholesale exchange market by requiring prior authorization for paying imports or financial commitments.

In addition, the government continued expanding the local bond market by diversifying the types of securities: fixed-rate bills and bonds in *pesos*, dollar-linked bonds settled in *pesos* and inflation-linked bonds. The role of the BCRA was important to boost those markets, for example, by making these new peso-denominated securities eligible for reserve requirements and BCRA repo operations. This institutional definition increased the return-at-risk on that securities perceived by commercial banks and, consequently increased their demand in the bond market. Since mid-May until the end of June, there was a relative stability in exchange markets: the implied exchange rate dropped 14 percent approximately and the BCRA accumulated foreign reserves. However, the pressures rose again in July and the BCRA had to deal with a period of increasing instability. Thus, the BCRA and the local security exchange commission (CNV, Comisión Nacional de Valores) implemented capital controls on implied exchange markets such as quantity-based restrictions or delaying the settlement date in order to increase the market risk of those operations. In addition, after the successful restructuring of the public debt denominated in foreign currency that finally occurred at the end of August 2020, the BCRA required a gradual restructuring of the private external debt to extend the maturity profile and reduce the short-term obligations.

However, the peak of the exchange market pressures was between September and October 2020 and the BCRA had to recalibrate the monetary policy in a context of lockdown relaxation and economic recovery. Broadly speaking, the BCRA reinforced the floor system by reducing the spread between the reverse repo policy rate and the market rate and initiated a rate hike cycle that increased the 1-day reverse repo rate from 19 to 32 percent, and to 36.6 percent in the case of the 7-day reverse repo rate, between October and November, that is, a return to the levels that existed previous to the big drop of March 2020. Also, it began to operate in the onshore dollar-denominated bond market to reduce the parallel exchange rates. The new official strategy on parallel markets was not only based on bond sales to withdraw liquidity but also simultaneous bond repurchases with dollars to keep stable the level of the public debt denominated in foreign currency held by third parties and, consequently, to not create an additional pressure on the country risk premium, the yield spread in dollar-denominated bonds between Argentina and United States. Note that these open market operations with dollars in the bond market were not unusual in recent central banking practices. For example, the Bank of Japan has been conducting dollar funds-supplying operations to ensure stability in financial markets, instead of exchange markets as in the case of Argentina.

This combination of rate hikes and open market operations created a conditional stability as the expectations on a collapse of the exchange rate framework were disappointed or at least temporarily postponed. The parallel exchange rate dropped 17 percent in the period October–November and it has been stable since then. In addition, the downward trend in the level of foreign reserves has been reversed since the beginning of December 2020. The worst of the crisis seems over, but many additional dangers lie ahead, not least the renegotiation with the IMF, which would be central for any significant program of recovery that hit Argentina strongly, and left the country with less fiscal space to respond.

BRIEF FINAL COMMENTS

Beyond the immediate dynamics of the crisis, the consequences of Macri administration mismanagement of the macroeconomic policy and the exchange rate crisis will be felt for a long time. In 2021, the low level of reserves and the high level of external debt, added to the uncertainty around the renegotiation of the IMF loan, have paralyzed the economy. The Argentine economy is dangerously close to a new *default*, and it is unlikely that it can be avoided without substantive support from the IMF. In the long term, the structural problems of the balance of payments, which have intensified during the Macri administration, are difficult to solve, both on the side of the substitution of basic imports, on the energy side in particular, and on the side of the diversification of exports, a perennial problem in Argentina, and in the peripheral countries in general.

The old Argentine pendulum, to which Diamand (1983, 38) referred, remains and, as he suggested, once again we find that: "the representatives of the local orthodox economic teams not only fully coincide with the 'efficient' demands of the Fund but even tend to be more enthusiastic about it." In the same way, Diamand (1983, 38) pointed out the inverse risk, according to which: "the popular current tends to adopt attitudes of repudiation of the recessive demands of the Fund [...] they reject the orthodox recession, but without promoting a coherent policy of the external sector that really replace its balancing effects." It is true that the latter is easier said than done, and that very few nations have been able to overcome the barriers of what is now called the middle-income trap (Vernengo, 2018). There is room for enormous pessimism about the possibilities of both a *default* and a prolonged period of stagnation, with the serious social consequences that this would have.

Furthermore, the change in the dynamics of global trade policy, with the intensification of the trade war between the United States and China, the renegotiation of several free trade agreements, and the relative ineffectiveness of the World Trade Organization (WTO), suggest that the industrial and export promotion policies of what was called the developmental state, and followed by several Asian countries such as Japan, South Korea, and now China, are still open to Argentina. Hope springs eternal.

NOTES

1.   Here it should be noted that debt in national currency is generally safe, once it can be monetized, and there is no possibility of *default* per se. Beyond that, this may be inflationary in the context of full employment, there is a marked difference with the external debt in dollars, which requires reserves to meet the payments. The theoretical foundations are related to what is called the theory of functional finance developed by Abba Lerner, and which have been rescued by the so-called Modern Monetary Theory (MMT). On the latter see Wray (2015).

2.   Between 2011 and 2015, the government had implemented strict quantity-based exchange controls to manage the chronic capital outflows. Consequently, in that period, there was an exchange rate gap between the official rate and a higher parallel rate that created distortive effects especially in financial markets.

3.   It should also be clear that the BCRA has the ability to control the interest rate on debt in *pesos*, intervening in the bond market. In addition, it should be noted that the vast majority of currency crisis models put the emphasis, when dealing with the fundamental causes, on the fiscal deficit as the main problem. For an alternative model that emphasizes external accounts, and shocks to trade and financial terms, see Cline and Vernengo (2016).

4.   For the risk of *default*, it is convenient to look at the relationship between short-term obligations, that is, interest on the debt, and international reserves. This measure is known in the literature as the Guidotti–Greenspan index. For the same diagnosis in 2014, near the end of the Cristina Fernández de Kirchner government, see Vernengo (2014).

5.   Here it is worth noting that there was distrust in the Kirchner governments with the strategy of using higher interest rates to attract funds and accumulate reserves, something that, as we noted, happened in Brazil. The idea was that the higher domestic rate would slow down credit and domestic growth, and the notion that the use of public banks to expand credit domestically in *pesos* was not pursued. On that see De Lucchi (2014) and Vernengo (2016b).

6.   Brazil had a longer trajectory of development of a market for public debt in domestic currency going back to the 1960s, during the last dictatorship. For a historical perspective see Pedras (2009).

7. For a discussion of capital flight in Argentina, see Bona (2018).
8. It should be noted that the Fund always maintained a Monetarist diagnosis of the functioning of the international economy, with the preponderance of the Polak model, which does not correspond to the dominant vision in the mainstream of the profession. For example, the view of Michael Mussa, the IMF's chief economist at the time, on the convertibility crisis presupposes that it was primarily a fiscal problem. There is no distinction between debt in domestic currency and in dollars, and there is no understanding of the structural problems of the balance of payments. See Mussa (2002).
9. It is important to note that parallel exchange rates are not only based on illegal or 'black' markets but also on financial markets through onshore–offshore operations in bond and stock markets: the ratio between the onshore price in *pesos* and the offshore (or onshore) price in US dollars of the same liquid financial asset creates an implicit exchange rate.

REFERENCES

Bank of International Settlements (BIS) (2017). "Recent trends in EME Government debt volume and composition". *Quarterly Review*, September.

Bhaduri, A. and Steindl, J. (1983). "The rise of monetarism as a social doctrine". *Thames Papers in Political Economy*, no 83/3.

Bona, L. (2018). "La fuga de capitalesen Argentina". *Documento de Trabajo*, no 24, Buenos Aires: Flacso.

Central Bank of Brazil (CBB) (2021). *Séries Temporais*, available at: http://www.bcb .gov.br, accessed December 18, 2021.

Central Bank of the Argentine Republic (BCRA) (2021). *Statistics*, available at: http:// www.bcra.gob.ar/PublicacionesEstadisticas/Principales_variables_i.asp, accessed December 18, 2021.

Cline, N. and Vernengo, M. (2016). "Interest rates, terms of trade and currency crises: Are we on the verge of a new crisis in the periphery?" In A. Gevorkyan and O. Canuto (eds), *Financial Deepening and Post-Crisis Development in Emerging Markets: Current Perils and Future Dawns*, pp. 41–62. New York: Palgrave Macmillan.

De Lucchi, J. M. (2014). "Macroeconomía de la deuda pública. El desendeudamiento argentino (2003–2012)". *Documento de Trabajo*, no 53, enero, cefid.ar.

De Lucchi, J. M. (2018). "La devaluación era evitable". *Página 12*, 28 de mayo.

De Lucchi, J. M. (2019). "When debt matters. Argentina's new debt trap and the return of the IMF". Public Seminar, The New School.

Diamand, M. (1983). "El pénduloargentino ¿Hasta cuándo?". *Cuadernos del Centro de Estudios de la Realidad Económica*, no 1.

Federal Reserve Bank (FED) (2021). *Data*, available at: https://www.federalreserve .gov/, accessed December 18, 2021.

Financial Times (2017). "How did Argentina pull off a 100-year bond sale?" June 20.

Instituto Nacional de Estadística y Censos (INDEC) (2021). *Estadísticas*, available at: https://www.indec.gob.ar/, accessed December 18, 2021.

Kriesler, P. and Lavoie, M. (2007). "The new consensus on monetary policy and its Post-Keynesian critique". February 2007, *Review of Political Economy*, 19(3), 387–404.

Ministry of Finance of Argentina (2021). *Macroeconomics*, available at: https://cbonds .com/macroeconomics/, accessed December 18, 2021.

Mussa, M. (2002). *Argentina y el FMI: del triunfo a la tragedia*. Buenos Aires: Planeta.

Pedras, G. B. V. (2009). "História da Dívida Pública no Brasil: de 1964 até os días atuais," In A. Silva, L. Oliveira de Carvalho, and O. Medeiros (eds), *Dívida Pública: A Experiência Brasileira*. Brasilia: Secretaria do Tesouro Nacional.

Reinhart, C. and Rogoff, K. (2009). *This Time is Different. Eight Centuries of Financial Folly*. Princeton: Princeton University Press.

Sturzenegger, F. (2016). "El uso del concepto de equilibrio general en su aplicación a la política monetaria". Academia Nacional de Ciencias Económicas, 16 de marzo. Disponibleen http://www.bcra.gob.ar/Pdfs/Prensa_comunicacion/Distertación_Stur -zenegger_Academia_NCE.pdf.

Taylor, J. B. (1999). "A historical analysis of monetary policy rules". In J. B. Taylor (ed.), *Monetary Policy Rules*. Chicago: University of Chicago Press, pp. 319–340.

Vernengo, M. (2014). "Argentina, vulture funds, and the American justice system". *Challenge*, 57(6), 46–55.

Vernengo, M. (2016a). "Neoliberalism resurgent in Argentina". *Dollars & Sense*, 332, 23–24.

Vernengo, M. (2016b). "Kicking away the ladder, too: Inside central banks". *Journal of Economic Issues*, 50(2), 452–460.

Vernengo, M. (2018). "¿La trampa del ingreso medio o el retorno de la hegemonía estadounidense?" *Coyuntura y Desarrollo*, 385, 171–178.

Wray, R. (2015). "Modern money theory". *The New Palgrave Dictionary of Economics*. London: Palgrave Macmillan.

8. The monetary circuit and the credit channel in Mexico[1]

Roberto Valencia Arriaga[2] and Santiago Capraro Rodríguez

INTRODUCTION

According to the New Macroeconomic Consensus (NCM), central banks are able to regulate the level of demand with interest rate adjustments. This is possible because this rate connects the monetary and real economy through different paths, known as the transmission channels of monetary policy. The connection is achieved thanks to credit. Among the different transmission channels, interest rates and credit are of particular relevance because, after a central bank rate change, the cost of credit can be modified, encouraging or discouraging its demand, and thus affecting both investment and output.

Acknowledging the importance of credit, it would be desirable to see a comprehensive explanation of credit within the NCM model. However, its operation can be known by way of simplifying that importance through the following causalities: interest rate–credit–investment–product. All this is summarized in an IS curve, where the product depends inversely on the real interest rate.

Given these weak assumptions, we embrace an unconventional framework in this paper in order to scrutinize the role of credit within the Mexican economy, and argue that the causalities that are attributed to the NCM framework are not established. Therefore, our goal is to develop a stock-flow model and a VAR that serve as a reference to discern the operation of the credit and interest rates channels in Mexico.

The principal results that we find are: (a) the interest rate channel is more relevant than the credit channel in the Mexican economy since credit has a very weak response to the variation of the monetary policy interest rate; and (b) investment causes credit not the other way around. The above is inferred from the results of the impulse-response and variance decomposition of the VAR model. The first point coincides with the post-Keynesian conjecture which states that a possible result of the increase in the interest rate of monetary policy is an increase in inflation and not a decrease, since the costs are higher and capitalists will try to transfer them to prices (Kaldor, 1980; Panico, 1988). Our second finding is consistent with the monetary theory of production, which states that it is not enough that the existence of money creates demand, it is necessary that the existence of demand creates money.

This chapter has three sections aside from the current one. In the second section, we present a brief theoretical discussion on the function of the interest rate and credit channels from the perspective of the NCM and Monetary Theory of Production (MTP). This discussion takes place within a Stock-Flow framework that allows for detailing the operation of the monetary circuit, permitting the rigor of these models to reveal the effects on income distribution of monetary policy, as a change in the interest rate does not have similar effects on the different economic agents. In the third section, we rely on the Stock-Flow model to carry out a first analysis on the role of credit and monetary policy in Mexico. The fourth section complements the analysis with a VAR model that covers the period 2002–2020, from which follows that the MTP is a better framework to understand the connection between the real and monetary economy in Mexico. Finally, the chapter closes with a brief section of conclusions.

THE THEORY BEHIND THE CREDIT CHANNEL IN A STOCK-FLOW FRAMEWORK

The key variable that connects the monetary economy with the real one is credit. However, within the NCM, this variable is not explicitly modeled, as can be seen in traditional macroeconomics manuals such as Galí (2008), and Carlin and Soskice (2006).

This omission has been implicitly remedied with the transmission mechanism of monetary policy, which shows the different paths or channels through which decisions of the central bank impact demand, supply and finally, inflation. For the purposes of this chapter, we will highlight the channels of interest rates and credit.

According to Galí (2008), through the channel of interest rates, the central bank has the ability to modify the consumption and investment decisions of households and companies intertemporally thanks to the rationality of the agents. Thus, a rise (fall) in the rate would increase (reduce) the opportunity cost for both entrepreneurs and households, causing them to decrease (increase) their investment and consumption spending in the current period, while increasing (decreasing) it during the following period.

Rochon (2019) shows that the credit channel has two components: a sub-channel via bank loans, and another that affects the balance sheet. Although in both cases these sub-channels seek to regulate the demand for credit, the primary objective is to impact the credit that is destined for invest-ment or consumption. So, an increase (decrease) in the central bank rate would raise (reduce) the rates that commercial banks charge for credit. The higher (lower) cost of financing would discourage (encourage) investment and con-sumption spending respectively, affecting the money supply.

On the other hand, the central bank also influences via the balance sheet, because a rise (fall) in its rate increases (decreases) the cost of debt. This would damage (improve) the balance sheets of companies, affecting their cash flows, and subsequently decrease (increase) their production. The increase (decrease) in the cost of debt would discourage (encourage) companies to demand more credit, but intended for the purpose of cleaning up this sheet. So, the impact on the balance sheet is an accelerator of the effect of monetary policy (Bernanke and Gertler, 1995), but with little impact on real investment.

Orthodox evidence that these channels work is shown in Sims (1992), Galí (1992) and Christiano, Eichenbaum and Evans (1999) in the case of the United States, and in Peersman and Smets (2003) in the case of the European Union.

A heterodox and explicit way to explain the role of credit as a connector between the monetary and real economy is found in the Monetary Theory of Production (MTP). This is a framework that Keynes began to develop in 1932 (Panico, 1988) and was taken up by the Franco-Italian school, combining both Marxist precepts and the original ideas of Keynes's own Treatise on Money (Pasarella, 2014).

In the MTP, it is argued that the connection between the monetary and real economy occurs through the so-called monetary circuit, which is composed of three phases: (a) *creation*, understood as the moment in which commercial banks request financing from the central bank to grant credit to the private sector, therefore creating money; (b) *circulation*, which occurs when employ-ers invest and pay wages to workers[3] and they deposit those wages into the commercial bank; and (c) *destruction*, which is when workers buy goods and services from companies, which pay the initial credit to the commercial bank, which finally pays the central bank financing, where the destruction of money occurs. However, it is possible to add one more phase: *motivation*, which is the reason why entrepreneurs go to commercial banks to apply for credit. This phase should take precedence over the others. Taking into account these four phases, we will expand the operation of the monetary circuit based on a Stock-Flow framework.

Stock Matrix

Following Godley and Lavoie (2007), we will begin by defining a matrix of stocks:

Table 8.1   *Stock matrix*

	Households	Enterprises	Banks	Government	Central bank	Total
Deposits	$+M_h$		$-M_b$		$-M$	0
Loans	$-L_h$	$-L_e$	$+L$			0
Capital		$+K$				$+K$
Bonuses	$+B_h$		$+B_f$	$-B$	$+REF$	0
Refinancing			$-REF$			0
Equity	V_h	V_e	V_f	V_g	V_{cb}	$-K$

Source: Authors' elaboration.

In Table 8.1, the columns show the following economic agents: (a) private sector, composed of Households and Enterprises; (b) financial sector, represented by commercial banks (Banks); and (c) state, composed of the Government and the Central Bank. We will omit the participation of the external sector because its inclusion would not produce results different from those intended in our objective. The variables of the economy are presented in the rows.

In Godley and Lavoie (2007), the monetary circuit begins with the creation of money. However, as noted above, it should begin with a *Motivation* phase, which is the reason that triggers the need and therefore demand for credit. This does not happen because of a change in the interest rate of the central bank, as is maintained in the NCM credit channel, since entrepreneurs are not waiting for a reduction in the rate before requesting credit from banks and investing. They invest when their businesses have been profitable (Kalecki, 1954), or when they find business opportunities that generate expectations of favorable future returns (Keynes, 1936). So, investment causes the demand for credit and not the other way around as advocated in the NCM.

Assuming that entrepreneurs have found a market opportunity, they would go to the banks to apply for credit. This operation is recorded in Table 8.1 with the label $(-L_e)$. Since both companies and households can apply for credit, this variable is also recorded in the Households column under the label $(-L_h)$. The sum of credit to businesses and households is the total credit granted by banks $(+L)$.

The demand for credit allows for the start of the Money Creation phase. Within this stage, unlike what is maintained in the orthodox approach of Loanable Funds, no prior bank deposits are required to offer credit, since at any time they will be able to request financing from the central bank.

In Mexico's case, the above has a legal basis within the Bank of Mexico Law and where the following objectives are expressed: (a) to provide the country with national currency; and (b) to promote the healthy development of the financial system (Banxico, 1993). The central bank, therefore, is obliged to provide the liquidity demanded by commercial banks, as the lack of it would affect the confidence of economic agents, causing a possible withdrawal of savings from the system. This legal requirement is compatible with the idea of Lavoie (2001), who points out that the central bank must constantly finance commercial banks, because as De Cecco (1999) argues, it is a lender of first instance.

Money creation is seen in the Central Bank column, which is a representation of the institution's balance sheet. Following Duwicquet and Mazier (2012), this operation is reflected by the label ($+REF$) and its counterpart is a money issue ($-M$).

Commercial banks receive resources from the central bank, which they record as ($-REF$). It should be noted that in the proposed system, banks have an alternative of funds in household deposits, so these will also be a liability of commercial banking ($-M_b$). However, it is imperative not to be confused with the postulate of Loanable Funds, since whether or not there are deposits, this does not condition the supply of credit. For ease, we will assume that deposits do not generate an interest.

The *Creation* phase is reinforced thanks to households being able to also apply for loans. Before being spent, these will be kept as bank deposits ($+M_h$).

It is worth noting that with the resources raised by Banks, they can offer credit. If they detect a risk in the investment projects that they do not want to assume, though, they could alternatively acquire government bonds ($+B_b$)

During phase three of the monetary circuit, *Circulation*, enterprises will create capital via investment. Capital creation will be the only source of wealth in the economy, so that the larger this acquis, the greater the potential for growth. This will be reflected on the companies' balance sheet by the label ($+K$). During this phase, companies will also pay wages to workers; however, we will see this in the flow matrix.

During phase four, *Destruction*, households would spend their resources either consuming goods and services or buying government bonds ($+B_h$). The former will be seen in the transaction matrix, while the balance of the latter is shown in Table 8.1.

It should be noted that the government participates within this circuit by spending, so it has the need to finance it with debt ($-B$) and taxes. The former can be purchased by both Households ($+B_h$) and Banks ($+B_f$), while the latter will be paid by the private and financial sectors.

As a general rule, both rows and columns must sum to zero with this methodology, so the Net Worth row is a column-level balance account. The only row that does not add up to zero is that of Capital because that would mean destruction of wealth.

Transaction Matrix

We will now look at the flow of money through the monetary circuit stages. For them, we will rely on Table 8.2, and from this the equations of agent behavior will be derived. The logic of the table is similar to the previous one, except that at the column level two types of accounts for both Enterprises and Banks will be identified: the current and the capital. In the first, the uses of resources will be reported, while the sources will be reported in the second.

As noted above, once there is motivation to demand credit, money creation comes via demand for credit. These transactions will be found in the Table 8.2 labels for Enterprises $(+\Delta L_e)$ and Households $(+\Delta L_h)$, where Δ denotes a change in the variable, since the sum of the loans taken in the current period plus the previous ones will give rise to the stock observed in Table 8.1. These resources will provide for the financial system, so that the current account of the Banks will be seen as $(-\Delta L)$. Now, it should be noted that the negative signs refer to a use of resources, while the positive ones to a source.

Table 8.2   Flow matrix

	Households	Enterprises		Banks		Government	Central bank	Total
		Current	Capital	Current	Capital			
Consumption	$-C$	$+C$						0
Investment		$+I$	$-I$					0
Government expenditure		$+G$				$-G$		0
Wages	$+W$	$-W$						0
Business Benefits	$+F_{he}$	$-F_e$	$+F_e$					0
Financial Benefits	$+F_{hf}$			$-F_f$	$+F_f$			0
Interest on loans	$-r_f L_h$	$-r_f L_e$		$+r_f L_h + r_f L_e - rREF$				0
Interest on bonds	$+rB_h$			$+rB_f$		$-rB_h - rB_f$		0
Change in credit	$+\Delta L_h$		$+\Delta L_e$	$-\Delta L$				0
Taxation	$-T_h$	$-T_e$		$-T_f$		$+T$		0
Change in deposits	$-\Delta M_h$				$+\Delta M_f$		$+\Delta M$	0
Change in bonuses	$-\Delta B_h$			$-\Delta B_f$		$+\Delta B$		0
Change in Refinancing					$+\Delta REF$		$-\Delta REF$	0
Save	S_h	0	0	0	0	0	0	S_t

Source: Authors' elaboration.

During the third stage, companies invest, as seen in the capital account ($-I$). Similarly, it appears in the current account since companies acquire capital goods from other companies. Following Kalecki (1983), the demand for capital goods will allow enterprises engaged in the production of these goods to demand employment (N) for which they will pay wages ($-W$). This income will allow workers to demand goods and services of salaried consumption ($+C$), so companies in this sector will need to increase their production, leading them to hire more labor for which they will pay new wages.

This demand will be reinforced by government spending ($+G$), resulting in the output level (Y). In the following four equations it is possible observe the determinants of output components:

$$Y = C + I + G \tag{8.1}$$

where Y = output level, C = consumption, I = investment, and G = government spending;

$$C = a_0 + a_1 YD, \quad a_0 > 0, 0 < a_1 < 1 \tag{8.2}$$

where C = consumption, a_0 = autonomous part, a_1 = marginal propensity to consumption and YD = disposable income;

$$I = \varphi F_{e-1}, \quad 0 < \varphi < 1 \tag{8.3}$$

where I = investment, φ = elasticity of investment to previous benefits, and F_{e-1} = previous period's benefits;

$$G = T + \Delta B - r_{-1} B_{-1} \tag{8.4}$$

where G = government spending, T = Taxes, ΔB = change of government bonds, and $r_{-1} B_{-1}$ = costs of past debt.

Following Keynes (1936), in equation (8.2) consumption will depend on an autonomous part and a marginal propensity which is a function of household disposable income. Also, according to Kalecki (1954), in equation (8.3) the investment depends of the previous period's benefits.

In equation (8.4) it is observed that government spending is financed by taxes and issuance of new debt. These revenues must be discounted from the costs of past debt.

Since companies finance their initial production with credit, we will pay interest on the resources requested during a previous period, so the difference between income and expenses will be business profits, which are distributed to households. Income results from multiplying the quantity of goods and services sold by the average price; while expenditures are composed of the payment of wages, financial expenses for credits taken in the past and taxes. Formally:

$$F_e = pQ - \left(W + r_{fe}L_{e-1} + T_e \right)$$ (8.5)

where F_e = business profits, p = average price, Q = quantity of goods and services sold, W = Wages, $r_{fe}L_{e-1}$ = interests paid on loans taken from previous periods, and T_e = paid taxes.

According to Rochon (2001), r_{fe}, that is, the interest rate charged by banks in period n to companies, is determined based on the rate fixed by the central bank plus a profit margin, as follows:

$$r_{fe} = r + \sigma$$ (8.6)

where r_{fe} = interest rate charged by banks to companies, r = rate fixed by the central bank, and σ = profit margin added by commercial banks.

As explained above, the demand for credit has two components, one for investment purposes and the other with the idea of cleaning up the balance sheet. This is expressed as follows:

$$L_e = \lambda_1 I - \lambda_2 r_{fe}, \quad \lambda_1 > \lambda_2 > 0$$ (8.7)

where L_e = credit demand of companies, λ_1 = elasticity of credit demand of companies to investment, I = investment, λ_2 = elasticity of credit demand of companies to its financial cost, and r_{fe} = interest rate charged by banks to companies.

From equation (8.7), interest rate changes, can affect demand for credit, but it does not move investment. Under these circumstances, the reduction in the interest rate charged by banks has a redistributive effect, as companies would use the new credit to pay for previous liabilities. Since consumers are accustomed to paying a price for the goods and services offered by companies, there would be no reason to lower prices despite the fact that the financial costs are minor. It should be noted that contrary to what is postulated in the NCM, the reduction of the interest rate does not increase Y and therefore inflation; rather, only greater benefit-sharing in the output would occur. In this way, the role of the interest rate is distributive (Panico, 1988).

Following Kalecki (1954), the average price will be determined by taking into account the unit prime cost to which companies will add a margin. In addition, companies will incorporate the financial cost. For simplicity, we will assume that the labor cost is the only cost. According to López and Valencia (2018), it is a quotient between wages and productivity. In addition, we will find that companies have a high degree of monopoly, so that they will be able to transfer all financial cost to households. The latter will be a ratio between the interest paid on loans taken from previous periods and productivity. Formally:

$$p = c(1+u) + ruf, u > 0 \qquad (8.8)$$

where: p = average price, c = unit prime cost, u = profit margin, and ruf = financial cost;

$$c = \frac{W}{q} \qquad (8.9)$$

where: c = unit prime cost, W = wages, and q = productivity;

$$ruf = \frac{r_{fe}L_{e-1}}{q} \qquad (8.10)$$

where: ruf = financial cost, $r_{fe}L_{e-1}$ = interest paid on loans taken from previous periods, and q = productivity.

With equation (8.8) it is possible to calculate the inflation rate or the growth rate of p, which, according to the NCM, depends on the inflation rate of the past period and the difference between the observed output (y) and the potential (y^*) usually named output gap, it is expressed in equation (8.11):

$$\pi = \pi_{-1} + \alpha(y - y^*) \qquad (8.11)$$

where: π = inflation rate, π_{-1} = inflation rate of the past period, α = elasticity of inflation rate to output gap, and $(y - y^*)$ = output gap.

It should be noted that the potential output (y^*) has been subject to various criticisms (Setterfield, 2006; Arestis and Sawyer, 2014; Levy, 2014) especially because of the difficulty calculating it and the assumptions behind it. Being consistent with a heterodox framework, we will approximate the potential output following Steindl (1976), whose mechanics are consistent with our Stock-Flow framework, and which could be approximated with K in Table 8.1. The reason is that a total use of productive capacity would imply the use of all capital goods available. This would trigger the supply peak of goods and services. If so, the demand for an additional good would be impossible to cover, as would be in the case of Kalecki (1954), where a rise in demand causes increases in prices owing to an inelastic supply.

However, since K depends on the investment, and this on past profits, investment growth constantly expands the potential output. Instead, a decrease in investment over a period will not necessarily contract K. It should also be noted that only in extreme situations will demand call for the full use of K.[4]

Turning to the behavioral equations of households, in equation (8.12) it is shown that the wages received ($+W$) depend on the amount of employment demanded by companies and the average wage, which will be determined exogenously to the model. Employment will be a function of investment. That is:

$$W = wN \tag{8.12}$$

where W = wages, w = average wage, and N = employment;

$$N = \mu I, \mu > 0 \tag{8.13}$$

where N = employment, μ = elasticity of employment to investment, and I = investment.

Since some individuals own businesses and banks, there will be some households that collect benefits at the end of the period from both companies ($+F_e$), and banks ($+F_f$). Households will be able to increase their disposable income by applying for credit from banks ($+ \Delta L_h$) which will depend on the disposable income of households from previous periods And as in the case of companies, households would seek to take advantage of a reduction in interest rates to clean up their balance sheets, so credit demand will weigh negatively on the changes in rates. Finally, households will save or spend their income in both goods and services ($-C$) and financial markets, where they can buy government bonds for which they will get a yield at the end of the period. The rate r will be the interest paid by the central bank on the bonds. In addition, households will pay taxes. In sum, household disposable income and their credit demand will be expressed as:

$$YD_h = W + F_e + F_f + \Delta L_h + rB - rL_h - T_h \tag{8.14}$$

where YD_h = household disposable income, W = wages, F_e = business profits, F_f = banks profits, ΔL_h = change in credit taken by households, rB = yield of government bonds, rL_h = financial cost of credit took by households, and T_h = taxes that households pay;

$$L_h = \rho YD_{-1} - \rho_1 r_{fh}, \quad \rho > \rho_1 > 0 \tag{8.15}$$

where L_h = household credit demand, ρ = elasticity of household credit demand to income disposable from previous periods, YD_{-1} = disposable income of households from previous periods, ρ_1 = elasticity of households credit demand to interest rate that households pay on loans, and r_{fh} = interest rate that households pay on loans.

The interest rate that households will pay on loans will be determined according to equation (8.16), where the margin charged to households (v) is added to the interest rate of the central bank, therefore:

$$r_{fh} = r + v, \quad v > 0 \tag{8.16}$$

where: r_{fh} = interest rate that households pay on loans, r = interest rate of the central bank, and v = margin charged to households.

Regarding banks, we will assume that their only cost is the interest rate they pay to the central bank for the requested financing ($-rREF$), while their income comes from the interest rate they charge households for the credit placed at the beginning of the period and the companies' credit. As discussed above, banks can also be funded through household deposits ($+\Delta M_f$). With the resources that banks get, they can choose between granting credit to the private sector or buying government bonds ($-\Delta B_f$). From the latter, banks will get a yield ($+rB_f$). Of course, they will have to pay taxes ($-T_f$). It follows that the net profits of banks are:

$$F_f = r_{fh} L_h + r_{fe} L_e + rB_f - rREF - T_f \tag{8.17}$$

where F_f = banks profits, $r_{fh} L_h$ = interest that banks charge to households for the credit, $r_{fe} L_e$ = interest that banks charge to companies for the credit, rB_f = yield of government bonds, $rREF$ = interest that banks pay to the central bank for the requested financing, and T_f = taxes that banks pay.

The government will fund all its spending by collecting tax (T) from companies, households and banks, and by issuing bonds. So, they have to pay the interest determined by the central bank to the owners of these bonds from previous periods ($-rB_{h-1} - rB_{f-1}$). The budget constraint of the government and tax collection are expressed as follows:

$$T + \Delta B = G + rB_h + rB_f \tag{8.18}$$

where T = taxes, ΔB = change of bonds, G = government spending, rB_h = yield that government pays to the household owners of bonds, and rB_f = yield that government pays to the bank owners of bonds;

$$T = \tau_1 F_{e-1} + \tau_2 W_{-1} + \tau_3 F_{f-1} \tag{8.19}$$

where T = taxes, $\tau_1 F_{e-1}$ = taxes from companies, $\tau_2 W_{-1}$ = taxes from households, and $\tau_3 F_{f-1}$ = taxes from banks.

Finally, the change in central bank flows can be seen as:

$$\Delta REF = \Delta M \tag{8.20}$$

where: ΔREF = change in refinancing, and ΔM = change in deposits.

CHANGES IN THE INTEREST RATE AND THEIR IMPACT ON CREDIT AND INTEREST RATE CHANNELS, AND OUTPUT

Once we have the whole system of equations, it is necessary to solve equations (8.2), (8.3) and (8.4), for which it is necessary use equations (8.5)–(8.19). Once we have solved, substitute equations (8.2), (8.3) and (8.4) into equation (8.1). After some algebraic simplifications, we reach:

$$Y = \left(rB_h + rB_f - rREF - \tau_3 F_{f-1} + Q\left(\frac{\mu\varphi F_{e-1}w(1+u)}{Q} + \frac{L_{e-1}(r+\sigma)}{Q} \right) - \tau_1 F_{e-1} + \Delta L_h - \tau_2 W_{-1} \right) a_1 +$$
$$a_0 + \varphi F_{e-1} - r_{-1}B_{-1} + \tau_2 W_{-1} + \tau_3 F_{f-1} + \tau_1 F_{e-1} + B_f + B_h \tag{8.21}$$

If we differentiate equation (8.21) with respect to the interest rate of the central bank, we obtain:

$$\left(B_f + L_{e-1} - REF + B_h \right) a_1 \tag{8.22}$$

We will use the result of equation (8.22) to explain the Mexican experience.

In equation (8.22) the channels of interest rates and credit appear implicitly and explicitly, respectively. About the second, it is observed that the credit that companies took in the previous period has an impact on the evolution of the output in the present. As shown in equation (8.7), credit depends on investment, and this on profits in the previous period (see equation (8.3)), so monetary policy would have to go a long way if it were to influence output through the credit channel. If we accept the Phillips curve of the NCM and tie it with this result, it will be easy to intuit that to impact the inflation rate, it will take at least two periods since the central bank interest rate is modified, but if and only if the credit demand from companies reacts to changes in the central bank rate. However, as stated above, during the first monetary circuit phase, and as formally observed in equations (8.3) and (8.7), investment needs cause demand for credit, not vice versa. Therefore, there is no reason to think that a reduction in the interest rate incentivizes investment. Evidence of this can be found in Mexico in 2020, when the central bank rate fell significantly, followed by commercial banks' rates. However, this does not encourage demand for credit from firms, as seen in Figure 8.1.

It shows the percentage of companies that requested new credit during 2020, the destination of this credit and the reasons why others did not request it. Regarding the first reference, there was a reduction from 24.2 percent to 18.5 percent of companies that applied for new credit between quarter one and four of this year. It is illustrative to note that during this period the central bank's interest rate had a significant contraction.

Additionally, about 60 percent of the companies said they did not demand credit due to the economic perception they had at that time, while approximately 50 percent justified zero demand for credit given the sales and profitability of their businesses.

Based on this, it can be concluded that the credit channel does not function as postulated in the transmission mechanism of NCM's monetary policy.

On the other hand, in equation (8.3) it can be seen that investment depends on previous profits, while in equation (8.5) it is shown that a decrease in the interest paid by the companies helps increase profits. This reasoning gives way to the channel of interest rates. Since it is clear from equation (8.6) that the rate charged by banks depends on the rate of the central bank, one might think that after a decrease of the latter, banks will respond in the same direction. If so, we

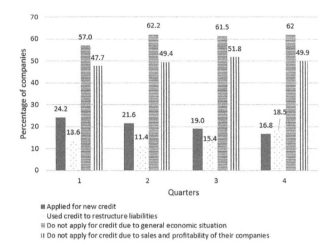

Source: Authors' elaboration with data from the short-term evaluation survey of the credit market (Banxico, 2021).

Figure 8.1   Credit market conditions in Mexico (2020)

would find two results: (a) an increase in company profits, which would cause investment to increase during the following period; and (b) since in equation (8.7) the demand for credit from companies also depends on the rate charged by banks, a rate fall will boost investment.

However, these conclusions should be taken cautiously. As seen in the previous section, what mainly motivates credit demand is a business opportunity that explodes in profits. This is confirmed by Figure 8.1. And while a fall in financial costs that increases profits could confuse our system of equations, the impetus to investment would be marginal since financial costs do not represent the largest outflow in companies. In addition, in equation (8.7) credit is observed to respond to the interest rate for the purpose of cleaning up company balance sheets. Evidence for this is shown in Figure 8.1, where, of the new credit demanded during the first quarter of 2020, 13.6 percent was used to restructure liabilities, while after the fall in the central bank rate, the percentage of companies that demanded credit to clean up their balance sheets was 18.5 percent.

Therefore, the credit requested as a result of the lower interest rate had no effect on the real economy, but rather only improved output profit-sharing.

In short, although it can be accepted that the interest rate channel works, the synchronous response in time and magnitude by the banks must be reviewed.

On the other hand, the credit channel only operates partially via the balance sheet, and therefore without effects on the real economy.

It also follows from equation (8.22) that, after a change in the interest rate, the effect on output will depend on the refinancing of the central bank (*REF*), the volume of government debt ($B_h + B_f$) and the marginal propensity to consume (a_1). It is interesting that an increase in refinancing does not guarantee an effect on the output. The reason for this is that we would be skipping the first phase of the monetary circuit, that is, the motivation to ask for credit. A greater injection of resources into the banks would have no outlet in the real economy, so this money would only find space by buying public debt. The year 2020 also provides evidence for Mexico, as the central bank launched a financing program for commercial banks with the idea that they would increase the credit for companies and consumers.[5] However, the program found no recipients, with the claim that banks were willing to lend, but that the private sector did not want the credit.[6]

EMPIRICAL EVIDENCE

In this section, we will present an econometric model for the Mexican economy referenced above. Given the characteristics of the series and, since it is a methodology used to understand the transmission mechanism of monetary policy (see, among others, González-García and Gaytán, 2006; Sidaoui and Ramos-Francia, 2008; Creel and Fontana, 2010), we have decided to estimate an Autoregressive Vector (VAR) model for the period 2002.4 to 2020.3 with quarterly data.

The model is formally expressed as follows:

$$X_t = \sum_{i=1}^{p-1} A_i X_{t-1} + \epsilon_t \qquad (8.23)$$

where X is a column vector that is composed of the following variables: r is the rate paid by government bonds and is a good proxy for the central bank reference rate; r_{fe} is the interest rate that commercial banks charge companies for credit; r_{fhc} is the interest rate that commercial banks charge households for consumer credit; r_{fhh} is the interest rate that commercial banks charge for mortgage loans; L_e is credit for businesses; ΔI is the growth rate of investment; Δy is the growth rate of GDP and π is the inflation rate.

The real variables are at 2013 prices and were transformed to logarithms, while the interest rates are nominal and did not undergo transformations.

In Table 8.3 it can be seen that Δy, ΔI and π are stationaries, so it was not necessary to take their first difference, while, due to the characteristics of the rest of the series, their first difference was obtained.

Table 8.3   *Unit roots test*

Variable	ADF			PP			KPSS	
	Nothing	Trend and intercept	Intercept	Nothing	Trend and intercept	Intercept	Trend and intercept	Intercept
r	0.2734	0.5716	0.3148	0.3252	0.5237	0.3191	0.1748	0.3577
Δr	0.0000	0.0000	0.0000	0.0000	0.0000	0.0000	0.0658	0.0622
Le	1.0000	0.9757	0.6842	1.0000	0.9696	0.6905	0.1870	1.1516
$[\![\Delta L]\!]e$	0.1168	0.0000	0.0000	0.0000	0.0000	0.0000	0.1386	0.2559
rfe	0.3073	0.2934	0.1140	0.3010	0.2934	0.1140	0.1289	0.3299
$[\![\Delta r]\!]fe$	0.0000	0.0000	0.0000	0.0000	0.0000	0.0000	0.0520	0.0592
$rfhc$	0.7630	0.5598	0.1165	0.7156	0.4966	0.1403	0.2865	0.3669
$[\![\Delta r]\!]fhc$	0.0000	0.0001	0.0001	0.0000	0.0001	0.0001	0.2728	0.3042
$rfhh$	0.7546	0.0240	0.0057	0.7245	0.0456	0.0057	0.2841	0.4419
$[\![\Delta r]\!]fhh$	0.0000	0.0000	0.0001	0.0000	0.0001	0.0001	0.1687	0.3036
ΔI	0.0027	0.0302	0.0355	0.0000	0.0001	0.0001	0.1884	0.4434
$\Delta\Delta I$	0.0000	0.0001	0.0001	0.0000	0.0001	0.0001	0.1376	0.1385
Δy	0.0009	0.0140	0.0052	0.0000	0.0001	0.0001	0.0987	0.1169
$\Delta\Delta y$	0.0000	0.0000	0.0001	0.0000	0.0001	0.0001	0.1259	0.1698
π	0.2482	0.0867	0.0430	0.0000	0.0001	0.0000	0.1141	0.4001
$\Delta\pi$	0.0000	0.0001	0.0001	0.0000	0.0001	0.0001	0.0609	0.0609

Note: For ADF and PP probabilities are reported. KPSS reference values: with trend 0.14600; with intercept 0.4630.
Source: Author' elaboration.

The model was estimated using three lags, according to Akaike and Schwartz's test. In addition, dummy variables were included for the periods 2003Q2, 2005Q1, 2006Q2, 2011Q2, 2012Q3, 2013Q4, 2017Q3, 2019Q4, 2020Q1.

Once the tests of correct specification and stability have been done, it can be seen that the model is well specified, as illustrated in Figure 8.2.

Supposed	Test	Prob.
Normality	Jarque-Bera	0.1102
Autocorrelation	LM1	0.4407
	LM2	0.0719
	LM3	0.0700
	LM4	0.1205
Heteroskedasticity	White (No Cross Terms)	0.2426

Source: Authors' elaboration.

Figure 8.2   *Credit market conditions in Mexico (2020)*

Impulse-response of the Interest Rate Channel

Based on the results of the accumulated impulse-response, we can identify that the channel of interest rates is partially met, because a crash of the central bank rate does have a long-term effect on the interest rate of company credit (panel A), while the cost of mortgage loans (panel B) and consumption (panel C) ends up dissipating over time (Figure 8.3).

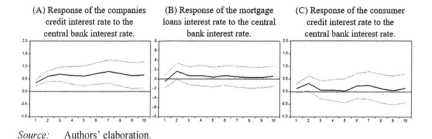

(A) Response of the companies credit interest rate to the central bank interest rate.

(B) Response of the mortgage loans interest rate to the central bank interest rate.

(C) Response of the consumer credit interest rate to the central bank interest rate.

Source: Authors' elaboration.

Figure 8.3   *Interest rate channel*

On the other hand, Figure 8.4 shows that assuming that there were changes in commercial bank rates, there is no investment effect, while the impact on GDP is limited.

The response of the variables in question to the central bank rate is shown in the first row of the figure. In the second the variables respond to the fee charged to companies, in the third, mortgage loans and in the fourth to the rate of consumption credit.

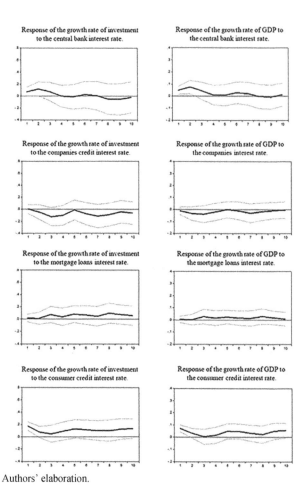

Response of the growth rate of investment to the central bank interest rate.

Response of the growth rate of GDP to the central bank interest rate.

Response of the growth rate of investment to the companies credit interest rate.

Response of the growth rate of GDP to the companies interest rate.

Response of the growth rate of investment to the mortgage loans interest rate.

Response of the growth rate of GDP to the mortgage loans interest rate.

Response of the growth rate of investment to the consumer credit interest rate.

Response of the growth rate of GDP to the consumer credit interest rate.

Source: Authors' elaboration.

Figure 8.4   Response of investment and GDP to interest rates

It is observed that investment only reacts persistently over time to the interest rate charged for consumption credit, although with a positive sign. While this result seems surprising, it is consistent with Sidaoui and Ramos-Francia (2008). They show that after an increase in the interest rate on consumer loans, loans also increase. If this is correct, there must also be a greater demand for goods and services, and therefore an increase in investment. So, our result is consistent with that of the authors, who attribute this rare effect to the shallowness of the credit market, and in particular to the market power of banks because they are able to raise the rate without slowing down the demand for credit.

In the first and fourth rows of second column, it is observed that the GDP growth rate reacts positively to the central bank rate and the consumer credit rate. With the first, there is a transitory effect, because in the long term it converges to zero. This result is contrary to the conventional precepts, but it does not follow the empirical evidence of those who adhere to this framework in Mexico. For example, González-García and Gaytán (2006) and Sidaoui and Ramos-Francia (2008) report similar results, although it is striking that they do not justify the reasons for this relationship. Using a different framework, López and Valencia (2015) and Caballero and López (2013) find a positive long-run relationship between the product and the interest rate, according to them, this result is due to the fact that a higher rate appreciates the exchange rate. This has two effects: on the one hand, it improves the share of wages within the output and stimulates consumption. On the other hand, it lowers the cost of foreign currency debt, which benefits the balance sheet. The appreciated exchange rate also lowers the cost of imported materials, which in economies such as Mexico has an important weight given the high imported content of export goods. Finally, the cost of imported machinery and technology is lowered. It is worth noting that the effect is very small, but it is consistent with Valencia, Capraro and Ortiz (2020) who report an elasticity of GDP to the exchange rate growth rate of –0.0142 percent.

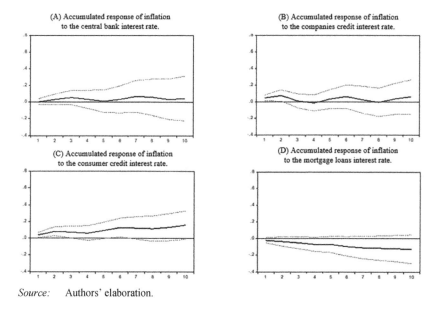

Source: Authors' elaboration.

Figure 8.5   *Inflation rate response to interest rates*

Regarding the response of GDP to the consumer credit rate, although it is higher, it is not as solid. It is consistent with the result of the response of investment to the same variable, as above.

Finally, Figure 8.5 shows the result of the inflation rate at the different rates. Panel A shows that there is no direct effect of the reference rate on inflation, which coincides with De Paula and Ferrari Filho (2010), who point out that in Latin American economies it is necessary to use other instruments to control inflation, such as the exchange rate. Panel B shows that there is a small but positive effect between inflation and the credit cost for businesses. The same is observed in Panel C regarding the consumer credit cost. In this sense, Taylor (2004) explains that under certain circumstances the increase in the interest rate increases costs and can generate inflation. This phenomenon was recorded by Kaldor (1980) during the monetarist experiment in the United Kingdom in the late 1970s.

Impulse-response Analysis of the Credit Channel

We will begin by analyzing the response of companies' credit to changes in interest rates (Figure 8.6).

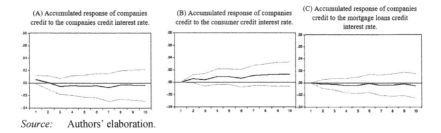

(A) Accumulated response of companies credit to the companies credit interest rate.

(B) Accumulated response of companies credit to the consumer credit interest rate.

(C) Accumulated response of companies credit to the mortgage loans credit interest rate.

Source: Authors' elaboration.

Figure 8.6 Credit response to interest rates

No significant response of credit to interest rates is observed. This result reinforces what is outlined with the Stock-Flow model, giving off the following premises: (a) in the face of an inflation shock, the central bank cannot control it through the credit channel, because although it increases in cost, the demand for credit will not react because, as was seen during the monetary circuit and in equation (8.7), its main trigger is investment; (b) in a situation of economic contraction accompanied by low inflation, the central bank cannot boost economic growth because credit is inelastic to its price; (c) an increase in the rate has redistributive effects, since given the market power of banks and companies, these would pass the cost on to households; and (d) after income redistribution and the negative impact on disposable income, as seen in equation (8.14), the effect on the real economy would be contractionary.

In short, a reduction in the interest rate does not encourage demand, but an increase does contract it. This is consistent with the following phrase recalled by Friedman during 1967: 'Monetary policy is like a loop, it serves to pull, but not to push' (Friedman, 1968, p. 1).

We will close this section with evidence that phase one of the monetary circuit is fulfilled in Mexico, that is, the demand for credit responds to investment needs (panel A), not the other way around (panel B). This is seen in Figure 8.7.

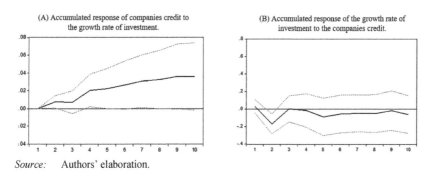

Source: Authors' elaboration.

Figure 8.7   *Response from credit to investment (A) and from investment to credit (B)*

The result of panel (B) is consistent with equation (8.22), since it is confirmed that a greater supply of credit, perhaps due to an increase in refinancing, is not enough to increase investment.

Finally, in Figure 8.8 we find that neither the growth rate of investment (panel A) nor of GDP (panel B) cause inflation, which it is also compatible with the post-Keynesian ideas that inflation is a problem of costs (Kalecki, 1954; Noyola, 1954) and not of demand.

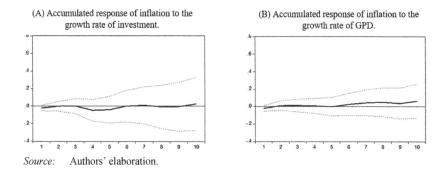

Source: Authors' elaboration.

Figure 8.8   Inflation response to ΔI (A) and ΔGDP (B)

Analysis of Decomposition of Variance

Following the structure of Reifschneider, Tetlow and Williams (1999) we present the results of the decomposition of variance after a change in the central bank interest rate. The variables were classified into two groups: those affected by the interest rate channel and those influenced by the credit channel. In addition, the effect on inflation is presented.

In the first group, it is shown that after a change in the reference rate, the rate that reacts immediately is the one charged for credit to companies, since 30.63 percent of it is explained by the rate of the Bank of Mexico. This effect begins to fade during the third quarter, while the rates for consumer and mortgage loans begin to be influenced to a greater extent, although not with the force of the first. It is notable that after 12 quarters, the effect on the cost of corporate credit persists, as almost a quarter of its variance is explained by the central bank rate.

Table 8.4   Decomposition of variance and response to the central bank rate (%)

Variable	Response in quarters					
	1	2	3	4	8	12
Interest rate channel						
Cost of credit for companies	30.63	31.69	29.2	28.2	24.65	23.24
Cost of consumer credit	2.45	4.28	7.16	6.43	7.21	7.32
Cost of mortgage credit	0.84	9.51	10.4	10.14	9.81	9.81
Credit channel						
Credit to the companies	3.33	6.39	6.34	6.68	5.46	5.36
GDP growth rate	5.02	4.27	4.07	5.69	6.39	6.57
Investment growth rate	11.47	8.27	8.15	9.22	9.37	8.94
Inflation rate	0.06	2.78	3.57	4.08	6.09	6.94

Source: Author' elaboration based on the results of the model.

Regarding the credit channel, the central bank rate explains the variance of credit to companies at just 3.33 percent during the first quarter, that of investment at 5.02 percent and GDP at 11.47 percent. The effect on the first two variables increases over time, but stabilizes around 5.3 percent and 6.5 percent respectively, while in the case of GDP it decreases to around 9 percent during the 12th quarter.

Finally, the rate of the monetary authority explains the inflation rate very little as, during the first year, it barely represents 4 percent.

CONCLUSIONS

Based on the monetary circuit, we have questioned the operability and causality of the channels of interest rates and credit in Mexico. Building a Stock-Flow model, we find that the interest rate channel works primarily via credit for firms. However, a change in the cost of this does not change the demand for credit or investment. Similarly, it follows that a reduction in the reference rate could benefit banks by obtaining cheaper resources, but it would not favor the real economy. On the contrary, a rise in the central bank rate would be harmful to the real economy since banks would pass these costs on to companies and eventually to households.

On the other hand, the credit channel cannot be explained by following the NCM, since its operation is more compatible with the Monetary Theory of Production. The reason is that, for investment, the existence of resources is not a sufficient condition, nor that they are cheap. Attractive projects that generate expectations of benefits are required.

These findings call into question the central bank's ability to regulate the level of demand and therefore inflation adjusting only the interest rate.

NOTES

1. This chapter is part of Project IA302122, 'Metas de inflación, apertura financiera y comercial, las restricciones al crecimiento en México', financed by DGAPA, UNAM.
2. I want to thank to Mariana Escobar Medina for her help in the construction of this chapter.
3. Complementarily, it could be seen as the time when all suppliers are paid.
4. An example happened during the COVID-19 crisis while on confinement in 2020, not only did the investment not grow, but there were some divestments in certain sectors of the economy (such as semiconductors), which reduced this potential product, causing that, during reactivation in 2021, demand will grow faster than supply.
5. See Banxico Press Release of April 21, 2020.
6. See Banks has 1.4 billion, but Mexicans demand less credits (forbes.com.mx) accessed August 18, 2021.

REFERENCES

Arestis, P. and M. Sawyer (2014), 'On the sustainability of budget deficits and public debts with reference to the UK'. In P. Arestis and M. Sawyer (ed.), *Fiscal and Debt Policies for the Future* (pp. 38–75). London: Palgrave Macmillan.

Banxico (1993), *Ley del Banco de México*. México: DOF.

Bernanke, B. and M. Gertler (1995), 'Inside the black box: The credit channel of Monetary Policy Transmission'. *Journal of Economic Perspectives*, 9(1), 27–48.

Caballero, E. and J. López (2013), 'Demanda efectiva y distribución del ingreso en la evolución reciente de la economía mexicana'. *Investigación económica*, 72(285), 141–163.

Carlin, W. and D. Soskice (2006), *Macroeconomics: Imperfections, Institutions, and Policies*. Oxford, UK: Oxford University Press.

Christiano, L., M. Eichenbaum and C. Evans (1999), 'Monetary policy shocks: What have we learned and to what end?' In J. Taylor and H. Uhlig (ed.), *Handbook of Macroeconomics*, (pp. 65–148). Amsterdam: North Holland.

Creel, J. and Fontana, G. (2010), 'Are the macro econometrics models of the Federal Reserve Board, the Bank of Canada, and the Sveriges Riksbank consistent with the new consensus macroeconomics model?' In G. Fontana, J. McCombie and M. Sawyer (ed.), *Macroeconomics, Finance and Money: Essays in Honour of Philip Arestis*, (pp. 3–18). London: Palgrave Macmillan.

De Cecco, M. (1999), 'The lender of last resort'. *Economic Notes*, 28(1), 1–14.

De Paula, L.F, and F. Ferrari Filho (2010), 'Arestis and Sawyer's criticism on the new consensus macroeconomics: Some issues related to emerging countries'. In G. Fontana, J. McCombie and M. Sawyer (eds), *Macroeconomics, Finance and Money: Essays in Honour of Philip Arestis*, (pp. 19–34). London: Palgrave Macmillan.

Duwicquet, V. and J. Mazier (2012), 'Financial integration and stabilization in a monetary union without or with bank rationing'. In D. Papadimitriou and G. Zezza (eds), *Contributions in Stock-flow Modeling: Essays in Honor of Wynne Godley*. London: Palgrave Macmillan.

Friedman, M. (1968), 'The role of monetary policy'. *The American Economic Review*, 58(1), 1–17.

Galí, J. (1992), 'How well does the IS-LM model fit postwar US data?' *The Quarterly Journal of Economics*, 709–738.

Galí, J. (2008), *Monetary Policy, Inflation and the Business Cycle: An Introduction to the New Keynesian Framework*. Princeton: Princeton University Press.

Godley, W. and M. Lavoie (2007), *Monetary Economics. An Integrated Approach to Credit, Money, Income, Production and Wealth*. New York: Palgrave Macmillan.

González-García, J. and A. Gaytán (2006), 'Structural changes in the transmission mechanism of monetary policy in Mexico: A non-linear VAR approach'. *Banco de Mexico Working Paper 2006–06*.

Kaldor, N. (1980), 'Monetarism and UK monetary policy'. *Cambridge Journal of Economics*, 4(4), 293–318.

Kalecki, M. (1954), *Teoría de la Dinamica Economica. Ensayo sobre los movimientos ciclicos dey a largo plazo de la economía capitalista*. México: Fondo de Cultura Económica.

Kalecki, M. (1983), 'Tres Sistemas'. *Investigación Económica*, 42(166), 19–40.

Keynes, J.M. (1936), *The General Theory of Employment, Interest, and Money*. New York: Harcourt Brace Jovanovich.

Lavoie, M. (2001), 'Kaleckian models of growth in a coherent stock-flow monetary framework: A Kaldorian view'. *Journal of Post Keynesian Economics*, 24(2), 277–311.

Levy, N. (2014), 'Monetary policy and economic growth: The reduction of the interest rate Reference Bank of Mexico'. *Economía Informa*, 387, 21–42.

López, J. and R. Valencia (2015), 'Macroeconomic effects of high interest rate policy: Mexico's experience'. *PSL Quarterly Review*, 68(274), 215–237.

López, J. and R. Valencia (2018), 'Fighting inflation in México: Theory and evidence'. *Journal of Post Keynesian Economics*, 42(9), 1–21.

Noyola, J. (1954), 'El desarrollo eonómicoy la inflación en México y otros países latinoamericanos'. *Materiales de Investigación Económica/Facultad de Economía UNAM*, 67–107.

Panico, C. (1988), 'Marx on the banking sector and the interest rate: Some notes for a discussion'. *Science and Society*, 52(3), 310–325.

Passarella, M.V. (2014), 'Financialization and the monetary circuit: A macro-accounting approach'. *Review of Political Economy*, 26(1), 128–148.

Peersman, G. and F. Smets (2003), 'The monetary transmission mechanism in the euro area: Evidence from VAR analysis'. *Monetary Policy Transmission in the Euro Area*, 36–55.

Reifschneider, D., R. Tetlow and J. Williams (1999), 'Aggregate disturbances, monetary policy, and the macroeconomy: The FRB/US perspective'. *Federal Reserve Bulletin*, 85, 1–19.

Rochon, L-P. (2001), 'Horizontalism: Setting the record straight'. In L-P. Rochon and M. Vernango (eds), *Credit, Interest Rate and Open Economy: Essays in Horizontalism*. Cheltenham, UK and Northampton, MA, USA: Edward Elgar Publishing.

Rochon, L-P. (2019), 'La política monetaria después de la crisis'. In I. Perrotini and J.A. Vázquez (orgs.), *Alternativas de política monetaria en la poscrisis*, (pp. 149–175). México: Facultad de Economía UNAM.

Setterfield, M. (2006), 'Is inflation targeting compatible with Post Keynesian economics?' *Journal of Post Keynesian Economics*, 28(4), 653–671.

Sidaoui, J. and M. Ramos-Francia (2008), 'The monetary transmission mechanism in Mexico: Recent developments'. *BIS Papers*, 35, 363–394.

Sims, C. (1992), 'Interpreting the macroeconomic time series facts: The effects of monetary policy'. *Yale University/Cowles Foundation Discussion Papers 1011*.

Steindl, J. (1976), *Maturity and Stagnation in American Capitalism*. New York: Monthly Review Press.

Taylor, L. (2004), *Reconstructing Macroeconomics: Structuralist Proposals and Critiques of the Mainstream*. Cambridge, MA: Harvard University Press.

Valencia, R., S. Capraro, and S. Ortiz (2020), 'Crecimiento guiado por exportaciones y metas de inflación en México: una apuesta en contra del crecimiento'. *Paradigma Económico*, 12(2), 63–91.

9. Monetary policy in Latin America during the COVID-19 crisis: was this time different?

Luiz Fernando de Paula, Paulo José Saraiva and Mateus Coelho Ferreira

INTRODUCTION

Emerging economies' central banks generally respond to financial and external crises by stemming massive capital outflows. The resulting sharp currency depreciation forced central banks in emerging economies to tighten monetary policy abruptly. For instance, this situation – that is, central banks' orthodox monetary as a response to financial and external crises – occurred during the Asian, Russian and Brazilian crises at the end of the 1990s. However, during the COVID-19 crisis, in general, the central banks of the main Latin American economies reacted somewhat differently, implementing quantitative easing policy, cutting policy rates and introducing some non-conventional monetary policy measures. Some findings indicate the reasons for that behaviour included: (i) the swift qualitative easing by the Fed and other advanced economy central banks calmed global financial conditions; (ii) the cyclical condition of Latin American economies at the time of the COVID-19 shock opened up more space for quantitative easing policy than in other crises; and (iii) the sharp drop in output and inflation that followed the COVID-19 shock compounded depressed business cycle positions and opened up space for quantitative easing policy.

It should be remembered that Latin America was the region of the world most affected economically and socially by the Coronavirus pandemic, largely as a result of its historical structural weakness, its limited fiscal space (as compared with most advanced economies), limited social protection coverage, highly informal labour market and its unequal and heterogeneous productive structure. These factors are fundamental to understanding its countries' difficulties in implementing policies to counter the effects of the pandemic on their economies.

This chapter examines the conventional and non-conventional monetary policy implemented by some major Latin American economies, such as Argentina, Brazil, Chile, Colombia, Mexico and Peru, during the COVID-19 shock, seeking in particular to answer the following questions: was this time different? Did these central banks apply non-conventional monetary policies? If so, what sort of non-conventional polices were implemented and for what purpose? What were the impacts?

The chapter is divided into four sections besides this introduction. The second section describes the main features of non-monetary monetary policy. The third section focuses on the experience of non-conventional monetary policy in the United States during the COVID-19 shock, as the Federal Reserve Bank's (FED's) monetary management is considered the 'benchmark' for non-conventional policies. The fourth section considers monetary policy in Latin American economies during the COVID-19 crisis. The fifth section concludes the chapter.

NON-CONVENTIONAL MONETARY POLICIES: AN INTRODUCTION

During financial economic crises, such as those seen in 2007–2008 and during the Coronavirus pandemic, conventional monetary policies (open market, rediscount and reserve requirements) have been less effective. This is because of, among other things, excessively volatile demand for reserves, extreme liquidity preference on the part of agents (households, firms and banks), a reduction in liquidity loans among depository institutions and the interruption of credit in various segments of the financial market, which limit the ability of the central bank to control long-term interest rates and prevent conventional monetary policies from being transmitted along credit, exchange, asset price and relative price channels (Cecioni et al., 2011).

This situation is aggravated when the short-term interest rate approaches the zero lower bound (liquidity trap). In this case, transmission mechanisms via the interest rate channel lose effectiveness and the central bank loses the ability to reduce long-term interest rate spreads, because it cannot flatten the interest rate maturity structure and risk premiums so as to stimulate aggregate demand and output (Blinder, 2010). As an alternative, non-conventional monetary policies are a set of instruments for central banks to intervene directly in specific financial markets to revert potential recession and asset deflation. These can be subdivided into balance sheet policies and signalling policies. Figure 9.1 shows the main transmission channels for nonconventional monetary policies. Through the signalling channel, the monetary authority communicates information to the public about what monetary policies intend to introduce, whether directed to the long-term interest rate, financial asset purchases, inflation or

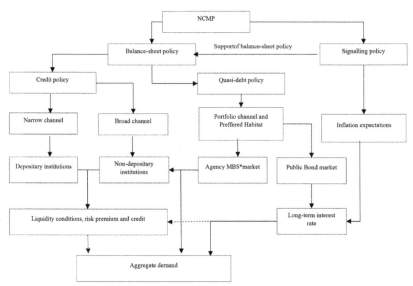

Note: (*) Agency MBS are mortgage-backed securities issued by the government-sponsored enterprises Freddie Mac and Fannie Mae.
Source: Authors' elaboration.

Figure 9.1   Non-conventional monetary policies (NCMP) transmission channels

other measures. Their effectiveness depends on the central bank's credibility and how market expectations and confidence affect financial and macroeconomic conditions. Note that, until the 2007 crisis, it was a widely accepted hypothesis that, in a situation of interest rates close to zero, the central bank would continue to influence long-term rates by way of expectations for the forward interest rate structure and to manage expectations through forward policy guidance (Eggertsson and Woodford, 2003).

Balance-sheet policies (as detailed in Table 9.1), can be subdivided into (i) exchange, (ii) quasi-debt management, and (iii) credit policies.

Table 9.1   Typology of balance sheet policies

		Impact on private sector balance sheet structure		
		Change in net foreign exchange exposures	Change in the composition and maturities composition of securities held by the public sector	Change in profile of private sector securities
Target-market	Exchange	Exchange policy		
	Public debt and securities		Quasi-debt management policy	
	Private credit and securities			Credit policy

Source: Borio and Disyatat (2009).

Each of a central bank's balance sheet policies involves a counterpart for the private sector balance sheet, the main characteristics of which are listed below.

(i)   *Exchange policy* operates directly on the foreign currency market and constitutes direct intermediation by the central bank between the domestic market and foreign sector. These measures improve domestic liquidity conditions and reduce the risk of private sector exposure to abrupt exchange rate variations. The central bank operates on the exchange market, buying and selling foreign currencies, exchange swap contracts etc., in such a way as to reduce the volatility and influence of foreign exchange prices at any given interest rate level.

(ii)   *Quasi-debt management policy* comprises central bank intermediation between the government and the private sector. These measures reduce risk premiums in relation to maturity and liquidity of public securities in private hands, so as to stabilise output. It is operationalised by purchasing public securities. Note that these assets are an important reference point for the market in that they correspond to a benchmark risk-free rate and, accordingly, affect financing costs and asset prices in general. For such policies to be effective normally requires purchases in substantial volume in order to produce any effect on asset yields.

(iii)   *Credit policy* acts on specific segments of the financial market (the interbank and non-bank markets), to alter the composition of the private sector balance sheet and so affect financing conditions. The operations performed by the central bank, which impact private debt and securities and alter balance sheets, are carried out in various manners, such as by alterations to collateral and maturities, counterparty terms on monetary operations, lending or private sector asset purchases. The objective is to relieve tensions on the interbank market, particularly maturities and spreads, and to improve conditions of credit to the non-bank sector. Such policies can produce indirect effects, in that the market on which they act plays an important financial intermediation role. Note also that these measures are applied directly to financial intermediaries, indirectly suggesting overall improvements to the market, by virtue of the role these institutions play. On specific markets, however, the central bank performs direct intermediation operations, without the participation of depository institutions, placing itself between investors and borrowers.

The theory underpinning non-conventional monetary policy can be divided into two groups. The first focuses on the effects of monetary policy on asset prices and imperfect substitutability on the asset side of the private sector balance sheet, and is referred to as the 'portfolio balance channel'. The central bank's purchasing of private sector portfolio assets, normally public and government agency securities, alters supply on these markets, leading to a more equitable redistribution of these securities' relative yields and maturities. For instance, the technical sources of reference here are Tobin (1969), Ando and Modigliani (1963) and Modigliani and Sutch (1966).

The second group emphasises imperfect substitutability on the liability side of the private sector balance sheet and is normally referred to as the 'credit channel'. In these operations, the central bank meets the need for loans directly, besides offering more attractive conditions (interest rates and maturities), with a view to improving financing conditions on the market, inducing credit expansion and raising asset prices. The main source authors here are Bernanke and Blinder (1989) and Bernanke and Gertler (1995).

NON-CONVENTIONAL MONETARY POLICY IN THE UNITED STATES

The rapid slowing of the USA economy due to the impact of the pandemic crisis was met by monetary and fiscal policy measures, particularly over the course of 2020, although they continued into 2021. Quickly recovering part of its arsenal of non-conventional monetary policies deployed during the 2007–2008 crisis, the FED, in cooperation with the Treasury, introduced new facilities to support the flow of credit to households and businesses, at the same time as fiscal measures were raised to new levels. FED Chair Jerome Powell (2020), in his Press Conference on April 29, 2020, made it clear how the FED intended to meet the COVID-19 crisis: "We are deploying these lending powers to an unprecedented extent [and …] will continue to use these powers forcefully, proactively, and aggressively until we are confident that we are solidly on the road to recovery".

Notwithstanding its powerful non-conventional monetary policy arsenal and it performing better than other advanced economies, the USA saw GDP shrink by 3.5 percent in 2020. On the labour market, over 20 million were unemployed, and in May 2020, unemployment stood at 14.7 percent, closing the year at 6.7 percent. On the financial market, in March 2020, the exchange swap spread of the dollar to other leading currencies (euro, yen, etc.) widened, as did spreads of corporate securities to what were considered zero-risk Treasury bonds.

Similarly on the stock market, the S&P500 dropped abruptly by 35 percent in just one month after 21 January 2020 and then rose strongly from then on, gaining 75 percent in just one year. That outcome indicated a certain confidence that the US economy would recover as a result both of the countercyclical measures introduced, including non-conventional monetary policies, and the return to normality of productive activities in the economy. One indicator was the 5.9 percent GDP growth forecast for 2021 (The Conference Board Economic Forecast, 2021).

The monetary policies introduced can be subdivided into conventional and non-conventional policies. As regards the former, from March 2020 the FED reduced the interest base rate (policy rate) by 50 base points on March 3, and on March 16 by a further 100 base points, to a range between 0.0 percent to 0.25 percent p.a. (Figure 9.2). The rate's return to zero marks the close of the conventional monetary policy management cycle.

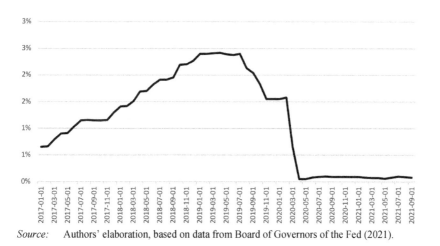

Source: Authors' elaboration, based on data from Board of Governors of the Fed (2021).

Figure 9.2   *Target interest rate for FED Funds – 2017–2021 (%)*

One of the FED's first non-conventional monetary policy measures was quantitative easing (QE), which became the main facility. Over the course of 2020 and by mid-2021, purchases of Treasury bonds had increased by just over US$2.9 trillion and, of mortgage-backed securities,[1] by approximately US$1.1 trillion. These measures contributed to a surge in central bank assets from US$4.3 trillion in March 2020 to US$8.5 trillion in September 2021, as Figure 9.3 shows.

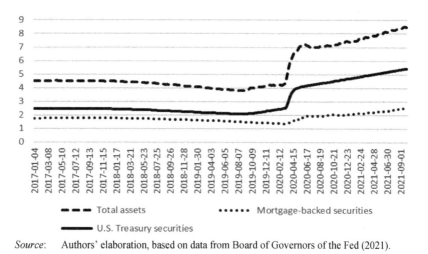

Source: Authors' elaboration, based on data from Board of Governors of the Fed (2021).

Figure 9.3   Quantitative easing, 2017–2021 (US$ trillion)

The first credit policy measure taken reintroduced the Commercial Paper Funding Facility (CPFF). Just as in 2007–2008, this facility was designed to ensure that companies could obtain funding for their payroll and financial liabilities, given that the credit market was paralysed. Another key purpose of that programme was to guarantee liquidity for papers traded on that market, reinforcing the secondary market. The amount earmarked for this programme was US$12.8 billion, more than 95 percent of which was Treasury capital managed by the FED. The programme was concluded on 31 March 2021.

A second credit policy, also revived from the previous crisis, was the Primary Dealer Credit Facility (PDCF). This programme was similar to a rediscount, facilitating overnight operations, which indirectly bolster the markets in credit to non-financial companies and households by providing liquidity to lenders. The FED thus offered loans to primary dealers with up to 90 days maturity at the overnight interest rate. The total financed by the FED was US$37.3 billion.

The FED's concern with Money Market Mutual Fund Liquidity Facility (MMLF) has to do with the fact that these money market funds, where the main investors are households and small businesses, feature high liquidity ('near money'). In order to prevent these funds from failing, as they do not have access to the 'discount window' available to depository institutions, the monetary authority launched a programme, jointly with the Treasury, to help meet investor demand for withdrawals and minimise losses, as well as to forestall the paralysis of this important market. The total amount involved was US$54 billion.

With a view to reinforcing consumer and corporate credit, on 23 March the FED and Treasury Secretary re-launched the Term Asset-Backed Securities Loan Facility (TALF). This programme enabled asset-backed securities to be issued, providing they were AAA rated. However, these measures were backed by the following assets: student loans, auto loans, credit card loans, loans guaranteed by the Small Business Administration (SBA), and certain other assets. The total provision for this facility was US$4.1 billion.

The Primary Market Corporate Credit Facility (PMCCF) was a new credit policy, especially developed for the COVID-19 crisis and designed to support issues of bonds and loans on the primary market to investment-grade non-financial companies. Initially developed for a four-year period, it operated jointly with the Secondary Market Corporate Credit Facility (SMCCF), which provided liquidity to the secondary market in corporate bonds, including on the stock exchange. The two programmes were launched on 23 March 2020, jointly representing US$800 billion in FED and Treasury Secretary funds, of which only US$70 billion was disbursed.

The Pay Check Protection Program Liquidity Facility (PPPLF) was put in place to bolster the Pay Check Protection Program (PCPP) by providing liquidity to participating financial institutions. Note that the main facility, the PCPP, is a programme not developed by the FED, but administered by the Small Business Administration (SBA), which received US$376 billion from the Treasury under the "CARES Act".[2] The main goal of the programme was to support small businesses and workers, and was developed particularly to protect employment by way of term loans.

The Municipal Liquidity Facility (MLF) represented support for state governments, counties with resident populations of more than 500,000 and towns with resident populations of more than 250,000. With support from the Treasury, the FED offered funds to support cash flow and also measures for companies and households.

This programme was allocated US$6.4 billion in all, with Eligible Notes[3] as collateral, and could include anticipation of taxes, revenues and bonds with maturities of no more than 36 months.

The Main Street Lending Program (MSLP) was established to support lending to small and medium-sized businesses that were in sound financial condition before the onset of the COVID-19 crisis. These gained access to loans with maturity of five years, deferral of principal payments for two years, and deferral of interest payments for one year. The programme executed US$16.4 billion. Five facilities were set up: the Main Street New Loan Facility (MSNLF), the Main Street Priority Loan Facility (MSPLF), the Main Street Expanded Loan Facility (MSELF), the Non-Profit Organization New Loan Facility (NONLF), and the Non-Profit Organization Expanded Loan Facility (NOELF).

Figure 9.4 shows the set of credit policies for the period from 2020 to mid-2021. The new facilities (PMCCF/SMCCF, PPLF, MLF and MSLP) stand out, totalling around 50 percent of the FED's operations. Of those originating with the 2007–2008 crisis, the MMLF and PDCF are of particular note.

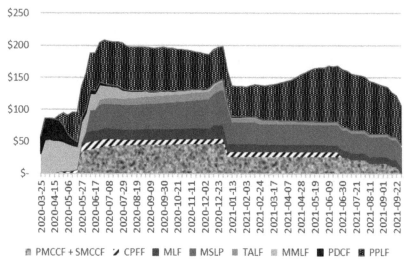

Source: Authors' elaboration, based on data from Board of Governors of the Fed (2021).

Figure 9.4   *Credit policies, March 2020 to September 2021 (US$ billion)*

Lastly, central bank liquidity swaps comprised permanent and temporary agreements between the FED and other central banks to establish US dollar exchange swaps to assure international liquidity. Exchange swap contracts expanded from US$18 billion in late February 2020 to US$448 billion by May.

MONETARY POLICY IN LATIN AMERICA DURING THE COVID-19 CRISIS

The COVID-19 Crisis in Latin America

The COVID-19 crisis hit the world economy hard, given the high degree of uncertainty as to the dynamics and evolution of the pandemic. International trade was badly shaken and commodity prices and capital flows fluctuated intensely, generating high levels of volatility on financial markets. In that context, the advanced economies implemented monetary and fiscal packages of unprecedented magnitudes, which produced high levels of liquidity at the global level in 2020 and 2021.

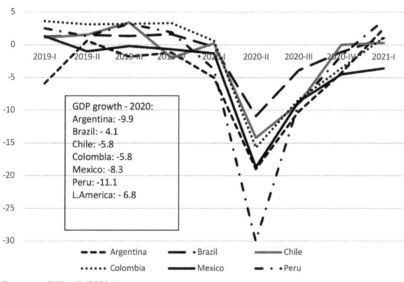

GDP growth - 2020:
Argentina: -9.9
Brazil: - 4.1
Chile: -5.8
Colombia: -5.8
Mexico: -8.3
Peru: -11.1
L.America: - 6.8

Source: ECLAC (2021a).

Figure 9.5   Year-on-year growth rates in GDP of the major Latin American economies

Latin America was the region of the world most affected economically and socially by the Coronavirus pandemic, largely as a result of its historical struc-tural weaknesses, limited fiscal space, limited social coverage, highly informal labour, and heterogeneous and unequal productive structure. These factors are fundamental to understanding the region's difficulties in implementing policies to counter the effects of the pandemic on the countries' economies and produce sustainable and socially inclusive economic recovery (ECLAC, 2021a).

As shown in Figure 9.5, all the major Latin American economies were abruptly shaken by the Coronavirus crisis, the worst affected in 2020 being Peru (–11.1 percent in real GDP), Argentina (GDP dropped 9.9 percent) and Mexico (GDP was –8.3 percent), with any recovery in 2021 resulting more from the statistical effect of the prior year's acute contraction. Particularly in 2020, negative GDP growth in Latin America overall (–7.0 percent) was far greater than the average for the advanced economies (–4.5 percent) and the emerging economies (–2.1 percent) (IMF, 2021).

This downturn in economic activity caused a strong rise in unemployment rates across Latin America in 2020 (averaging 10.5 percent) – most markedly in Colombia (15.1 percent), Brazil (13.5 percent) and Argentina (11.5 percent) – a marked drop in labour force participation and considerable increases in poverty and inequality, worsening the region's structural problems (Figure 9.6). Vulnerable groups, particularly informal workers, young people, workers with little education, women and immigrants, were the worst harmed by loss of work (ECLAC, 2021a).

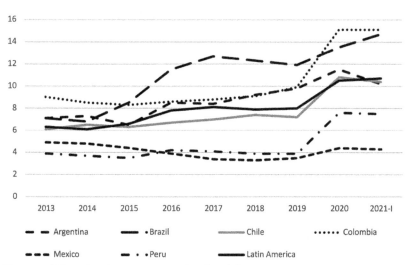

Note: * Unemployed as a percentage of total work force.
Source: ECLAC (2021a).

*Figure 9.6   Unemployment in the major Latin American economies**

It is important to emphasise that the instability of the international financial market resulting from the pandemic, combined with uncertainty on commodities markets, led first to strong exchange devaluation in response to capital flight. This has now been followed ever since by intense exchange rate volatility. The central banks of Brazil, Chile, Colombia and Mexico expanded the scope of their interventions in the exchange market, using a series of instruments, including futures contracts and exchange swaps, to provide liquidity to this market. Many Latin American countries also used monetary agreements with the International Monetary Fund (IMF) and FED to open up contingent credit lines with a view to reinforcing their exchange reserves.

Despite strong exchange devaluation at the onset of the Coronavirus pandemic, inflation in 2020 remained at its historically low levels as a result of the acute contraction of aggregate domestic demand, which reached an average accumulated rate of 3.0 percent in the 12 months to December 2020. In 2021, however, inflationary pressures on the cost side, particularly prices of food, energy and other production inputs, in addition to greater exchange volatility, led to an overall tendency for inflation rates to rise, most adversely in Brazil (8.3 percent) and Mexico (5.9 percent), to an accumulated average of 5.4 percent in the region in June 2021 (ECLAC, 2021a).

It was in this context of economic downturn and falling inflation in 2020 that many Latin American central banks deployed their conventional and non-conventional monetary policies so as to avert a liquidity crisis in the banking sector, any sharp fall in financial asset prices and contraction of credit supply, with a view to stimulating economic activity overall. In particular, many central banks used non-conventional instruments, which included purchasing securities held by banks, setting up financing programmes (jointly with the Treasury) for households and firms and even, in some cases, financing governments directly (ECLAC, 2021b). This subject will be discussed in the next sub-section.

Non-conventional Monetary Policy in Latin America during the COVID-19 Crisis

In the recent literature (Aguilar and Cantú, 2020; Arslan et al., 2020; ECLAC, 2020; Server et al., 2020), the monetary and fiscal policy responses by emerging countries (including Latin America) to the COVID-19 crisis in early 2020 are being regarded as an advance over the implementation of countercyclical macroeconomic policies in the Great Recession of 2008, particularly as regards preserving levels of income and employment in a global crisis. This shift in economic policy postures was crucial in support of measures to restrict population mobility, such as lockdown and social distancing, which were necessary to contain the advance of the Coronavirus and ensure health systems had capacity to meet demand for beds, to provide care for those infected. These measures paralysed various sectors of the economy, except those considered essential. The scenario caused by the pandemic called for an effective fiscal and monetary policy response in order to prevent a more precipitous fall in incomes. There was a consensus that these policies were necessary to avert a probable financial crisis due to erosion of company cash flows and mounting default on the part of households as a result of the economic crisis triggered by the Coronavirus pandemic.

In fiscal policy, the measures introduced in Latin America consisted mainly of deferring payment of income and value added taxes (in some cases, reaching 1 percent of GDP) and in increasing the share of direct cash transfers to households, sub-national units and also to companies to enable them to maintain their employees for specific periods. ECLAC (2021a, p. 84) reported:

> primary expenditure – which excludes interest payments – has grown significantly, with real increases above 10% in several countries (and more than 20% in some cases) in January–September 2020 relative to the same period in the 2019. This growth is largely explained by higher spending on current transfers (subsidies, retirement and other pensions, and social benefits, among other items), which influence the level of disposable income and thus consumption by families and businesses.

Considered against historical patterns, this level of public spending was significant, even though much lower than in the advanced countries (ECLAC, 2021b). Note that the scenario of slow economic growth prior to the pandemic and Latin American countries having higher public debt/GDP ratios than those of other emerging countries did not significantly hamper fiscal expansion in the period. The public debt/GDP ratio rose an average of 7.4 percent in the region between year-end 2019 and September 2020, to higher levels in Brazil (14.8 percent), Colombia (12.5 percent) and Paraguay (8.0 percent) (ECLAC, 2021a, p. 90). As a result, greater coordination with monetary policy was required in order to reduce this fiscal cost to the Treasury, as well as to prevent higher exchange risk from public debt denominated in foreign currency, especially for countries such as Argentina, Paraguay, Uruguay and Venezuela, where this represented around 80 percent of their total public debt.

The monetary policy response to the COVID-19 crisis was to introduce greater flexibility to traditional interest-rate based monetary policy, despite a movement towards capital flight: "In the first ten months of 2020, the domestic currencies of 17 of the region's economies lost value against the dollar relative to their end-2019 exchange rate, recording an average depreciation of 16.3%" (ECLAC, 2021a, p. 98). Most Latin American countries reduced interest rates during the period, even to levels close to the zero lower bound. In Brazil, for instance, the interest rate was brought down to levels around 2 percent at year-end 2020, while Peru set even lower levels (0.25 percent) (ECLAC, 2021a, p. 93). The average reduction for the region was considerable against historical patterns: 2.05 percent in 2020, with Mexico and Paraguay introducing cumulative reductions of 3.0 percent and 3.25 percent, respectively, over the course of the year (ECLAC, 2021a, p. 94). Venezuela was the only country in the region to apply a restrictive policy during 2020, but there the scenario prioritised combating hyperinflation (ECLAC, 2020).

During the Great Recession, the overall trend in the emerging economies, including Latin America, was for the base interest rate to be raised to offset the movement towards capital outflows and its adverse effects on the economy caused by exchange devaluation (Aguilar and Cantú, 2020). In that period, the region's central bank aimed to avoid raising inflationary expectations and missing inflation targets as a result of a supply shock under the pass-through effect of import prices on production costs. Another key concern was to avoid increasing systemic risk to economic agents' balance sheets denominated in foreign currency. Arslan et al. (2020) explained that this response to the COVID-19 crisis constituted a paradigm shift for emerging country central banks in that it made it possible to address what is known as the 'fear of floating'[4] (Calvo and Reinhart, 2002).

Figure 9.7 lists the monetary policy interest rates of Latin American countries that set inflation targets between 2007 and 2021.

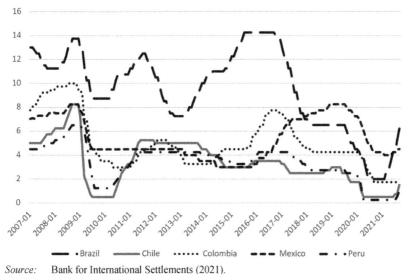

Source: Bank for International Settlements (2021).

Figure 9.7   *Policy rate (%), Selected Latin American countries, 2007–2021*

Aguilar and Cantú (2020, p. 1) offer some reasons why this space opened up for countercyclical policies during the COVID-19 crisis. As most emerging countries posted GDP growth below potential, there thus existed a negative gap, which enabled aggregate demand to expand without causing immediate inflationary pressures. They had also introduced structural changes that expanded anchorage of inflationary expectations and helped them administer inflation target regimes, also reducing their exchange risks by maintaining larger portions of their long-term debt denominated in local currency, combined with significant build-up of international reserves. Another point was the support derived from the speed with which advanced economies' central banks implemented their non-conventional monetary policies, leaving ample leeway for maintaining liquidity available to emerging countries at the outset of the COVID-19 crisis and reducing the pressure expected from non-resident outflows from their financial markets. Another reason was the complementary measures implemented by central banks and governments, such as lowering of reserve requirements, more active intervention in the exchange market, capital controls, specific policies on credit for the private sector and strengthening of macro-prudential regulatory measures (ECLAC, 2021b). Aguilar and Cantú (2020, p. 4) argue that:

> In addition to cutting rates, EME central banks implemented domestic lending operations and funding facilities to reduce illiquidity risks. They established direct lending to private sector to ease financing conditions and intervened in FX markets to reduce currency volatility. Together with supervisory authorities, they eased prudential regulations to increase banks' capacity to lend.

As already highlighted, the FED once again opened up its exchange swap line broadly for Latin American countries at the start of the COVID-19 crisis.[5] Thus,

> These two factors made a coordinated policy response between fiscal and monetary authorities in most EMEs possible – even with limited fiscal space. So far, monetary and fiscal policy easing have complemented each other in supporting the flow of credit and aggregate demand. (Aguilar and Cantú, 2020, p. 1)

However, the most significant change in monetary policy in emerging countries was the introduction of non-conventional monetary policies during the COVID-19 crisis – an avenue not explored in response to the previous global crisis. Arslan et al. (2020) explain that most of these measures were carried out by way of asset purchases by central banks on the long-term public and private securities markets, either by 'Operation Twist' methods or by quantitative easing. Some countries, Brazil among them, had to modify their legislation in order to purchase securities on the secondary market. The Central Bank of Colombia announced bank and public securities purchases of around 0.8 percent of GDP, while in Chile, the amount was 2.8 percent of GDP in private bank securities alone (Arslan et al., 2020, p. 2). The monetary base of countries operating inflation target regimes expanded by an average of 7.4 percent in the first three quarters of 2019, but by 19.7 percent in the same three quarters of 2020 (ECLAC, 2021a, p. 95). To a lesser extent, other non-conventional monetary policies were used, such as forward guidance, consisting of the central banks announcing that, for a certain period, they would hold monetary policy at a constant interest rate or to some specific condition, so as to affect market expectations for the long-term interest rate curve (Campbell et al., 2012). The Central Bank of Brazil (BCB) opted for a policy of this type between August 2020 and March 2021 (BCB, 2021).

At the time of writing, there appear to be no broad empirical studies of the outcome of non-conventional monetary policies in Latin America. However, empirical study findings in the literature do show non-conventional monetary policies to have had significant positive impact in affording emerging countries greater economic policy space, if less so than to the advanced countries. Sever et al. (2020), using an impulse response and local projections method on high-frequency daily data for purchases of long-term public and private securities, demonstrated that, close to the dates of the central banks' announcements, these measures led to reductions of up to 25 base points in these securities' yields. Arslan et al. (2020) reported similar findings, noting that this impact may vary among emerging countries, depending on the starting conditions. Neither of these studies found any significant or persistent effect on exchange rates. Accordingly, Arslan et al. (2020, p. 6) wrote:

> The absence of such effects probably reflects the clearly defined scope of the programmes, which explicitly aimed at restoring confidence in markets rather than at providing monetary stimulus, let alone the monetary financing of fiscal deficits. That said, by serving to contain the rise in bond yields, the measures also provided useful support to EME economies during the pandemic shock.

Lastly, BCB (2021) identified a significant negative effect of the forward guidance announcement on yields from public securities with two-year maturities. Table 9.2 summarises the distribution of non-conventional monetary policies introduced in some Latin American countries, such as the purchase of public and private securities from financial institutions, public sector credit co-financing programmes and direct financing by central banks of public sector expenditure.

Table 9.2   *Non-conventional monetary policies in Latin America during the COVID-19 crisis*

	Economies with inflation targeting	Economies controlling monetary aggregates		Economies with other arrangements
Exchange type	Flexible	Flexible	Intermediate	
Central banks that announced purchases of public and private securities from financial institutions	Brazil, Chile, Colombia, Paraguay, Mexico and Peru	Argentina and Uruguay	Bolivia	
Central banks co-financing public sector credit programmes	Brazil, Chile, Colombia, Paraguay, Mexico and Peru		Bolivia	
Central banks financing the public sector directly	Paraguay	Bolivia		Venezuela

Source: Adapted from ECLAC (2020, p. 137).

CONCLUSION

The rationale offered by emerging countries, including Latin America, for applying non-conventional monetary policy was that such policies were necessary to correct any possible dysfunctions and assure liquidity on the public and private securities market, so as to restore international investor confidence by their central banks' acting as buyers and sellers of last resort (Aguilar and Cantú, 2020; Arslan et al., 2020). It is to be emphasised that this pattern of rationale was expressed by most Latin American countries (ECLAC, 2020). Thus, these countries' non-conventional monetary policies were considered quantitatively more modest and temporary and designed not to interfere in price formation by the private market. In Latin America, the region most affected economically and socially by the Coronavirus pandemic, the productive and social heterogeneity typical of the region, plus its structural weaknesses, hindered the implementation of more robust countercyclical policies, among them non-conventional monetary policies.

In any case, over and beyond these significant differences in how non-conventional monetary policies were conducted, emerging countries can be seen to have shifted from their conventional policy posture when the economy reopened and after the persistent external shocks on the exchange market, with some countries – contrasting with the resilience of advanced countries – rapidly raising their interest rate levels over the course of 2021 in order to respond to rising inflationary expectations. The most emblematic case in Latin America was Brazil's central bank, which started 2021 with a short-term interest rate (policy rate) at its historical minimum of 2 percent, but raised the rate to pre-pandemic levels over the course of the year. That abrupt change may undermine economic recovery after the pandemic and seems to indicate that, despite the advances during the COVID-19 crisis, Latin American countries have a long way to go in conducting economic policy in such a way as to support sustainable economic growth with greater social equity.

NOTES

1. Mortgage-backed security is a type of asset-backed security, which is secured by a mortgage or collection of mortgages.
2. Coronavirus Aid, Relief, and Economic Security (CARES).
3. "Eligible notes are tax anticipation notes (TANs), tax and revenue anticipation notes (TRANs), bond anticipation notes (BANs), revenue anticipation notes (RANs), and other similar short-term notes issued by Eligible Issuers, provided that such notes mature no later than 36 months from the date of issuance." (Federal Reserve, 2020).
4. Fear of floating is said to exist when a country officially adopts a floating exchange rate regime, but in practice the central bank intervenes in foreign exchange markets to avoid currency volatility.
5. ECLAC (2021a, p. 101) reported: "The capacity of the region's monetary authorities to protect their currencies in 2020 has been strengthened by the agreements reached by a number of Latin American central banks with the International Monetary Fund (IMF) and the United States Federal Reserve System."

REFERENCES

Aguilar, A. and C. Cantú (2020), "Monetary policy response in emerging market economies: Why was it different this time?" Basel: Bank for International Settlements, *BIS Bulletin* no. 32.

Ando, A. and F. Modigliani (1963), "The 'life cycle' hypothesis of saving: Aggregate implications and tests". *American Economic Review*, 53(1), 55–84.

Arslan, Y., M. Drehmann, and B. Hofmann (2020), "Central bank purchases in emerging market economies". Basel: Bank for International Settlements, *BIS Bulletin* no. 20.

Bank for International Settlements (2021), Available at https://www.bis.org/statistics/cbpol.htm?m=6_382_679. Accessed 20 October 2021.

Bernanke, B. and A. Blinder (1989), "Credit, money and aggregate demand". *American Economic Review*, 78(2), 435–439.

Bernanke, B. and M. Gertler (1995), "Inside the black box: The credit channel of monetary policy transmission". *Journal of Economic Perspectives*, 9(4), 27–48.

Blinder, A. (2010), "Quantitative easing: Entrance and exit strategies". *CEPS Working Paper, no 204*. Brussels: Centre for European Policy Studies.

Board of Governors of the Fed (2021), Available at https://www.federalreserve.gov/data.htm. Accessed October 19, 2021.

Borio, C. and P. Disyatat (2009), "Unconventional monetary policies: An appraisal". *BIS Working Paper 292*, November.

Calvo, G. and C. Reinhart (2002), "Fear of floating". *Quarterly Journal of Economics*, 117(2), 379–408.

Campbell, J.R., C.L. Evans, J.D.M. Fisher and A. Justinian (2012), "Macroeconomic effects of federal reserve forward guidance". *Brookings Papers on Economic Activity*, 42(1), 1–80.

Cecioni, M., G. Ferrero and A. Secchi (2011), "Unconventional monetary policy in theory and in practice". *Bank of Italy, Economic Outlook and Monetary Policy Research Department*, September.

Central Bank of Brazil (BCB) (2021), "Estimação dos efeitos de *forward guidance* na curva de juros". Brasília: Banco Central do Brasil, *Estudo Especial* no. 101.

ECLAC (Economic Commission for Latin America and the Caribbean) (2020), *Economic Survey of Latin America and the Caribbean, 2020* (LC/PUB.2020/12-P), Santiago.

ECLAC (Economic Commission for Latin America and the Caribbean) (2021a), *Preliminary Overview of the Economies of Latin America and the Caribbean, 2020* (LC/PUB.2020/17-P/Rev.1), Santiago.

ECLAC (Economic Commission for Latin America and the Caribbean) (2021b), *Economic Survey of Latin America and the Caribbean, 2021* (LC/PUB.2021/10-P/Rev.1), Santiago.

Eggertsson, G. and M. Woodford (2003), "The zero bound on interest rates and optimal monetary policy". *Brookings Papers on Economic Activity*, 34, 139–211.

Federal Reserve (2020), "Municipal liquidity facility". Available at https://www.federalreserve.gov/newsevents/pressreleases/files/monetary20200409a3.pdf. Accessed October 21.

IMF (International Monetary Fund) (2021), *World Economic Outlook, October 2021*. Available at https://www.imf.org/en/Publications/WEO/Issues/2021/10/12/world-economic-outlook-october-2021. Accessed October 15, 2021.

Modigliani, F. and R. Sutch (1966), "Innovations in interest-rate policy". *American Economic Review*, 56(1), 178–197.

Powell, A. (2020), Transcript of Chair Powell's Press Conference, Available at https://www.federalreserve.gov/mediacenter/files/FOMCpresconf20200429.pdf. Accessed 20 October 2021.

Sever, C., R. Goel, D. Drakopoulos and E. Papageorgiu (2020), "Effects of emerging market asset purchase program announcements on financial markets during the Covid-19 pandemic". *IMF Working Paper* no. 292, December.

The Conference Board Economic Forecast (2021), Available at https://www.conference-board.org/research/us-forecastacessado. Accessed October 2021.

Tobin, J. (1969), "A general equilibrium approach to monetary theory". *Journal of Money Credit, and Banking*, 1(1), 15–29.

10. The Central Bank of Brazil in the face of the COVID-19 economic crisis

Isabela Andrade do Carmo and Fábio Henrique Bittes Terra

INTRODUCTION

The Coronavirus crisis reached global dimension fast. At the beginning of 2020, just after the pandemic was declared by the United Nations World Health Organization, the World Bank said that developing and emerging countries would be affected through three channels: (1) supply restrictions, because production stopped due to social distancing and lockdowns; (2) a fall in trade terms because of diminishing prices of commodities; and (3) a liquidity shortfall owing to liquidity preference of investors. Following (3), the intense reflux of capital from developing and emerging markets resulted in higher interest rates for external borrowing, depreciated exchange rate and higher costs of imported inputs. Moreover, these two last factors would result in higher inflation (World Bank, 2021) – this is actually happening; for instance, in Brazil the Consumer Price Index amounted 10 percent in October 2021.

In this critical scenario, countries quickly adopted fiscal and monetary measures to mitigate the impacts of the COVID-19 economic crisis. In Brazil, these impacts appeared in the first quarter of 2020, with a GDP fall of 1.5 percent. In 2020, the country's GDP fell 4.4 percent, unemployment rose from 12 percent to almost 15 percent, poverty grew, the exchange rate depreciated more than 20 percent, and inflation was above its target in both 2020 and 2021.

In particular, the Central Bank of Brazil (CBB) had an important role, and for the first time in history it was allowed to undertake a wide range of unconventional monetary policies, including large-scale asset purchase and quasi-debt public debt management. These measures sought to stabilize the financial markets so that they kept financing economic activity. Unconventional monetary policy was first undertaken in the 2008 crisis and, since then, it has been somehow managed, but the CBB kept following the conventional path of only using the policy rate as the main tool. However, so great was the COVID-19 economic crisis that more than just the conventional was needed in Brazil too.

Considering this, this chapter presents and analyses the monetary policy of the CBB during the COVID-19 economic crisis – that is, from the first quarter of 2020 to the end of 2020. In 2021 the CBB did not renew most of the unconventional measures and even started a restrictive monetary policy, trying to confront a nearly 10 percent consumer inflation.

This chapter has six sections. After this introduction, there is a short analysis of the Brazilian economy in 2020 to show the economic consequences of the COVID-19 pandemic. The third section describes the conventional monetary policy of central banks whereas the fourth section reviews the unconventional monetary policy. The fifth section recalls and summarizes the actions of the CBB against the COVID-19 economic crisis. The final section concludes.

THE ECONOMIC CONSEQUENCES OF COVID-19 IN BRAZIL

The social distancing required to contain the contagious virus interrupted supply chains and stopped economic activity worldwide. To the World Bank (2021), the economic impact of the pandemic is the greatest global event since World War II. The recovery of economic activity in some economies that dealt well with the virus, such as China, Japan, Korea, Germany and some others, has been faster than expected; still, the recovery is heterogeneous and faces challenges such as high unemployment, rising energy prices, scant supply of inputs produced by the manufacturing industry, and the global disorganization of transport logistics.

World Bank (2021) shows that the world GDP fell nearly 3.5 percent in 2020, a softer decrease when compared with the –4.9 percent estimated by the IMF (2020) in October 2020. Whereas the IMF (2020) expected –5.8 percent in Brazil in October 2020, the country also surpassed expectations and GDP dropped – 4.4 percent in 2020. This lower decrease of the Brazilian GDP was due to the measures the Government undertook to confront the COVID-19 crisis, including those monetary ones that are the object of this chapter.

The pandemic in Brazil started with strong effects on the main economic aggregates, with some reaching their worst level or variation ever. The CBB's monthly indicator of economic activity went down 12.7 percent in April 2020 over March 2020 whereas, if compared on a year-on-year basis, the decrease was 14.7 percent. The April to June GDP was down 9.7 percent. Household consumption, gross formation of fixed capital, commerce, and services dropped 13.5 percent, 15.2 percent, 14.1 percent and 11.1 percent, respectively, in comparison with the same quarter of 2019.

Some sectors showed some improvement in the second semester of 2020. Industrial activity grew 2.6 percent in September 2020 over August 2020. The manufacturing industry grew more than the whole industry in this period: 3.9

percent. In the year-on-year comparison, industry went down 3.4 percent in September, a smaller decrease when compared with April and May 2020, 21.8 percent and 27.6 percent, respectively. Data of the aggregate economic activity shows that after the minimal low in April, it grew 1.9 percent in October. In turn, GDP data shows a recovery in the third quarter: 7.7 percent growth after a fall of 9.7 percent in the second quarter.

Although some sectors and the aggregate GDP reported improvement from the third semester on, the recovery is heterogeneous between economic sectors; for example, services as well as the labor market did not improve in 2020. Unemployment went from 11.9 percent in December 2019 to 14.6 percent in the third quarter of 2020, improving a little in the last quarter of the year, but ending 2020 in 13.5 percent, with an annual average of 13.5 percent.

The Brazilian National Treasury and CBB's countercyclical measures, such as the emergency income, postponement of taxes, measures to assist firms, etc., helped the Brazilian financial system to end the first semester of 2020 in the same position as at the end of 2019. The set of liquid assets held by the biggest banks[1] of the country was R$420 billion in June 2020, significantly higher than the R$206 billion of December 2019 (CBB, 2020a).

The Liquidity Index of the banking system had its lowest level (1.95) in March 2020, which was the worst moment of the crisis for the financial system. However, the CBB measures to furnish liquidity had good results and by June the Liquidity Index was 2.43, while the Index's average over 2015–2019 was 2.17.

The Liquidity Coverage Ratio (an Index that estimates the short-term liquidity of financial institutions) resembled that of the Liquidity Index. It ended the first semester of 2020 at 237 percent (CBB, 2020a) well above the minimum mandatory level of 100 percent. The long-term liquidity presented a similar trend, although it fewer fluctuations when compared with the Liquidity Coverage Ratio and the Liquidity Index. The Structural Liquidity Index ended the first semester of 2020 at 1.17, after being 1.12 in March – the 5-year average was 1.11 (CBB, 2020a). The increase in the Structural Index resulted from the more stable deposits that banks started gathering during the crisis.

Although the base Selic rate was at its lowest level ever in 2020, 2 percent per year, crises make financial institutions more risk averse, which results in higher spreads charged on loans. Because of the rising loans granted by government-owned banks, the fall in household borrowing was eased at the beginning of the crisis and, in the first semester of 2020, there was only a small reduction of 0.5 percent in this type of bank loans (although in some specific types of household borrowings the decrease was greater, for instance credit card operations dropped 16.90 percent from January to June 2020).

Loans to firms had another trend in the period. Because of the social distancing and lockdown measures, there was a huge fall in firms' sales, strongly reducing their revenues. Thus, firms demanded bank loans, which rose by 60 percent in March 2020. The aggregate credit in Brazil was raised by 4.3 percent between December 2019 and June 2020. Credit to households rose by 1.2 percent in the period while loans to firms increased by 8.6 percent. In June 2020, one quarter after the commencement of the crisis, the credit furnished to firms expanded by 11.5 percent, especially to micro, small, and medium size businesses, whose borrowings were 14.7 percent bigger that month (CBB, 2020a).

Moreover, credit renegotiation, a measure the CBB stimulated, rose in the first semester of 2020. In April, the renewed credit totaled R$475 billion, a number much larger than the R$67 billion reissued in February 2020. Loans granted to households were the main type of credit renewed.

Other important data of the first semester of 2020, the crisis' acutest period, was the reduction of financial institutions' cost to raise funds (CBB, 2020a). Three reasons explain that: (1) the reduction of the Selic rate; (2) the credit renegotiation program, which reduced credit default and consequently avoided higher spreads; and (3) all the measures the CBB undertook to avoid banks restricting credit.

Inflation has been in a dubious trend. Throughout 2020 it behaved well, with deflation in April and May. However, because of the impacts of the exchange rate depreciation and the rising prices of commodities, the Brazilian main consumer price index, called IPCA, finished 2020 at 4.52 percent, a bit above the target but still within the superior margin of the inflation target (the aim was 3.75 percent and the range 2.5 percent to 5.5 percent). In 2021 the situation became concerning: the IPCA ran all year long above the superior margin of the inflation target (the aim was 3.50 percent and the range 2.25 percent to 5.25 percent) and reached 10 percent in October 2021.

To sum up, COVID-19 hit Brazil strongly. Its effects were felt more in the real sector of the economy, with GDP decreasing by 4.4 percent in 2020 and unemployment being on average 13.5 percent throughout 2020, the highest level ever. The financial system has somehow suffered less than the economic real sector. The largest financial impact of the pandemic crisis happened in commence in March and April 2020. After that, there was a recovery and different indexes reported that the situation got better than that at the beginning of the crisis. Undoubtedly, the fast and unconventional monetary policy the CBB undertook played a role in that.

THE CONVENTIONAL MONETARY POLICY OF THE CBB

The CBB is responsible for formulating, executing, overviewing, and controlling the monetary, exchange rate, credit, and financial policies in Brazil.

The Bank organizes, rules, and polices the Brazilian financial system, as well manages the national payment system and the system of means of payment (CBB, 2015). To supervise the Brazilian financial system, the CBB creates rules, such as the number of participants in the market, the minimum capital requirement to enter into the financial system, the minimum levels of solvency and liquidity, among others.

Besides this regulatory scope of action, the CBB has three macroeconomic goals under its responsibility, namely fighting inflation, softening economic cycles, and reaching the lowest possible unemployment. However, by law, the main assignment of the CBB is securing the purchasing power of the Brazilian national currency, *Real*, by controlling price levels.

To execute monetary policy, the CBB conventionally manages three tools: (1) compulsory deposits; (2) a discount window for loans of last resort; and (3) open-market operations. In October 2021, the actual rate of a compulsory deposit was 21 percent on checking accounts and 17 percent on saving deposits. In turn, the discount window has not been significantly used in the last two decades.

The main monetary policy tool in Brazil is the open market operation, because it is flexible, agile and has a broad reach. Open market operations in Brazil are made every weekday, they only use public debt as collateral and seek to maintain the Selic base rate at the target announced by the CBB Monetary Policy Committee, to converge the effective IPCA to the target.

In a normal context, the CBB manages the monetary policy using the above-described tools, especially open market operations, in pursuit of fixing the short-term interest rate by controlling the liquidity of the economy. The CBB's final aim is controlling inflation, which is the monetary anchor of the Brazilian economy. By means of the transmission channels of the monetary policy, changes of the Selic base rate affect financial assets' prices, availability of credit, liquidity level, and economic activity.

However, in crisis moments these transmission channels are disturbed and limit CBB's management of monetary policy which, in turn, might result in a higher longer-term interest rate, debt deflation and credit restriction, destabilizing the financial system and worsening the crisis. The loss of efficacy of the conventional monetary policy makes central banks pursue unconventional monetary policies (Bank of Portugal, 2015). Central banks of advanced economies, including the supranational European Central Bank, have adopted these unconventional measures since the 2008 Great Financial Crisis, yet the CBB only fostered them during the COVID-19 crisis.

THE UNCONVENTIONAL MONETARY POLICY

There is no consensus on the definition of unconventional monetary policy (UMP), and on which are its transmission channels. Borio and Disyatat (2009) say that the main aspect of the UMP is that central banks use their balance sheet to influence prices and conditions of financial markets. Moreover, the UMP would consist of policies that go further than the conventional base rate policy. These unconventional measures both drive the market's expectations about long-term interest rates and affect credit availability via channels others than the short-term interest rate (Peersman, 2011).

Potter and Smets (2019) argue that the UMP enables central banks to influence a broad set of financial activities, to solve transmission channel issues of the monetary policy, and to grant additional monetary stimulus in a zero lower bound context. The UMP is implemented when the disturbance of the transmission channels of monetary policy is such that the traditional tools are no longer effective. The measures of the UMP are usually temporary. Their use is often made during and in the aftermath of a crisis. Nevertheless, since 2008 the UMP is implemented time and again and because of the consequences of the COVID-19 pandemic it assumed an unprecedented scale.

It is worth noting that the unconventional tools of monetary policy are not totally strange to conventional monetary policy. What really differs between both is the use of the available tools, the intensity of the use of these tools, the motive to adopt them, and the wide range of sectors and actors upon which the measures are aimed. Nevertheless, what is unconventional in one country might not be so elsewhere. Thus, the 'unconventional' depends on each country's particular monetary policy framework and on the instruments that can be added to it.

IMF (2013) classifies the UMP channels as (1) a signaling channel, (2) a scarcity channel, and (3) a duration channel. The first refers to the communication between the central banks and the agents to transmit credibility and anchor expectations regarding the future of the monetary policy. The scarcity channel is the impact that big players such as central banks can cause on financial assets' prices. As big buyers, central banks can largely change the supply and demand for financial assets, changing their price. The duration channel is the capacity of central banks to modify the financial system yield curve by purchasing financial assets in large scale – it can be understood as a generalized type of the scarcity channel. When buying in large scale, central banks absorb and reduce risks and alter the duration of assets. Since the purchase of asset by central banks makes the portfolio of investors safer, the latter are expected to accept a lower risk premium, so possibly reducing the financial system yield curve.

Some authors join these two last channels – scarcity and duration – into one, called the balance sheet channel. This channel gathers measures to grant liquidity to financial institutions, to buy public and private assets, to furnish credit to both financial and non-financial institutions, and it also encapsulates the management of exchange rate reserves.

Borio and Disyatat (2009) and Cecioni et al. (2011) present two main mechanisms through which the UMP works. The first is the signaling channel and refers to the communication of the central bank to the public to restore the confidence of market players and direct their expectations. The signaling policy can back the monetary policy and has a strong utility in economies where the zero lower bound has been reached. The second mechanism is the balance sheet or portfolio channel. It is used when central banks wish to act in specific markets, furnishing liquidity and altering yield curves.

Balance sheet policies modify the size and the composition of balances of both banks and non-banking agents. They can be classified in four categories, namely the policies of (1) exchange rate; (2) quasi-debt management; (3) credit; and (4) bank reserves (Borio and Disyatat, 2009; Cecioni et al., 2011; Saraiva, 2014).

The exchange rate policy works through central banks purchasing external currencies. It aims to influence the variance (volatility) and the price (level) of the exchange rate (Borio and Disyatat, 2009). It works by central banks managing foreign reserves to administer the exchange rate market's liquidity. Exchange rate policy is already common in emerging and developing economies, such as Brazil and Mexico, to try to offset the effects of international capital flows entering and leaving the country.

Quasi-public debt management is the purchase of government bonds in the portfolio of private agents. When central banks buy bonds of different maturities, they alter the risk premium and the yield curve of the public debt trying to stabilize the service of the debt over time (Borio and Disyatat, 2009; Saraiva, 2020). It is called 'quasi-debt' management because public debt management is usually a task of national treasuries, but as in this case it is undertaken by central banks, the 'quasi-debt' appears.

The efficacy of this measure relies on purchasing public bonds in a volume large enough to reduce their availability in the market and so influence the market price of the public debt. Those with public bonds on their portfolios would have greater wealth by means of the wealth effect due to decreasing interest rates emerging from central banks' quasi-debt management. Rising face value asset holders can be stimulated to borrow to finance new investment projects or even to sell their appreciated assets to consume with their greater purchasing power. In both ways, the quasi-debt policy dynamizes economic activity. Furthermore, once public bonds set the financial market benchmark interest rate, variances of the public debt yield curve change financial markets' financing conditions (Borio and Disyatat, 2009).

The credit policy consists of measures directed to specific segments of the economy. These are intended to assuage the scant liquidity of the crisis period, reduce the spread charged at the interbank market, and have better credit granting. These measures enlarge the exposition of central banks to other actors. Nevertheless, this is the expected outcome of this policy, and it means central banks deleveraging and cleaning these actors' balance sheets. Although central banks increase their risk exposure, their power of issuing reserves enables them to be the greatest risk carrier of any economy. Credit policy practices this power to de-leverage the financial system and build financial stability.

The bank's reserves policy is pursued to fix a target to the aggregate level of bank reserves. It aims to both promote the stability of banks to foment social confidence in them (a kind of prudential measure) and build greater incentives for bank lending. Although the control of the variation of money supply is a monetary anchor that is no longer used, some sorts of bank reserves policies are still in place, such as the CBB's historically adopted compulsory deposits.

THE CBB UNCONVENTIONAL MONETARY POLICY TO CONFRONT THE ECONOMIC IMPACTS OF THE COVID-19 PANDEMIC

When the economic impacts of the COVID-19 pandemic started in the Brazilian economy, the CBB began taking measures, including some that were unconventional. The CBB purposed to: (1) keep the banking system liquid and stable; (2) guarantee the normal level of capital of the financial system and the proper functioning of the credit channel; (3) offer special conditions for debt refinancing of sectors affected by the crisis; (4) maintain the proper work of the exchange rate market; and (5) help revive economic growth after the pandemic, in which the credit channel was seen as the means to push economic activity.

Given the dimensions of the crisis, the CBB understood that other tools rather the traditional ones were needed. Therefore, the UMP would be a stronger and faster response to the crisis. The CBB's strategy to confront the impacts of the pandemic was twofold. On the one hand, it took measures to grant liquidity to the financial system; on the other hand, it moved to free or reduce capital requirements. Both sets were aimed at all financial institutions, but they especially looked at banks, because the Brazilian financial system is extensively bank-based. The first group of procedures sought to preserve the liquidity of financial markets. The second group of measures aimed at freeing resources to banks, increasing their available resources.

In view of that, the CBB was trying to make the financial system retain sufficient liquid resources to assist the higher liquidity demand from the financial system itself as well as from non-financial actors, which was expected in the pandemic crisis. Moreover, the Bank was also planning to leave the banking system with enough resources to lend because firms needed to borrow money in order to survive while they were in lockdown.

The Measures to Grant Liquidity

One of the main actions the CBB took to widen the liquidity provision was the flexibilization of the compulsory deposit. By the end of 2019, the compulsory deposit ratio was, on average, 25 percent on saving deposits and 31 percent on current account deposits. In February 2020, the CBB reduced the quota of compulsory deposits, with an effective start on March 16, 2020. However, the pandemic begun in between these dates and the CBB made a larger cut in the quota, bringing them to, on average, 18.5 percent on saving deposits and 21 percent on current account deposits. In October 2020 the CBB renewed these quotas until the end of 2021 (CBB, 2020c). If, on the one hand, the CBB relaxed compulsory requirements, on the other hand it ruled that 5 percent of the freed resources needed to go to micro and small businesses until August 10, 2020, and on top of that another 5 percent up to September 8, 2020.

The CBB also changed the calculation of the Liquidity Coverage Ratio, the short-term liquidity that financial institutions mandatorily reserve. The CBB authorized that the resources of compulsory requirements should no longer fulfill 15 percent, but instead 30 percent of the Liquidity Coverage Ratio. Thus, when collecting their compulsory reserves, banks were already accounting for a greater part of the Liquidity Coverage Ratio. Lower compulsory requirements on both current account and saving deposits plus the allowance for greater use of compulsories to form the Liquidity Coverage Ratio released R$264.4 billion to the banking system from March 2020 to the end of 2021 (CBB, 2020b).

Within its UMP, the CBB created three special lines to furnish liquidity to financial institutions. They were called the Special and Temporary Liquidity Lines (LTEL, for the Portuguese *Linhas Especiais Temporárias de Liquidez*) and they innovated in the collaterals asked by the CBB for lending. These LTEL were (1) loans warranted by Guaranteed Financial Bills (LGF, for the Portuguese *Letras Financeiras Garantidas*); (2) new term deposits with special guarantees (NDPGE, for the Portuguese *Novo Depósito a Prazo com Garantias Especiais*); and (3) loans backed by private debentures.

With the loans warranted by Guaranteed Financial Bills, the CBB lent to financial institutions that used financial bills backed on their credit portfolio to warrantee the borrowings. This measure contributed to correcting some dysfunctions of the credit market due to the rising borrowing demand of households and firms. The CBB allowed the entrance of several types of financial institutions in the program, such as commercial, multiple and investment banks. The LFG could last from 30 to 359 days and, to mitigate the risk it was taking, the CBB rated the financial bills and lent in accordance with this credit risk assessment. The program's potential resources were estimated at R$670 billion. However, as the whole set of measures the CBB undertook were enough to stabilize the financial market and to normalize the credit supply to the economy, only R$105 billion were contracted (CBB, 2020b).

The NDPGE was an additional source of resources accessible to all financial institutions that were members of the Credit Guarantor Fund – a fund that guarantees small amounts of specific investments of financial institutions which are components of the Fund. The NDPGE enabled bigger loans to a single borrower and the lender would not have to make the fiduciary assignment of their receivables. The program focused on medium and small financial institutions. The estimated potential of loans of this program was R$200 billion, but loans reached only R$20.8 billion (CBB, 2020b).

The loans Backed by the Private Debentures Program allowed the CBB to lend to financial institutions taking private bonds as collateral. The program was intended to secure the proper operation of the secondary debentures market without risking the cash flow of financial institutions. If financial institutions defaulted on a loan, the CBB could have taken the due amount by taking either some assets or part of the compulsory reserves of the defaulting institution (Silva, 2020). The measure was little used, only R$3 billion out of R$91 billion potentially loanable; nevertheless, CBB (2020a) estimated that the program resulted in spreads 30 percent lower in the secondary debentures market.

In terms of liquidity support, there were two other measures. First, more flexible rules for Bills for Agribusiness Credit (LCA for the Portuguese *Letras de Crédito do Agronegócio*). With this measure, financial institutions with total assets up to R$1.5 billion could keep getting funds through LCA, up to R$100 million, without needing to lend to the agribusiness. Conventionally, 35 percent of funds gathered with LCA go to rural businesses (Silva, 2020). This unconventional act contributed to increase credit to small firms and stimulated small financial institutions to issue LCA. In addition, the CBB (2020b) estimated the impact of the measure to be R$2.2 billion and this was actually its outcome.

Second, the program 'One-year Foreign Repurchase Agreements Backed by Brazilian National Treasury Bonds' was aimed at furnishing liquidity in foreign currency to Brazilian financial institutions. With the program, the CBB borrowed foreign money through repurchase agreements and transferred the funds raised to Brazilian financial institutions, strengthening their position in external resources. In turn, financial institutions underwrote the loans with their public bonds. The CBB (2020b) pointed out that up to R$ 50 billion could be raised in this program, but it lent R$23.2 billion.

To sum up, the measures to furnish and secure liquidity to financial institutions were new. If seen as a whole, they had built, although temporarily, a new framework for the Brazilian monetary policy. These measures are unconventional because they (1) were not base-rate oriented monetary policy; (2) were something exceptional, not previously adopted; (3) were a strong framework, that gathered a substantial sum of resources; and (4) were, at least some of the policies, oriented to specific segments of financial markets.

Capital Relief Measures

Capital reliefs measures temporary modified regulatory capital requirements that form the minimum capital buffer required for the operation of financial institutions. Different from the measures to furnish credit and liquidity which changed norms set by the CBB itself, capital relief measures altered the requirements set and overviewed by the Basel Accords. For instance, the CBB regulated compulsory deposits, however they are not part of the Basel Accords. This kind of measure was pursued to supply relief resources to financial institutions and, consequently, to augment the credit granted to the economy.

The biggest act within this category of unconventional measures was the reduction in the Additional Principal Capital (ACP) factor, which amounted to a discharge of R$620 billion to banks (CBB, 2020b). The ACP is a Basel Accords ruled mechanism that seeks to construct a capital buffer that financial institutions employ during crises; when recurring to this buffer, the financial institutions do not need to restrict credit to improve their financial conditions. After the resolution was taken, the CBB noticed some resistance of the financial institutions to reduce their buffer. Hence, the CBB reduced even more the ACP ratios and set a gradual step back to the normal aliquots, which goes until April 2022.

The second biggest measure in terms of resources relieved became known as an 'overhedge'. It removed the obligation of banks to deduce from their capital provision the taxes charged on their operations with foreign money intended to finance Brazilian external investments. Banks make an 'overhedge' because their gains or losses are taxed. Hence, if they make an additional hedge, greater than what is really needed, they can compensate both the exchange rate variation and the tax charged on the operation.

However, in a period of a short international liquidity like crisis, the institutions reduce their foreign financing, and dismissing these operations exacerbates the volatility of the exchange rate. The CBB changed the rules regarding the 'overhedge' to both diminish the volatility of the exchange rate, already augmented because of the crisis, and keep normal the flux of domestic financial institutions lending to Brazilian external investments. This act released R$520 billion (CBB, 2020b).

Another measure that the CBB had never used before but practiced during the COVID-19 crisis was granting working credit to firms. The program 'Working Capital for Business Preservation' (the acronym was CGPE for the Portuguese *Capital de Giro para Pequena Empresa*) was complementary to the fiscal policy programs made by the Brazilian National Treasury. CGPE exclusively lent working capital to micro, small, and medium businesses – that is, firms annually billing up to R$400 million. In order to make resources available to financial institutions, the measure allowed them to use part of their regulatory capital in loans. With this measure, temporary fluctuations of the regulatory capital could be used for granting credit, although restricted to small-size firms. The program amounted R$14.4 billion of credit granted, but the estimated potential was R$127 billion (CBB, 2020b).

There were three further acts within the capital relief category. First, there was also an 85 percent reduction in the Risk Factor Weighting of the capital requirement for credit operations to small and medium enterprises. This lasted only until the end of 2020 but it was a success: the total estimated, R$35 billion, was furnished. Second, the minimum capital required by financial institutions exposed to Term Deposits with Special Guarantees was reduced. This prudential measure diminished from 50 percent to 35 percent the Risk Factor Weighting of this capital requirement and it relieved R$2.3 billion out of a R$12 billion potential (CBB, 2020b). Third and finally, the CBB also reduced the capital requirement for the smallest group of financial institutions in the Brazilian financial system (called Segment 5, known by the acronym S5) which has simpler risk calculations in the system because the business range is not broad. The Risk Factor Weighting for capital requirement was reduced from 12 percent to 10.5 percent to cooperative credit societies and from 17 percent to 15 percent to the other S5 financial institutes. CBB (2020b) pointed out that R$16.5 billion were discharged by this measure and that this had been its estimated potential.

Table 10.1 summarizes the measures described in the two categories, namely liquidity provision and capital relief. The table shows that, especially in the liquidity provision category, the effective amount used, R$427.1 billion, was smaller than the potential of R$1,264 billion. The table also shows that the main measures in terms of resources were those of capital relief, in that R$1,225.2 billion out of a potential R$1,348.2 billion were effectively raised by the financial institutions. The reason for this difference is twofold. On the one hand, the whole set of measures showed itself to be bigger than what was needed to return the Brazilian financial system to normality after the initial pandemic shock. On the other hand, the category capital relief furnishes resources to financial institutions that are not borrowed from the CBB as the measures to furnish liquidity. Capital relief measures raise capital that enters into the regular cash flow of financial institutions, coming from their typical funds raising. Therefore, financial institutions preferred them to borrowing liquidity from the CBB.

Table 10.1   *Liquidity provision and capital relief measures (2020 and 2021, in R$ billion)*

Measure	Potential impact	Implemented
Liquidity Support		
Changes in compulsory reserves requirements	R$255.8	R$269.4
Additional reduction in reserve requirements	R$70	R$70
Flexibilization of LCA regulation	R$2.2	R$2.2
Loan backed by LFG credit operations	R$670	R$105.1
One-year term repos backed by federal government bonds	R$50	R$23.2
New Term Deposit with Special Guarantees (NDPGE)	R$200	R$24.2
Loans backed by debentures	R$91	R$3
Subtotal	R$1.274	R$427,1
Capital Relief		
Overhedge	R$520	R$520
Reduction of ACP	R$637	R$637
Reduction in the capital requirement for credit operations for small enterprises	R$35	R$35
Reduction in capital for S5 segment	R$16.5	R$16,5
Reduction in capital for DPGE exposures	R$12.7	R$2,3
Working capital for business preservation	R$127	R$14.4
Subtotal	R$1,348.2	R$1,225.2
Total	R$2,622.2	R$1,652.3

Source: CBB (2020b, 2021b).

The literature on UMP has not seen regulatory measures as a sort of monetary policy tool. However, the measures of capital relief were relevant during the COVID-19 crisis, and they deserve to be considered as an important auxiliary instrument in the pursuit of financial stability. Strauss-Khan (IMF, 2008) says that a policy that cyclically alters the aliquots of capital requirements are key in a crisis. Moreover, the coordinate action between the monetary and regulatory authorities (most of times they are the same, but not always) is very important to identify and control risks (IMF, 2008).

The Quasi-debt Management Policy

Central banks' actions in the public and private debt markets became quite common in the aftermath of the 2008 Great Financial Crisis, chiefly in the advanced economies, such as the United States of America, Japan, and the European Central Bank. However, the CBB was not allowed to carry out this measure. Nevertheless, Constitutional Amendment 106, approved in May 2020 (Brasil, 2020), provided the CBB with the power to manage public debt, accompanied with that already made by the Brazilian National Treasury.

The large-scale asset purchase that the CBB was permitted to undertake enabled the Bank to engage in this balance sheet policy. The purchase of assets would affect the yield curve of the financial system as well as furnish liquidity to the public and private debt markets. Notwithstanding these benefits, the CBB did not undertake any measure it was permitted. It only defined how its purchases would be done and tested the electronic purchasing system. But no acquisition of private or public bonds was done. Hence, this powerful tool was in place to confront the effects of the COVID-19 crisis.

The CBB Forward Guidance

The forward guidance policy intends to enhance the communication between the central banks and the agents, in that it aims to strengthen the transparency and predictability of central banks' future steps. Potter and Smets (2019) argue that forward guidance is a historical policy of central banks, because orienting agents' expectations is a common practice of monetary authorities. The novelty of forward guidance in the context of the UMP is that central banks have a rather more direct and explicit intention of guiding private sector's expectations when compared with tranquil times.

The literature on UMP splits forward guidance into two main categories. The first, called Delphic Forward Guidance, is applied when the monetary authority intends to enhance the communication with the public to improve the efficacy of monetary policy. When using this type of forward signaling, central banks indicate which is the likely future of the monetary policy, subject to some conditions which are of well-known public knowledge. The second type is the Odyssian Forward Guidance, employed when central banks desire to introduce an additional monetary stimulus. This second type is usually implemented in a crisis due to the need for more economic incentives than those offered by the conventional tools of the monetary policy, especially when the economy is at the zero lower bound.

The Delphic Forward Guidance can either be quantitative or qualitative. In the former, the central bank offers outlooks to the economic variables that drive the bank's actions, detailing the assumptions as well as the probabilities applied to each scenario. This is the most restrictive sort of forward guiding. In turn, the more flexible qualitative forward guidance reveals only partial information regarding the future measures of the central bank, indicating in a vaguer manner the future acts of the bank. In the Odyssian Forward Guidance the central bank attaches the end of the monetary stimulus to some clear criteria, either a state of the economy (state-contingent forward guidance) or a time limit (time-contingent forward guidance).[2]

There are three transmission channels from the forward guidance to the economy. The first is the impact of forward guiding on short and long-term interest rates. The second is their capability to reduce the volatility of the markets, which might even culminate in lower risk premiums. Finally, the forward guidance is believed to increase the sensibility of agents to some specific data because the tool emphasizes a set of economic indicators and variables. Moreover, apart from the type of forward signaling, the central bank must communicate well with the public and should create no disturbing noise. The efficacy of the instrument is directly related to the credibility of the central bank and anything that bothers it can raise problems to the forward guidance efficiency.

Along with as the other tools of the UMP, the forward guidance was implemented by many central banks, including those anchored to the inflation targeting regime. However, the instrument gained credence after the 2008 Great Financial Crisis, when markets faced large instability and central banks encountered their zero lower bound. Nevertheless, Brazil just used the tool during the COVID-19 crisis, and only for a period as short as the second half of 2020.

In the 232nd meeting of the Committee of Monetary Policy, August 4 and 5, 2020, the Committee announced the implementation of a future prescription as an additional tool of monetary policy. The proceedings of the meeting explicitly said that the Committee was willing to drive agents' expectations and to provide for inflation targeting the correct monetary stimulus, given the turbulent context imposed by the pandemic (CBB, 2020d). Then, there was a fear of deflation, quite different from in 2021, when inflation surpassed the superior margin of the target.

In the proceedings of the meeting, the Committee pointed out some challenges of forward guidance in developing countries such as Brazil. These economies have greater vulnerability in their fundamentals and are more exposed to the effects of external crises. However, the Committee concluded that the forward guidance, even not being as powerful as in advanced economies, could bring benefits to the Brazilian monetary policy. It could enable the

CBB to better communicate its future actions, helping to adjust expectations and to manage the financial system yield curve.

The forward guidance implemented in Brazil was asymmetrical – that is, it would work only during the period when the Selic base rate could be pushed downwards. Moreover, the trigger for dismissing the forward signaling would be the dealignment between agents' expected inflation and the actual inflation target. When expectations of future inflation were above the actual target (that is, the target itself and not the margin around the target) the CBB would stop future signaling.

The Committee also attached the maintenance of the forward guidance to two other factors: (1) the maintenance of the fiscal regime (saying that if the fiscal regime was changed, the structural interest rate would change); and (2) the expectations of long-term inflation. The CBB (2020e) estimated the impacts of the forward guidance on the Selic rate and shows that on the day after the announcement of the implementation of the forward guidance, when a cut of 25 basis points also occurred in the base rate, the two-year interest rate fell from 3.41 percent per year to 3.30 percent.

The Monetary Policy Committee of the CBB decided to dismiss the forward guidance in the first Meeting of 2021, which occurred on 19 and 20 January. The Committee's argument that, although the fiscal regime was kept and future expected inflation was anchored, short-term expectations of inflation for 2021 and 2022 were quite close to the target (in addition, the CBB's own outlooks were seeing the projected inflation to be close to the target in 2021 and 2022 (CBB, 2021a)). Therefore, the context was suggesting some increase in the Selic rate soon, so the forward guidance would not fit anymore. The first rise in the Selic rate happened at the beginning of March 2021 and, in all meetings of the CBB Committee of Monetary Policy in 2021, the Selic rate was raised – it rose from 2 percent in March to 7.75 percent in October.

FINAL REMARKS

This chapter has synthesized the measures the CBB adopted during 2020 and 2021 to ease the economic effects of the COVID-19 pandemic. It has also tried to interpret these acts considering the literature on UMP. This was necessary because Brazil has never adopted UMP, whereas advanced economies have been undertaking UMP, although in a changing scale, since the 2008 Great Financial Crisis.

The UMP framework available to the CBB in this crisis was bigger than in any other crisis, whether domestic or external. While in the 2008 Great Financial Crisis the CBB implemented measures to provide liquidity equal to 3.5 percent of the GDP, in the measures throughout the COVID-19 crisis, with some of them continuing until 2022, the total liquidity provision was 17.5

percent of the GDP. Capital relief measures were not made in 2008, but in the COVID-19 crisis they totaled 15.8 percent of the GDP.

Finally, this UMP framework was important to the fast recovery of the Brazilian financial system in 2020. After the great shock in March and April, the Brazilian financial system recovered in the second semester of 2020. For instance, the liquidity and solvency indicators of the domestic banking system were better in the second semester of 2020 than by the end of 2019, prior to the crisis. The widened toolkit of the CBB, empowered with the UMP, was key in this process, in such a way that R$1.666 out of R$2.652 trillion potentially available were deployed. The UMP enlarges the CBB's capacity to act to surpass crises and minimize the damages they cause. It should not be something sporadic, but a permanent part of the CBB toolkit, as it has been to the central banks of the advanced countries for almost 15 years now.

NOTES

1. These are called the S1 financial institutions. They are the most important and biggest financial institutions of the Brazilian financial system with a size greater than 10 percent of the GDP and they make important external activities.
2. This is not the only definition of forward guidance. Filardo and Hofmann (2014) present another categorization of the instrument dividing it in (1) qualitative forward guidance; (2) threshold (quantitative) forward guidance; and (3) calendar-based forward guidance.

REFERENCES

Bank of Portugal (2015). 'Política monetária não convencional do BCE: o que foi feito e que impacto teve?' *Boletim Econômico*, 27–48.

Brasil (2020). 'Emenda Constitucional no. 106, de 07 de maio de 2020. Institui regime extraordinário fiscal, financeiro e de contratações para enfrentamento de calamidade pública nacional decorrente de pandemia'. *Diário Oficial da República Federativa do Brasil*, 87, Seção 1, 1–2. Brasília: Imprensa Nacional.

Borio, C. and Disyatat, P. (2009). 'Unconventional monetary policies: An appraisal'. *BIS Working Papers*, 292, Basel: Bank of International Settlements.

Cecioni, M., Ferrero, G. and Secchi, A. (2011). 'Unconventional monetary policy in theory and in practice'. *Bank of Italy Occasional Papers*, 102.

Central Bank of Brazil (CBB) (2015). *Regimento Interno do Banco Central do Brasil.* Brasília. 103p. Available at: https://www.bcb.gov.br/content/acessoinformacao/ Documents/regimento_interno/RegimentoInterno.pdf. Accessed October 24, 2021.

Central Bank of Brazil (CBB) (2020a). *Relatório de Estabilidade Financeira – Outubro de 2020.* Available at: https://www.bcb.gov.br/content/publicacoes/ref/202010/ RELESTAB202010-refPub.pdf. Accessed October 24, 2021.

Central Bank of Brazil (CBB) (2020b). *Medidas de Combate aos efeitos da Covid-19.* Available at: https://www.bcb.gov.br/conteudo/home-ptbr/TextosApresentacoes/ Apresentacao_RCN_TCU_17.8.20.pdf. Accessed October 24, 2021.

Central Bank of Brazil (CBB) (2020c). *Assuntos de Política Monetária – Propõe alteração provisória na alíquota do recolhimento compulsório sobre recursos a prazo.* Available at: https://www.bcb.gov.br/pre/normativos/busca/downloadVoto .asp?arquivo=/Votos/BCB/202066/Voto_do_BC_66_2020.pdf. Accessed October 24, 2021.

Central Bank of Brazil (CBB) (2020d). *Ata da 232° Reunião do Comitê de Política Monetária (Copom) do Banco Central do Brasil: 4 e 5 de agosto.* Brasília: Banco Central do Brasil. Available at: https://www.bcb.gov.br/content/copom/atascopom/ Copom232-not20200805232.pdf. Accessed October 24, 2021.

Central Bank of Brazil (CBB) (2020e). 'Estimação dos efeitos do forward guidance na curva de juros'. *Estudos especiais do Banco Central.* Brasília: Banco Central do Brasil.

Central Bank of Brazil (CBB) (2021a). *Ata da 236° Reunião do Comitê de Política Monetária (Copom) do Banco Central do Brasil: 19 e 20 de janeiro.* Brasília: Banco Central do Brasil. Available at: https://www.bcb.gov.br/publicacoes/atascopom/ 20012021. Accessed October 24, 2021.

Central Bank of Brazil (CBB) (2021b). *Central banking in Brazil in times of Covid-19.* Seminar presented at the Chicago Booth School of Business. Available at https:// www.bcb.gov.br/conteudo/home-ptbr/TextosApresentacoes/Apresentação_RCN _Chicago_4.3.21.pdf. Accessed October 24, 2021.

Filardo, A. and Hofman, B. (2014). 'Forward guidance at the zero lower bound'. *BIS Quartely Review*, 37–53.

International Monetary Fund (2008). *'The IMF and its Future'.* A speech by Dominique Strauss-Kahn. International Monetary Fund.

International Monetary Fund (2013). *Unconventional Monetary Policies – Recent Experience and Prospects.* Washington: International Monetary Fund.

International Monetary Fund (2020). *World Economic Outlook, October 2020: a long and difficult ascent.* Washington: International Monetary Fund.

Peersman, G. (2011). 'Macroeconomic effects of unconventional monetary policy in the Euro area'. *European Central Bank Working Paper Series*, 1397. Frankfurt: European Central Bank. Available at: https://www.ecb.europa.eu/pub/pdf/scpwps/ ecbwp1397.pdf. Accessed October 24, 2021.

Potter, S. and Smets, F. (2019). 'Unconventional monetary policy tools: A cross-country analysis'. *Committee on Global Financial System Papers*, 63. Basel: Bank for International Settlements.

Saraiva, P. J. (2014). *Três debates sobre os rumos da Política Monetária pós-crise, à luz d experiência americana: a revisão do Novo Consenso Macroeconômico, as políticas não convencionais e a crítica keynesiana.* PhD Dissertation presented at the Post Graduate Program in Economics of the Economics Institute of the Federal University of Rio de Janeiro, 243p. Rio de Janeiro: Instituto de Economia da Universidade Federal do Rio de Janeiro. Available at: https://www.ie.ufrj.br/images/ IE/PPGE/teses/2014/Paulo%20Jose%20Saraiva.pdf. Accessed October 24, 2021.

Silva, M. S. (2020). *Política econômica emergencial orientada para a redução dos impactos da pandemia da Covid-19 no Brasil: medidas fiscais, de provisão de liquidez e de liberação de capital.* Brasília: Instituto de Pesquisa Econômica Aplicada.

World Bank (2021). *World Bank Open Data.* Washington: The World Bank Group. Available at: https://data.worldbank.org/. Accessed October 24, 2021.

11. The financial aspects of the COVID-19 crisis in Brazil: a Minskyan approach

Norberto Montani Martins, Ernani Teixeira Torres Filho and Luiz Macahyba

INTRODUCTION

The COVID-19 crisis is a crisis like no other (Georgieva, 2020). In the absence of vaccines in 2020, the solution found by health authorities was to prevent person-to-person contagion, introducing social isolation measures and lockdowns. Such measures and the uncertainty that surrounded the pandemics prompted, as result, a strong economic recession, marked by the shutdown of factories and businesses, a huge increase in unemployment and the collapse of aggregate demand.

Although not a financial crisis in its inception, the COVID-19 crisis can be analyzed through its financial dimensions. The events that took place in March 2020, when global financial markets almost collapsed, as in 2008 (Tooze, 2020), reinforces this analytical possibility. In this chapter we use a Minskyan framework to discuss how the COVID-19 crisis unfolded in Brazil. We then analyze the measures put forth by the Central Bank and the Ministry of the Economy to deal with the crisis in 2020 and 2021. Finally, we discuss the impacts of those policies on the financial system, firms and families from the viewpoint of financial fragility and instability, aiming to assess the forms a potential economic recovery can take.

The rest of the chapter is divided as follows. The next section sets the analytical framework, inspired by Minsky's analysis of financial fragility, instability and crises. The third section describes the main effects of the COVID-19 shock on Brazilian financial institutions, firms and families. The fourth section provides an overview of policy responses, focusing on those that impact financial fragility and instability. The fifth section ends the chapter and discusses the prospects of the Brazilian economy with Minskyan lenses. Final remarks are given in the sixth section.

THE COVID-19 CRISIS THROUGH MINSKYAN LENSES

From a Minskyan perspective, families, corporations, and governments (except for the Central Bank) look similar in one main feature: they always have to manage cash flows. "Each economic unit – be it a business firm, household, financial institution, or government – is a money-in-money-out device" (Minsky, 1980, p. 212). This obligation has to follow a very strict rule that Minsky called the survival constraint: every economic unit always has to command an amount of money (cash or demand deposits) equal or larger than the total value of their due financial obligations (Mehrling, 1999; Papadimitriou, 2004; Neilson, 2019). Otherwise, companies could face the penalties associated with bankruptcy, and families may become unable to pay for their basic needs.

As economic units are mainly financial devices, Minsky (1967, p. 33) claims that "capitalism is essentially a financial system, and the peculiar attributes of a capitalist economy center around the impact of finance upon system behavior." In other words, capitalism is finance and one cannot comprehend the behavior of the economic system, particularly its crises, without considering finance.

This statement helps to illuminate the 2008 global meltdown. This crisis originated in the US financial system, fueled by a decentralized scheme of credit origination, exploitative loans, leveraged positions of subprime borrowers, and structured investment vehicles (Dymski, 2010). The collapse of Lehman Brothers, a major dealer bank on Wall Street, epitomized the financial debacle, which had serious consequences for the economy and the people all around the world.

However, a first glance at the COVID-19 crisis reveals a very different picture. This economic shock is unprecedented in several ways, and its origin has no relationship with a particular failure of a financial institution or to prior degradation of cash flows and balance sheets, as in 2008. However, it clearly has a financial dimension, as global financial markets almost collapsed in March 2020 and even the US Treasury market, which has long been viewed as the world's safest haven, suffered from major turmoil (Duffie, 2020; Tooze, 2020). In this chapter, we use Minskyan lenses to help in illuminating the financial dimensions of the current crisis.

To tackle the new coronavirus, governments have imposed lockdowns and other severe limitations to gathering in public, transportation, shops, and offices. These measures inflicted a large, unpredicted loss of cash inflows all over the economy. The uncertainty sparked a flight to safety in financial markets, depressing liquidity and asset prices, and putting pressure on the balance sheets of banks and other financial institutions. Firms saw their revenues evaporate and many had to close their doors. Households lost jobs and saw their wealth plummet. In sum, the shortfall of money led many economic units to face, in a very short period, a more severe Minskyan survival constraint.

Therefore, the real effects of the pandemic had vast financial consequences. The COVID-19 shock is not a typical 'Minskyan moment' in which financial fragility builds up and turns into instability. However, it was a 'moment' that led the economy to the edge of instability. Minsky´s insights also help map the financial consequences of the pandemic (Burlamaqui and Torres Filho, 2020). First, it is important to distinguish between two different financial processes – financial fragility and financial instability – even though Minsky often used these terms interchangeably.

Financial fragility, the first process, refers to an economy in which more and more units are being exposed to a more intense survival constraint. From this point of view, Minsky suggested a taxonomy composed of three classes of economic units. The more robust ones – hedged – have net earnings large enough to pay for the service of all their debts. They most probably survive even if they face a severe shortfall in the money they are expecting to come in.

The second class is the speculative units. They can pay all amortization installments with their net earnings, but not all the interests due. In compensation, they believe they will be able to refinance their liabilities in the future in favorable terms. Therefore, they are riskier than the hedged units are as they may face a difficult time if the liquidity of the financial market evaporates. However, they probably would not go bankrupt. The third class includes the riskier units, which Minsky called Ponzis. Their cash earnings are insufficient to pay for more than the interests due, and therefore their debts tend to escalate. They have minimum chances to survive a difficult financial environment.

From a macroeconomic perspective, an economic system is more fragile the more populated it is with speculative and Ponzi units. It reflects the "history of the economy and the effect of historical developments upon the state of long-term expectations" (Minsky, 2016, p. 109). It is a long-lasting feature.

Financial instability, the second process, emerges when increasing financial fragility makes the system dysfunctional. After this 'Minsky moment', financial systems are unable to perform systemic functions such as providing liquidity, pricing assets, and providing credit for companies and families. It is a dangerous process, and usually short-lived, in the sense that instability can trigger a fully-fledged crisis if the State is unable to intervene. According to Burlamaqui and Torres Filho (2020, p. 4): "contagion is the crucial event in producing a generalized credit freeze, which morphs into a run for liquidity inside the financial system, an asset fire sale and – in the absence of central bank intervention – to an asset price collapse and a financial crash".

Minsky's well-known *financial instability hypothesis* (FIH) posits that "the economy has financing regimes under which it is stable, and financing regimes in which it is unstable" and that "over periods of prolonged prosperity, the economy transits from financial relations that make for a stable system to financial relations that make for an unstable system" (Minsky, 1992, pp. 7–8). Therefore, FIH is "a function of the decreasing ratio of cash inflows to out-flows (debt commitments) for every agent in the system except sovereign governments" (Burlamaqui and Torres Filho, 2020, p. 4). In other words, stability is destabilizing, and the 'music stops' when the mix of financial positions is not validated by the financial system anymore.

The usual FIH is not the cause of the COVID-19 crisis. However, the impact of the health measures to contain the contamination and the uncertainty unleashed by the duration of the pandemic sparked financial instability as defined herein. The unexpected and generalized loss in cash earnings put over-whelming pressure on the previous financial structure, accelerating financial fragility in the whole economy.

Adding to these two processes, there is also a third one, which is also relevant to understanding the current crisis. Different from the others, it is an extension of the conventional Minskyan framework. It is the concept of balance sheet restructuring or an "asset-liability restructuring process", in the terms of Burlamaqui and Torres Filho (2020, p. 5). It refers to the con-sequences of the persistence of more critical balance sheet unbalances, such as a large population of negative net worth but positive cash flow units. This situation demands a long-lasting rebuilding of margins of safety. This concept relates directly to Koo's (2003) idea of a 'balance sheet recession,' in which potential bankruptcy and insolvency are permanent features of a given system.

Minsky did not explore in detail the aftermath of crises, focusing instead on the cyclical upward movement towards speculative and Ponzi positions. However, recessions also have feedbacks on financial fragility that could last longer than the initial shock, be it exogenous or endogenous to the economic system. An 'insolvency flood' could give room to a depression: "Depending on how [this insolvency issue] unfolds, the outcome can boomerang back to the financial system, restating the dangers of financial instability and its degen-eration into a financial crisis, followed by a deep recession or depression" (Burlamaqui and Torres Filho, 2020, p. 8). Indeed, the stock of financial assets and wealth in general at stake could be problematic, and the politics underlying recovery programs is inexorably difficult.

Summing up, although the COVID-19 crisis is not a typical financial crisis, one cannot ignore its financial dimensions. Therefore, the current crisis could be analyzed through a framework inspired by the works of Minsky, which puts finance center stage. In the following sections, we use the concepts of *financial fragility*, *financial instability*, and *balance sheet restructuring* to understand how the COVID-19 crisis unfolded in Brazil and how the Brazilian authorities responded to it.

A MINSKYAN ANALYSIS OF THE COVID-19 SHOCK IN BRAZIL

The quick spread of COVID-19 around the globe and the escalation in the number of hospitalizations and deaths injected a great dose of uncertainty in the global economy. Different from the typical Minskyan script, *financial fragility* did not build up gradually until it morphed into an unstable regime. There was a huge shock in the system prompting the release of a process of *financial instability* in global financial markets. Financial conditions, which had been easing during 2019 and the onset of 2020, tightened sharply in March 2020 after the World Health Organization declared that COVID-19 could be characterized as a pandemic (IMF, 2020).

The uncertainty that surrounded that development prompted major financial disruptions, as summarized by Tooze (2020):

> [G]lobal financial markets came as close to a collapse as they have since September 2008. The price of shares in the world's major corporations plunged. The value of the dollar surged against every currency in the world, squeezing debtors everywhere from Indonesia to Mexico. Trillion-dollar markets for government debt, the basic foundation of the financial system, lurched up and down in terror-stricken cycles.

The picture was troublesome, as even the US government bonds market was under huge pressure and subject to serious liquidity risks:

> [T]he COVID-19 crisis triggered heavy investor trade demands that overwhelmed the capacity of dealers to intermediate the market. Over several tense days, yields rose sharply, calling into question the longstanding view that Treasuries are a reliable safe haven in a crisis. (Duffie, 2020, p. 2)

Amid this context, emerging markets witnessed massive portfolio outflows, the more pronounced and with the largest breadth since the 2008 global financial crisis, especially because "many of the emerging market and frontier economies [were] now much more reliant on foreign portfolio investors and external funding" than in the past (IMF, 2020, p. 24) – a process named 'original sin redux' by Carstens and Shin (2019).[1] In Brazil, the behavior of capital flows resembled its pairs: there was a huge capital flight, which prompted a strong depreciation of the domestic currency.

Tectonic plates moved in asset markets, and there was a major reallocation of portfolios towards highly liquid financial assets. Assets were liquidated in the stock and fixed-income markets, sold both by foreign and domestic investors, giving room to short-term government bonds or repurchase agreements. *Financial instability* hit hard on stocks and corporate bonds, the riskier asset classes, but a fully-fledged crisis was avoided due to policy interventions. The effects of the initial shock in asset prices are summarized in Table 11.1, in which the numbers register the percentage change accumulated in the quarter.

Table 11.1   *Selected financial and economic indicators (% change QoQ)*

	Asset prices					Other macroeconomic indicators				
	Interest rate	Govt bonds	Corporate bonds	Stocks	FX (USD)	GDP	Sales	Unemployment	Real salaries	Inflation
Q4.2019	1.2	1.9	0.7	10.4	−3.2	1.6	1.0	11.0	1.9	1.8
Q1.2020	1.0	−1.0	−4.1	−36.9	29.0	−0.3	−1.2	12.2	−1.3	0.5
Q2.2020	0.8	2.9	3.5	30.2	5.3	−10.9	−1.8	13.3	−5.6	−0.4
Q3.2020	0.5	0.5	2.8	1.6	3.0	−3.9	8.3	14.6	0.1	1.2
Q4.2020	0.5	2.9	2.5	25.8	−7.9	−1.1	−4.8	13.9	0.2	3.1
Q1.2021	0.5	−1.3	0.8	−2.0	9.6	1.0	−1.0	14.7	−1.5	2.1
Q2.2021	0.8	1.5	2.2	8.7	−12.2	12.4	3.5	14.1	−0.6	1.7
Q3.2021	1.2	−0.5	1.4	−12.5	8.7	n.a.	n.a.	n.a.	n.a.	3.0

Source: Anbima (2021) and Ipeadata (2021).

In the real sector, the combination of lockdowns and the uncertainty about the severity and length of the pandemics fostered supply and demand shocks. In the supply side, businesses and firms have been persuaded to shut their doors, logistical routes were put in stand-by and credit vanished. On the demand side, people were obliged to stay at home, investment and consumption plans were postponed, and incomes and wealth shrunk. Indexes of economic activity, sales, earnings and employment plunged in the first and second quarters of 2020 (Table 11.1).

The environment of depressed aggregate demand fostered a frustration of expected revenues and affected the state of expectations. In a blink of an eye, cash flows evaporated, engendering a massive increase in the *financial fragility* of firms. Companies needed to adjust their expenditures quickly in order to maintain themselves operational. Survival constraints were squeezed. A typical response was to reassess firms' production levels and therefore adjust the demand of labor. In turn, the financial flows to families were impacted, resulting from the increase in unemployment, the decrease in incomes and asset deflation.

The strangulation of cash flows associated with the coronavirus crisis had a major impact on the *financial fragility* of firms and households, which in turn reinforced the pressures on survival constraints in the financial system. Such effects do not have the same temporality that *financial instability* issues had, but were also fundamental to determine the evolution of the systemic financial fragility, understood herein as the materialization of a fully-fledged crisis. In other words, in the absence of government intervention, 'fragilization' tends to be a long-lasting process. 'Ponzification' of households, firms and financial institutions could follow, reinforcing the original processes of instability and 'fragilization'.

The particularities of the COVID-19 crisis are illustrated in Figure 11.1. It depicts a schematic representation of the typical Minskyan scheme on the left side (a): "financial fragility, which is a prerequisite for financial instability, is, fundamentally, a result of internal market processes" (Minsky, 2008, p. 280). On the right-hand side (b), financial fragility does not precede instability; financial instability takes place and squeezes survival constraints, with negative feedback loops (2) that induce further instability and the 'Ponzification' of economic units.

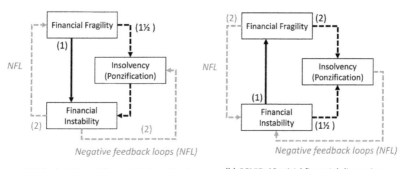

(a) Minsky's financial instability hypothesis   (b) COVID-19 crisis' financial dimensions

Source: Authors' elaboration.

Figure 11.1   *A schematic representation of Minsky's financial instability hypothesis and the COVID-19 crisis' financial dimensions*

Returning to Table 11.1, despite the pressure on the agents' survival constraints, one can see that the original negative shock was reversed in a relatively short period of time. In asset markets, the recovery was set in motion in the second quarter of 2020. Real macroeconomic indicators took more time to recover, but there was a sign of improvement in the third and fourth quarters of 2020. To understand why and how this recovery took place we need first to understand the measures adopted by Brazilian authorities.

AN OVERVIEW OF POLICY RESPONSES

From the viewpoint of the COVID-19 crisis' financial dimensions, economic policies put forth by Brazilian authorities aimed to relax the survival constraints of financial institutions, firms and households, through different channels. Although the major goals of the policies were not set in these terms, their financial impact was of paramount relevance to restore a relative normality in financial markets, to keep firms' doors open and to provide a relief for the unemployed.

In this section we will analyze such policies according to the Minskyan framework set in the second section. From the start, it is relevant to notice that all the policies adopted suffered from one major setback: Brazilian authorities thought that by December 31, 2020 the virus would be tamed.[2] Moreover, there are clear signs of a lack of coordination in the implementation of several measures, and some dose of conflict between the Executive and the Congress, as highlighted by Paula (2021). Despite this, the Congress, the Central Bank of Brazil (CBB) and the National Treasury were able to set a policy response that avoided a fully-fledged crisis, controlled *financial instability* and mitigated *financial fragility* – at least in 2020.

Table 11.2 shows another set of selected financial and economic indicators that influenced the design of countercyclical policies. From the fourth quarter of 2019 to the first quarter of 2020, there was a sudden drop in the average liquidity index of Brazilian banks, measured by the ratio between highly liquid assets and short-term liabilities. The average Basel's core capital index of the banking system and the average profitability of banks, measured by return-over-equity (RoE), also decreased in that period. Alongside the stress in financial asset markets, such developments set the scene for the intervention of the CBB.

Table 11.2   Selected financial and economic policy indicators

	Banks' soundness (%)			Target Selic rate (%)**	Loans (QoQ % growth)				Fiscal support (BRL billion)	
	RoE	Core capital	Liquidity*		Households	Firms	SMEs	Total	Emerg. Aid	Guarantees
Q4.2019	18.0	9.3	242.7	4.5	3.9	2.3	3.6	3.2	–	–
Q1.2020	16.8	8.9	195.4	3.8	1.6	5.2	1.1	3.1	–	–
Q2.2020	14.7	8.9	241.9	2.3	–0.4	3.1	1.6	1.1	121.5	20.9
Q3.2020	13.0	9.1	274.5	2.0	4.0	7.2	21.0	5.4	115.4	22.0
Q4.2020	12.3	8.9	285.8	2.0	5.6	4.9	6.4	5.3	56.2	15.2
Q1.2021	13.0	9.0	246.8	2.8	2.5	1.6	3.7	2.1	0.7	–
Q2.2021	15.0	9.4	231.7	4.3	4.4	0.5	2.2	2.7	26.7	–
Q3.2021	n.a.	n.a.	n.a.	6.3	5.7	4.3	9.5	5.1	25.1	5.0

Notes: * Measures the ratio between highly liquid assets and short-term liabilities.
** Percent per annum.
Source: CBB (2021) and Brazilian National Treasury (2021).

In order to contain asset deflation and restore liquidity and the normal functioning of financial markets, the Monetary Policy Committee (Copom) of the Central Bank cut the basic interest rate and the National Monetary Council (CMN)[3] reduced reserve requirements and provided a regulatory relief to the liquidity coverage ratio (LCR) of systemically important banks.[4] The basic interest rate dropped 2.25 percentage points from February to August 2020, reaching its historical nominal floor (2.0 percent). The funding costs of the financial system are highly sensitive to this rate and dropped accordingly.

In turn, the newly available liquidity in the system, promoted by the cut from 31 percent to 17 percent in reserve requirements on time deposits (and later by the additional release of savings deposits requirements in July), could be reallocated from Central Bank reserves to any other classes of assets at the discretion of banks. Given the uncertainty and liquidity preference, the natural candidates were repo and interbank markets, but there were spillovers to public and corporate bond markets, as well as other assets. Therefore, banks were able to fund themselves without major disruptions and asset prices benefited from the easing of financial conditions.

A second set of actions concerns the provision of liquidity assistance programs by the Central Bank and the creation of special funding instruments for financial institutions, especially mid-level banks, which are not systemically important. Two types of Special Temporary Liquidity Lines (LTEL) were created, one backed by guaranteed financial bonds and the other by corporate bonds (debentures). CMN also re-edited the term deposit with a special deposit insurance scheme from the Brazilian Credit Guarantee Fund (FGC), which allowed larger limits of insurance in order to attract investors. All those measures aimed to facilitate the rollover of liabilities of financial institutions, especially mid-sized banks, which faced several difficulties in accessing adequate funding in 2008 (Mesquita and Torós, 2010).

Liquidity ratios and asset prices increased in the months following the CBB and CMN measures – see Table 11.1 for asset prices and Table 11.2 for liquidity – re-establishing the good functioning of financial markets and avoiding *financial instability* morphing into a fully-fledged crisis. In Minskyan terminology, *financial instability* was successfully contained due to 'Big Bank' actions in Brazil.

The measures described above had a dual nature as, while they were focused on taming *instability*, they also contributed to mitigating the *financial fragility* of financial institutions. Regarding firms and households, the sudden increase of *financial fragility* was fought with a different set of measures, with the credit market playing the leading role in the response. It is relevant to notice that, unlike previous experiences, especially the 2008 financial crisis, most of the credit support measures adopted by the Brazilian government in the current crisis were orientated by the criteria and allocative decisions of the 'market', not the Brazilian Development Bank.

We can identify three main groups of measures: (i) a relaxation of capital requirements; (ii) an easing of regulatory requirements for loans, including credit provisioning rules; and (iii) the creation of special lines to SMEs backed by public guarantees. The first two groups operated through CMN and CBB financial regulation, including the Basel 3 macroprudential framework. The third one, in turn, combined resources from the National Treasury, guarantee funds that already exist but were dormant, and the engagement of the public and a few major private banks.

The relaxation of capital requirements was intended to encourage banks to expand their assets, loans included. There was no 'injection' of government funds into banks, but a reduction in the cost of capital and the creation of room on banks' balance sheets in order to accommodate more lending and foster the demand for financial assets. CBB estimations were that the cut in capital requirements would make room for an expansion of loans and assets of BRL1.2 trillion, around one third of the total amount of credit outstanding in February 2020.

In addition, the authorities exempted the institutions from increasing the provisioning for renegotiated loans and allowed the classification of such new loans according to pre-crisis parameters (credit scores). Such measures were intended to provide incentives to new loans and reduce their 'cost' in terms of banks' capital. However, to effectively generate new loans, the first two groups of policies were mediated by banks' preferences, especially the lack of appetite of financial institutions to accept more credit risks in an environment of great uncertainty.

In practice, good borrowers such as large firms were able to access more credit as a result of regulatory incentives, while borrowers of lower credit scores, such as SMEs and households, demanded a set of additional measures that will be detailed further ahead (Netto et al., 2021). The growth rate of total outstanding loans slowed down in the first quarter of 2020, though the growth of loans to firms accelerated if we compare with the fourth quarter of 2019 (Table 11.2). Despite the risks posed by the increase in *financial fragility*, large firms were able to access bank loans as an alternative to turbulent capital markets. Indeed, in the years before COVID-19, there was a major reconfiguration of financial markets in Brazil: public and development banks shrunk, especially the National Development Bank (BNDES), as a deliberate policy choice, and capital markets flourished, a process that augmented the procyclicality to which firms' balance sheets are subject (Torres Filho, Macahyba and Martins, 2021). The access to new loans, however, was limited to larger firms: loans to SMEs and households lost momentum, and the second quarter of 2020 was marked by a decrease in the outstanding amounts of personal loans.

One might say that there was a *heterogeneous and unequal credit freeze* in the COVID-19 crisis.

In order to meet the demand for cash from SMEs, the Brazilian government made use of public guarantee funds to foster the credit supply. Operations with guarantees can drastically reduce uncertainties regarding the ability of beneficiary firms to honor their obligations and, from the point of view of financial institutions, the use of guarantees also prompts discounts in capital requirements (credit risk mitigating instruments) and reduces the levels of provisioning. From the point of view of public finance, guarantee programs require fewer resources than other mechanisms for directing credit.[5]

The Brazilian authorities structured three different guarantee-based programs focused on SMEs with special interest rates and grace periods: (i) the Emergency Employment Support Program (Pese), which provided loans linked to the maintenance of jobs and payroll bills; (ii) the National Program to Support Micro and Small Businesses (Pronampe), which used Banco do Brasil's Guarantee Fund for Operations (FGO) to provide loans without a previously specified use to micro and small firms; and (iii) the Emergency Credit Access Program (Peac), which used the BNDES Guarantee Fund for Investments (FGI) to provide loans to SMEs. They became operational in the third quarter of 2020, fostering a 21.0 percent growth QoQ in outstanding loans to SMEs (Table 11.2).

It is relevant to notice that despite BNDES not being center stage of the Brazilian government's response to COVID-19, public banks were very important in channeling guaranteed loans to SMEs due to their capillarity and former experience with such clients, especially to micro and small firms (Mendonça, Cubero and Nappi, 2021). Private banks were more relevant in Peac, which targeted mid-size firms.

Finally, the main pressure on *survival constraints* was set at households. The word 'survival' here not only refers to the Minskyan theoretical construct, but also means survival in the context of the COVID-19 and the following famine. People lost their jobs, saw their incomes disappear, and also needed to stay home to avoid death. In a country such as Brazil, in which 23 million people lived below the poverty line before the pandemics (Landim, 2021), *financial fragility* is directly associated with deprivation.

The Brazilian Congress set-up an unconditional cash transfer program, the Emergency Aid, directed to families with incomes lower than three minimum wages (BRL3,300). The program provided relief to the unemployed, the self-employed and informal workers, and also encompassed beneficiaries of other social programs such as Bolsa Família. The emergency aid transferred BRL600 to its beneficiaries (some families were able to accumulate more than one beneficiary) in the first five months of the program, and then another round of four BRL300 instalments in 2020. The transfers were suspended in the onset of 2021, despite the second wave of the virus, and then re-established in mid 2021.

According to Paula (2021, p. 192), that program "contributed to rapid improvement in income distribution, offsetting low-income families' loss of income, particularly for those earning less than half a minimum wage". It was a relief in terms of households' cash flows, but the lower values transferred in the second and third rounds of the aid limited their positive impact on families' financial conditions – and poverty. Many households demanded new loans at the end of 2020 and the beginning of 2021, as a form to deal with financial needs, pressuring indebtedness to its higher historical levels.

Figure 11.2 summarizes the policies adopted by Brazilian authorities and depicts their effects according to a schematic representation of different sectors – financial system, firms, and households – and variables of interest. It shows the direct impacts of policy measures, such as lower interest rates' effect in lowering banks' funding costs, and the indirect financial developments on firms' and households' financial conditions. For the sake of simplicity, we did not explore in that picture the potential feedback effects of firms' and house-holds' *financial fragility* on *financial instability*.

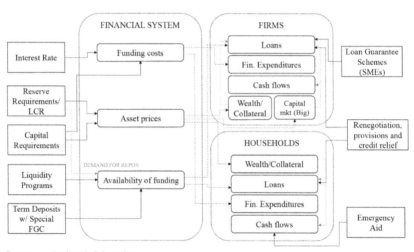

Source: Authors' elaboration.

Figure 11.2   *Policy interventions and their effects on financial instability and fragility*

The set of measures deployed by CMN, CBB and other Brazilian authorities played a relevant role in preventing the global liquidity shock and the increased liquidity preference in the domestic market, central elements of *financial insta-bility*, morphing into a fully-fledged crisis, in which the Brazilian financial system could have become dysfunctional. Nevertheless, the COVID-19 impact on *financial fragility* will be long-lasting and the erratic support to business and households may not be sufficient to avoid a massive decrease in the margins of safety of such agents. The recovery was clearly unbalanced: asset prices surpassed pre-crisis levels, but SMEs and households were still under pressure by a depressed aggregate demand and a challenging labor market.

PERSPECTIVES FOR FINANCIAL FRAGILITY AND INSTABILITY IN THE BRAZILIAN ECONOMY

Policy measures were successful in creating a cash flow relief for financial institutions and promoting the smooth functioning of financial markets for a while. The efforts seem to have succeeded in preventing *financial instability* to disseminate and prompt a full-blown financial crisis. After a first period of turbulence, liquidity in financial markets returned to normal levels, albeit under a different portfolio configuration from the period immediately prior to the shock. Asset prices recovered and there were no reports of serious prob-lems within the Brazilian financial system. The wealthiest were the ones that most welcomed that results.

The set of measures designed to induce banks to maintain the flow of credit created room in balance sheets and reduced the costs of transactions through a regulatory swipe. The voluntary action of large banks was the backbone of the policy response, the allocation of resources being determined by market criteria. The initial strategy via market incentive mechanisms did not deliver good results, except to large firms, and several imbalances had built up in balance sheets of smaller firms and households. The response to such agents' cash flow issues required, therefore, a more interventionist action of the State, via guarantee funds and the Emergency Aid.

The economic recovery process was thus unbalanced. Data on financial institutions provided in Table 11.2 show that banks' profitability recovered and their average core capital position is very comfortable. Table 11.3 shows that large public firms were able to navigate the COVID-19 crisis without major setbacks: profitability recovered and surpassed pre-crisis numbers; such firms are in a more comfortable position in terms of their ability to pay interest on their outstanding debt, as measured by the interest coverage ratio; and the net debt to earnings before interest, taxes, depreciation and amortization (EBITDA), a measure of leverage, is now lower than pre-crisis levels.

Although there are no comparable data to SMEs available, one can see that households face a very different picture. Brazilian families were able to save more with the Emergency Aid in place, but their income suffered a lot in 2021.

Table 11.3   *Selected financial indicators of public (large) firms and households*

	Listed firms (%)				Households (%)		
	Interest cov. ratio	Net debt/ EBITDA	RoE	Debt serv. ratio	Indebtedness	NPL	Saving deposits*
Q4.2019	4.6	2.1	7.9	28.9	48.8	3.5	3.4
Q1.2020	4.1	2.4	6.9	30.1	49.4	4.0	0.4
Q2.2020	4.2	2.4	5.5	28.8	49.4	3.6	11.2
Q3.2020	4.4	2.1	5.8	30.1	52.2	3.2	6.1
Q4.2020	4.6	1.8	8.0	31.2	56.5	2.9	3.4
Q1.2021	5.9	1.8	9.5	30.5	58.0	2.9	−2.2
Q2.2021	6.5	1.7	12.0	30.1	59.6	2.9	1.7
Q3.2021	n.a.	n.a.	n.a.	n.a.	n.a.	3.0	0.1

Note: (*) QoQ % growth.
Source: CBB (2021).

In this context, the debt service ratio, the part of their disposable income in the last 12 months dedicated to service debts, and the debt-to-income ratio increased substantially this year – 59.6 percent is the highest historical level of households' indebtedness.

The strategy of Brazilian authorities in 2021 seems to be very different from the previous year. As highlighted by Paula (2021, p. 177) it seems the "federal government has no coherent economic recovery strategy for 2021 and beyond." First, there was the catastrophic strategy to deal with SARS-CoV-2 in Brazil, which ignored the possibility of a second wave and put the country at the top of the death toll ranking (adjusted by population). Second, the ability to give a structured and permanent response to *financial fragility* was undermined by a premature turn to fiscal austerity, which limited the resources directed to guarantee funds and unconditional cash transfers. Third, due to inflationary pressures, the Central Bank started to promote interest rate hikes and the basic rate reached 7.75 per annum at the end of October 2021 – 4.0 percentage points above the level in the first quarter of 2020.

Amid all this, Brazilian households are being squeezed by a staggering labor market, lower incomes and earnings, higher interest rates and higher indebtedness – not to mention inflation. Their financial positions are deteriorating and soon *financial fragility* might transform into higher levels of non-performing loans (NPLs), putting some pressure on loan markets and banks' profitability. Poverty and food insecurity are now a reality, which could become even worst as the current government decided to change the structure of social assistance and replace Bolsa Família with a new and misty program of conditional cash transfers called Auxílio Brasil, or 'Brazil Aid' (Campello, 2021).

The progressive reversal of monetary and financial measures, beyond interest rate levels approaching two digits, probably will not engender a situation of *financial instability* in the absence of a turbulence in global financial markets. However, tighter financial conditions may accentuate the *financial fragility* of non-financial units, bringing to the fore balance sheet imbalances. So far, insolvency issues have been solved in the private sphere – with the exception of airline companies and other specific situations. It is not a coincidence that capital concentration is a new feature brought by the crisis: in Brazil, "the volume of mergers and acquisitions grew eightfold in the first half of 2021 compared to the same period last year, to BRL56.8 billion, while equity offerings totaled BRL15.3 billion, an increase of 55 percent" (Reuters, 2021).

Inflation, economic stagnation and some domestic turbulence on financial markets due to fiscal hawks and the mismanagement of interest rates by the Central Bank are now the main challenges that will set the scene for the unfolding of financial fragility in subsequent years. This scenario reflects the perception pointed out by Burlamaqui and Torres Filho (2020, p. 22) that: "The COVID-19 crisis is in fact an extremely challenging cluster of crises, and its financial dimension, though contained for now, is likely to become more complex and multilayered". The authors advocate it is necessary that 'Big Bank' and 'Big Government' policies are combined to provide "a decent livelihood, financial security, and social justice," and an analysis of the Brazilian experience shows that such goals will hardly be achieved in the near future under the current policy setting.

At the end of the day, the COVID-19 crisis is not solved and it will bring new challenges in the near future, demanding new responses and measures from the Brazilian authorities. The odds are in favor of an uneven, unbalanced recovery that could take the form of a depression or stagflation. While banks and large firms may be able to navigate such troubled waters, smaller firms and the population may face a challenging situation. To paraphrase Minsky, the current crisis showed that if stability is destabilizing, instability is even further destabilizing. To succeed in achieving a decent livelihood, financial security, and social justice, a major policy change will be needed and we advocate that the Minskyan framework could provide a useful guide for the adoption of alternative policies.

FINAL REMARKS

This chapter developed a Minskyan framework to analyze how the COVID-19 crisis unfolded in Brazil and to comprehend the measures adopted by the Brazilian government between March 2020 and March 2021 and their consequences on economic units and the general economy. We argued that although the COVID-19 crisis is not a typical financial crisis, one cannot ignore its financial dimensions: financial fragility, financial instability and the risk of an insolvency flood are insightful ideas to understand what happened in 2020 from our perspective.

First, the Brazilian financial system was shaken by the global financial turmoil of March 2020, with several consequences for the liquidity of banks and domestic financial markets. Second, there was an uneven and heterogeneous credit freeze, which impacted most micro, small and medium firms and families. Third, the macroeconomic impacts of the COVID-19 shock created huge pressures on the cash flows of individuals. To deal with those consequences, Brazilian authorities adopted a set of policies targeted to contain liquidity pressures on financial institutions, re-establish the flow of credit to SMEs, and compensate the evaporation of household's incomes.

Our analysis points out that liquidity measures adopted by Brazilian authorities contributed to avoiding *financial instability* prompted by the COVID-19 crisis morphing into a fully-fledged crisis. The support to small business via loans based on guarantee funds and households via the Emergency Aid in 2020 was sufficient to prevent the dissemination of financial fragility in the most critical period of the crisis.

However, the reversion of such policies in 2021 and the erratic response of Brazilian authorities after the recovery of asset prices and the demise of financial instability may not be sufficient to avoid a massive increase in financial fragility in the Brazilian economy in the following years. Financial conditions are now tightening and there were no visible silver linings at the time this chapter was written (October 2021). As Minsky points out in his book *Stabilizing an Unstable Economy*:

> If we are to do better in the future, we must launch a serious debate that looks beyond the level and the techniques of fiscal and monetary policy. Such a debate will *acknowledge the instability of our economy and inquire whether this inherent instability is amplified or attenuated by our system of institutions and policy interventions*. (Minsky, 2008, p. 320, our emphasis)

In order to avoid an unbalanced recovery, or a depression or stagflation, with serious consequences for firms' and households' financial positions, and therefore for financial stability as a whole, the Brazilian authorities need to pursue a different policy agenda, tailored to provide a decent livelihood, financial security, and social justice. As suggested by Burlamaqui and Torres Filho (2020), Big Government and Big Bank policies will need to turn now into a targeted set of stimulus packages and grants to help the post-pandemic expansion of strategic sectors, the conversion of the employment-relief schemes already in place into a robust job guarantee program, and a robust income program to assist informal, unemployed, and unemployable workers, not to mention a set of initiatives to tackle the climate crisis.

NOTES

1. See Paula, Fritz and Prates (2020) for a detailed analysis of the changes in external vulnerability of emerging economies.
2. Not to mention the denial of the COVID-19 by the chief of the Executive, President Jair Bolsonaro, and high-level officials in Brazil, which jeopardized lockdowns, favored off-label untested and ineffective treatments, and delayed the development and distribution of vaccines. See for instance Londoño (2021).
3. The National Monetary Council is formed of the head of the CBB, the Ministry of the Economy and the Special Secretary of Finance from the Ministry of the Economy.
4. The liquidity coverage ratio is a regulatory limit that aims to promote the short-term resilience of a bank's liquidity risk profile. See BIS (2019) for a detailed explanation.
5. This is because, on the one hand, public guarantees are able to mobilize (leverage) a volume of market resources several times greater than the state's contribution. On the other hand, there is the possibility of collecting premiums from the insured, compensating part of the losses that may eventually occur if the borrower does not honor its obligation.

REFERENCES

Anbima (2021), *Dados e Estatísticas*, available at: https://www.anbima.com.br, accessed October 15, 2021.

BIS (2019), *Liquidity Coverage Ratio: LCR10 Definitions and Application*. Basel: Bank for International Settlements.

Brazilian National Treasury (2021), *Estaísticas e Finanças Públicas*, available at: https://www.gov.br/tesouronacional/pt-br, accessed October 15, 2021.

Burlamaqui, L. and E. T. Torres Filho (2020), 'The COVID-19 crisis: A Minskyan approach to mapping and managing the (western?) financial turmoil'. *Levy Economics Institute Working Paper no. 968.*

Campello, T. (2021), 'Auxílio Brasil: Um engodo'. *Focus Brasil*, n.29, Fundação Perseu Abramo, September 27.

Carstens, A. and H. S. Shin (2019), 'Emerging markets aren't out of the woods yet'. *Foreign Affairs*, March 15.

Central Bank of Brazil (CBB) (2021), *Séries Temporais*, available at: http://www.bcb .gov.br, accessed on October 25, 2021.

Duffie, D. (2020), 'Still the world's safe haven? Redesigning the U.S. treasury market after the COVID-19 crisis'. *Hutchins Center Working Paper no 62.*

Dymski, G.A. (2010), 'Why the subprime crisis is different: A Minskyian approach'. *Cambridge Journal of Economics*, 34(2), 239–255.

Georgieva, K. (2020), 'A global crisis like no other needs a global response like no other'. *IMF Blog*, April 20.

IMF (2020), 'Global Financial Stability Overview: Markets in the Time of COVID-19'. *Global Financial Stability Report.* Washington: International Monetary Fund, 1–37.

Ipeadata (2021), *Séries Históricas*, available at: http://www.ipeadata.gov.br, accessed October 25, 2021.

Koo, R. (2003), *Balance Sheet Recession: Japan's Struggle with Uncharted Economics and its Global Implications.* New York: John Wiley & Sons.

Landim, R. (2021), 'Quase 28 milhões de pessoas vivem abaixo da linha da pobreza no Brasil'. *CNN Brasil*, October 07.

Londoño, E. (2021), 'Unvaccinated and defiant, Bolsonaro pushes back against criticism in his U.N. speech'. *New York Times*, September 21.

Mehrling, P. (1999), 'The vision of Hyman P. Minsky'. *Journal of Economic Behavior & Organization*, 39, 129–158.

Mendonça, A. R. R., Cubero, M. C. and J. F. Nappi (2021), 'Medidas de enfrentamento da crise econômica gerada pela COVID-19 no Brasil em 2020: Uma análise dos efeitos sobre o crédito'. In A. W. Palludeto, G. C. Oliveira and S. Deos (orgs.), *Economia Política do Novo '(A)normal' do Capitalismo: Pandemia, Incertezas e Novos Paradigmas.* Curitiba: Editora CRV.

Mesquita, M. and M. Torós (2010), 'Considerações sobre a atuação do Banco Central na Crise de 2008'. *Central Bank of Brazil Working Paper Series no 202.*

Minsky, H. P. (1967), 'Financial intermediation in the money and capital markets'. In G. Pontecorvo, R. P. Shay and A. G. Hart (eds.), *Issues in Banking and Monetary Analysis.* New York: Holt, Rinehart and Winston, 33–56.

Minsky, H. P. (1980), 'Finance and profits: The changing nature of American business cycles'. *Hyman P. Minsky Archive, paper 63*, available at: http://digitalcommons .bard.edu/hm_archive/258/, accessed October 25, 2021.

Minsky, H. P. (1992), 'The financial instability hypothesis'. *Levy Economics Institute Working Paper no 74.*

Minsky, H. P. (2008), *Stabilizing an Unstable Economy.* New York: McGraw Hill.

Minsky, H. P. (2016), *Can "It" Happen Again? Essays on Instability and Finance.* New York: M. E. Sharpe.

Neilson, D. H. (2019), *Minsky.* Cambridge: Polity Press.

Netto, M., Viturino, C., Pereira Porto, R. and A. Slivnik (2021), 'Apoio às MPMEs na crise da COVID-19: desafios do financiamento para resiliência e recuperação'. *IADB Monograph n. 893.*

Papadimitriou, D. B. (2004), *Induced Investment and Business Cycles.* Cheltenham, UK and Northampton, MA, USA: Edward Elgar Publishing.

Paula, L. F. R. (2021), 'The COVID-19 crisis and counter-cyclical policies in Brazil'. *European Journal of Economics and Economic Policies: Intervention*, 18(2), 177–197.

Paula, L. F. R., Fritz, B. and D. Prates (2020), 'The metamorphosis of external vulnerability from "original sin" to "original sin redux": Currency hierarchy and financial globalisation in emerging economies'. *IE/UFRJ Working Paper no 33.*

Reuters (2021), 'Mergers and acquisitions grow eightfold in Brazil'. *Reuters Latin America Business Stories*, July 2.

Tooze, A. (2020), 'How coronavirus almost brought down the global financial system'. *The Guardian*, April 14.
Torres Filho, E.T., Macahyba, L. and N.M. Martins (2021), 'Crédito Corporativo de Longo Prazo no Brasil: do BNDES à Intermediação Privada?' *IE/UFRJ Working Paper no 12.*

Index